The Legal Order

First published in 1917 (Part 1) and 1918 (Part 2), with a second edition in 1946, this is the first English translation of Santi Romano's classic work *L'ordinamento giuridico* (*The Legal Order*). The main focus of *The Legal Order* is the notion of institution, which Romano considered to be both the core and distinguishing feature of law. After criticizing accounts of the nature of law centred on notions of rule, coercion or authority, he offered a compelling conception, not merely of law as an institution, but of the institution as 'the first, original and essential manifestation of law'. Romano advanced a definition of a legal institution as any group that shares rules within a bounded context: for example, a family, a firm, a factory, a prison, an association, a church, an illegal organization, a state, the community of states, and so on. Therefore, this understanding of legal institutionalism at the same time provides a ground-breaking theory of legal pluralism whereby 'there are as many legal orders as institutions'. The acme of a jurisprudential current long overlooked in the Anglophone environment (Romano's work is highly regarded in France, Germany, Spain and South America, as well as in Italy), *The Legal Order* not only proposes what Carl Schmitt described as a 'very significant theory'. But, more importantly, it offers precious insights for a thorough rethinking of the relationship between law and society in today's world.

Santi Romano (1875–1947) was one of the key figures of Italian legal scholarship in the twentieth century. He was professor of Administrative Law and Constitutional Law at many prestigious Italian universities and was the President of the Italian Council of State, the highest legal-administrative body ensuring the legality of public administration.

Mariano Croce is Assistant Professor of Political Philosophy at Sapienza – Università di Roma, Italy. His research includes theory of the state, legal and political institutionalism, legal pluralism and LGBTQIA studies. Among his books are *The Legal Theory of Carl Schmitt* (Routledge, 2013, with A. Salvatore) and *Undoing Ties: Political Philosophy at the Waning of the State* (Bloomsbury Academic, 2015, with A. Salvatore).

Law and Politics: Continental Perspectives

Series Editors

Mariano Croce
Sapienza – Università di Roma, Italy
and
Marco Goldoni
University of Glasgow, UK

A core legacy of the Continental juridico-political tradition is the methodological commitment to the idea that law and politics are inextricably tied to one another. On the one hand, law has to be studied in the light of the concrete political dynamics, social forces, and societal movements that make law what it is. On the other hand, the analysis of political processes should be coupled with the study of the legal techniques through which politics exerts its effects on social reality.

The series aspires to promote works that use the nexus 'law & politics' as a prism that allows understanding societal dynamics beyond the deep-seated borders separating purely legal from purely political methodologies. It welcomes theoretically informed and empirically grounded analyses that foster the development of theory in the study of juridico-political processes.

The qualifier 'Continental' signifies not so much a geographical or socio-historical feature as a methodological one. The approach that the series aims to promote, regardless of the nationality of prospective authors, materializes at the intersection between the vocabularies and methodologies of legal and political theories. In other words, the starting point of this approach is that the interplay between legal and political processes provides a precious lens to observe and comprehend contemporary societal phenomena.

Titles in this series
Ethics of Hospitality
Daniel Innerarity (Translated from the Spanish by Stephen Williams and Serge Champeau)

Forthcoming titles in this series

The Anthropological Paradox
Niches, Micro-worlds and Psychic Dissociation
Massimo De Carolis

Temporal Boundaries of Law and Politics
Out of Joint
Luigi Corrias and Lyana Francot (eds)

Foucault's Politics of Philosophy
Power, Law and Subjectivity
Sandro Chignola

The Legal Order

Santi Romano

Edited and translated by
Mariano Croce
with a foreword by Martin Loughlin
and an afterword by Mariano Croce

Routledge
Taylor & Francis Group

LONDON AND NEW YORK

First published 2017 by Routledge

2 Park Square, Milton Park, Abingdon, Oxfordshire OX14 4RN
52 Vanderbilt Avenue, New York, NY 10017

Routledge is an imprint of the Taylor & Francis Group, an informa business

First issued in paperback 2018

English language translation © 2017 Mariano Croce

British Library Cataloguing-in-Publication Data
A catalogue record for this book is available from the British Library

Library of Congress Cataloging-in-Publication Data
Names: Romano, Santi, 1875–1947, author. | Croce, Mariano.
Title: The legal order / Mariano Croce. Other titles: Ordinamento
    giuridico. English
Description: [Second edition]. | Abingdon, Oxon [UK] ; New York :
    Routledge, 2017. | Series: Law and politics: continental perspectives |
    Includes bibliographical references and index.
Identifiers: LCCN 2017001651 | ISBN 9781138280991 (hbk)
Subjects: LCSH: Law—Philosophy. | Jurisprudence.
Classification: LCC K230.R642 A3613 2017 | DDC 340/.1—dc23
LC record available at https://lccn.loc.gov/2017001651

ISBN: 978-1-138-28099-1 (hbk)
ISBN: 978-0-367-18080-5 (pbk)

Typeset in Baskerville
by Apex CoVantage, LLC

MIX
Paper from
responsible sources
FSC
www.fsc.org
FSC™ C013985
Printed in the United Kingdom
by Henry Ling Limited

Contents

Editor's acknowledgements

I first came across *The Legal Order* when I was rummaging in my father's personal library. He had died years before, and we hardly had the opportunity to discuss my discovery. So, I would like to dedicate my translation to his memory. A special thank you to Alberto Romano, renowned professor of Administrative Law and Santi's grandson, who enthusiastically supported the idea of bringing *The Legal Order* to the attention of an Anglophone audience: his writings on Santi Romano provide an invaluable source for all those who have an interest in him. I benefited from the substantial help of Martin Loughlin and Marco Goldoni. Martin's commitment to the project was admirable as he revised the draft, provided precious comments and engaged in inspiring exchanges. Marco, not only as the co-editor of our series 'Law & Politics', but as an irreplaceable collaborator and dearest friend, patiently double-checked my translation from the Italian and discussed the host of doubts, whether linguistic or theoretical, that haunted my work from the very beginning. It was particularly gratifying to know that such towering figures as Sabino Cassese and Paolo Grossi wholeheartedly approved of this translation.

A big thank to Colin Perrin, commissioning editor at Routledge, for his unswerving support of Marco and my project of heightening the intellectual exchange between Continental and Anglophone scholarship.

This cultural enterprise would not have been possible if Alberto and Francesca Romano had not generously granted the right to translate *L'ordinamento giuridico* into English.

Santi Romano and the institutional theory of law

I. Introduction

The five decades stretching from the 1880s through to the 1920s constitute a remarkably rich period in the history of European legal thought. The dynamic forces of industrialization and urbanization had loosened many traditional communal bonds, generating new forms of functional interdependencies. But towards the end of the century the destructive creativeness of laissez-faire capitalism was giving way to a new stage of organized capitalism.

As the need for more extensive state regulation over economic and social activity acquired a broader acceptance, west European states began to assume a different institutional shape. Under the prevailing tenets of classical liberalism, improved well-being had remained a matter of individual responsibility and governmental intervention was mainly confined to the prevention of harm. But during this transitional period, political movements emerged that challenged these assumptions and projected alternative conceptions of the nature of the relationship between the individual and the state. These movements gradually had an impact on public policy, leading in turn to basic reforms in the state's governing arrangements. These various changes in socio-economic organization, state form, and social philosophy had a profound impact on the prevailing patterns of legal thought. The period is commonly regarded as marking a pinnacle in the development of positivist legal science. But what makes it an especially rich period in the history of jurisprudence is that this moment of hegemony of legal positivism was simultaneously one in which many of legal positivism's underlying assumptions were subverted by innovative jurists who sought to draw more radical implications about the nature of law in the modern world that was now unfolding.

Santi Romano's book on *The Legal Order* is an example of the innovative jurisprudence of the period. It is of the first importance because it provides the most rigorous account of the institutional theory of law that emerged at that time. Yet Romano's innovative contribution to legal scholarship has failed to attract much attention in the English-speaking world. Notwithstanding its appearance in German, French, Spanish and Portuguese, it was never translated into English. For this reason alone, the present publication of *The Legal Order* is to be greatly welcomed, not least because it might encourage a new generation of legal scholars to reflect on the significance of institutional jurisprudence. But the book is not merely of historical interest. Romano's book remains unsurpassed to this day as a study of the essential elements of institutional jurisprudence. At a time when institutional theories are gaining renewed attention and scholarly debates over the plurality of legal orders has assumed a heightened intensity, the publication of this study in English reminds us of how much English-language scholarship has lost through the relative inaccessibilty of Romano's work.

Because this English translation comes a century after its first publication, it is appropriate that this introduction should not confine itself to a consideration of the main themes of Romano's legal thought. It is imperative both to situate his account in the context of his times and to offer some reflections on the work's continuing importance. Before highlighting the main themes of the book, I will sketch the intellectual context within which Romano was writing and, after introducing the work, I will consider its continuing significance in contemporary legal thought.

II. Intellectual context

The rapid advances in scientific and technological knowledge during the nineteenth century had had a perceptible influence on social thought. Social thought moved away from the transcendental search for eternal truths towards a growing recognition that in the social context truth was a quality validated through experience and testing. This shift was most clearly marked in the innovative work of the French positivist scholars, Henri de Saint-Simon and Auguste Comte. Saint-Simon's stridently expressed conviction that social thought must always be guided by scientific principles was moulded into a more systematic method by his faithful disciple, Comte. Comte maintained that human knowledge moves through three developmental stages – the theological, the metaphysical, and the scientific (or positive) – and only in the nineteenth century was this scientific stage of human knowledge beginning to emerge. Earlier modes of thinking had thus become anachronistic and needed to be supplanted. Metaphysics had to be replaced by 'social physics' or what Comte called 'sociology'.[1] Legal scholars are invariably followers rather than innovators, and it was not long before this scientific re-orientation of social philosophy began to permeate jurisprudential thought.

Saint-Simon and Comte had argued that the theological foundations of classical natural law and the metaphysical abstractions of natural right must be overcome in order to discover, by observation and inductive reason, the laws governing all social phenomena. One manifestation of their influence in jurisprudence was

---

1 See A. Comte, *Cours de philosophie positive* (Paris: Ballière, 2nd edn. 1864); G. Lenzer (ed.), *Auguste Comte and Positivism: The Essential Writings* (New York: Harper, 1975), 254–255.

the emergence and eventual dominant status within the legal academy of legal positivism. Following Comte's lead, legal positivists began to devise a science of law based on empirical investigation into the nature of positive laws. Their investigations rested on three basic contentions. The first is that laws are nothing other than the commands of the sovereign within a state. It was claimed, secondly, that this sovereign was not some mystical or transcendental being but simply a special category of legal person who could be identified through sociological observation, that is, by identifying that person whose commands are habitually obeyed and who does not habitually obey any other. And thirdly, it was maintained that subjects obey these laws not from some metaphysical sense of duty, but essentially because otherwise the sovereign might inflict a sanction. Once these basic claims of legal positivism had been adopted, the scholarly study of law was quickly transformed. The appropriate role of the professor of law, it was asserted, was neither to venerate nor to criticize the law: it was to expound. The professor's primary duty was to explain in rational and systematic form the structure and logical relations of the enacted laws of the state.

By adopting this positive analytical method, legal scholars were able to ensure that law maintained its status within the field of scientific inquiry as a discrete category of human knowledge. But certain jurists of the period soon recognized that this autonomy was acquired at the cost of unduly narrowing the subject's disciplinary boundaries, thereby altering its character. Rather than being a cultural artefact studied in order to gain insight into a society's evolution and its collective values, law was being represented merely as a kind of technical knowledge, a technique by which the modern state could carry out its various tasks.

As the school of legal positivism increased its sway during the latter half of the nineteenth century, its hegemony was challenged by a set of jurisprudential theories that drew different conclusions from the growing influence of scientific principles. These alternative modes of legal thought shared a deep scepticism over the assumption that the individual could be extracted from history and culture to be reconstituted as an isolated datum of social or legal analysis. In place of the Newtonian physics on which legal positivism seemed to rest its scientific claims, they drew their jurisprudential ideas from Darwinian biology. Law, they maintained, is not a data set to be analysed but an organic arrangement of interacting parts whose structure continuously adapts to its social and political environment. Rejecting the atomistic basis of legal positivism, these jurists asserted the critical importance of *experience*, that is, of acquiring a practical understanding derived from living within a specific social milieu.[2] Since society is an organism and individual life has an inherently social character, it follows

---

2   As one contemporary jurist famously put it: 'The life of the law has not been logic; it has been experience. The felt necessities of the time, the prevalent moral and political theories, intuitions of public policy, avowed or unconscious, even the prejudices which judges share with their fellow-men,

(they claimed) that experience precedes any formal distinction that might be drawn between subject and object.

From this alternative scientific perspective, the human sciences aim not so much to gain objective knowledge but to acquire understanding; in William James' language, they are 'tender' rather than 'tough' disciplines.[3] We acquire insight into a field such as law through a hermeneutical exercise in which we attain a certain level of understanding of the subject through a detailed study of its parts and further understanding of the parts through a provisional grasp of the nature of the whole. Such a circular exercise seeks 'to understand life in its own terms'.[4] Life and experience, Dilthey explains, 'contain the framework which we find in the forms, principles, and categories of thought'.[5] This vitalist approach, founded on 'lived experience' (*Erlebnis*), deploys a historical method and remains sceptical of the value of abstract conceptual thinking.[6]

In this approach, the study of law involves a continuous search for meaning: it evolves as we acquire a worldview (*Weltanschauung*), a (provisional) sense of how things hang together. Legal knowledge is not acquired by the mind joining together discrete bits of data like particular rules; it consists in attaining an understanding of legal relations acquired through experience. This hermeneutical method underpins many of the more sociologically-orientated jurisprudential ideas of the time. It exerted a particular influence on jurists who developed the institutional theories of the period. These theorists accepted the basic account of human development portrayed by Comte but at the same time they rejected what Dilthey called his 'crude naturalistic metaphysics', that is, his attempt to present a sociology based on the natural sciences rather than on the distinctiveness of the human sciences.[7] In their various ways, these institutional theories sought to manage rather than overcome the tensions between monism and pluralism, idealism and materialism, rationalism and empiricism.[8] But what remains of overriding importance in their work is the necessity of relating text to context, norms to life.

---

have had a good deal more to do than the syllogism in determining the rules by which men should be governed.' O.W. Holmes, Jr, *The Common Law* (London: Macmillan, 1887), 1.

3   W. James, *Pragmatism and Other Essays* [1907] (New York: Washington Square Press, 1963), Lct.1.

4   W. Dilthey, *Introduction to the Human Sciences: An Attempt to Lay a Foundation for the Study of Society and History* [1883] R.J. Batanzos trans (London: Harvester Wheatsheaf, 1988), 12.

5   Dilthey, ibid.

6   This vitalist approach is one that Dilthey shared with many other philosophers of his generation, including Bergson, Nietzsche and Schopenhauer.

7   Dilthey, ibid. 140.

8   On the affinities in western thought see J.T. Kloppenberg, *Uncertain Victory: Social Democracy and Progressivism in European and American Thought, 1870–1920* (New York: Oxford University Press, 1986).

III. Institutional theory

The earliest exponent of institutional theory of this period was the French legal scholar, Maurice Hauriou (1856–1929). Appointed to a chair in administative law at the University of Toulouse in 1888, he stayed there for the rest of his career, producing a series of leading treatises on public law which secured him pre-eminent status as a legal scholar.[9] By the beginning of the 20th century, he had also acquired an international reputation as one of France's leading legal philosophers. Hauriou's distinctive philosophy of law came from thinking systematically about the implications of the recent growth of public law for general jurisprudence. This line of thought culminated in his 'theory of the institution'. Although he produced various studies from the 1890s that were illustrative of his philosophy,[10] only in 1925 did he publish a comprehensive statement of institutional theory.

Hauriou's institutional theory entailed a shift from conceptual to phenomenal thinking, from formalism to realism. On the nature of legal order, he disagreed both with legal positivists, who treated the sovereign as the source of law, and with contemporary sociologically-oriented jurists such as Léon Duguit, who (following Comte and Durkheim) founded law on social fact. For Hauriou, normative order could not be derived solely from the sovereign or from social fact; it derived from an amorphous metaphysical source that was better able to incorporate the dynamic aspects of social life into its framework of understanding.

In his mature statement of the theory, Hauriou maintained that institutions constitute the juridical basis of state and society.[11] States and societies are founded not on violence but on power, a power that builds its authority through a gradual social acceptance by its subjects. Critical to this process is the formation of institutions. Institutions, which express 'duration, continuity and reality', are the true repositories of the creative power of societies.[12] Consequently, and contrary to legal positivist theories, it is not law that creates institutions, but institutions that make law.[13] Legal rules are secondary phenomena. Lawyers often mistake the legal rule for action, but in reality the legal rule is an element of reaction.

---

9 Maurice Hauriou, *Précis de droit administratif* (Paris: Larose et Forcel, 1892); id., *Principes de droit public* (Paris: Larose et Tenin, 1910); id., *Précis de droit constitutionnel* (Paris: Sirey, 1923).

10 See, e.g., M. Hauriou, *La science sociale traditionelle* (Paris: Larose, 1896). The 6th edition of his administrative law treatise, published in 1907, first introduced the idea that institutions had superseded sovereignty in performing the key role in the foundation of the modern state: see M. Hauriou, *Précis de droit administratif et de droit public* (Paris: Larose et Tenin, 6th edn. 1907), viii–ix, ch. 1.

11 M. Hauriou, 'The Theory of the Institution and the Foundation: A Study in Social Vitalism' in A. Broderick (ed.), *The French Institutionalists: Maurice Hauriou, Georges Renard, Joseph T. Delos* (Cambridge, Mass.: Harvard University Press, 1970), 93–124 [translation of 'La théorie de l'institution et de la fondation' (1925) 4 *Cahiers de la nouvelle journée* 2–45]. Its sub-title displays the influence of the Bergson's philosophy (cf. n.6 above).

12 Ibid. 93.

13 Ibid. 97, 123.

This is because rules invariably operate to limit the powers of individuals and institutions,[14] whereas it is individuals and institutions that constitute the creative forces in society.

Hauriou defines the institution as 'an idea of a work or enterprise that is realized and endures juridically in a social milieu'.[15] In order for this idea to be realized 'a power is organized that equips it with organs'.[16] With respect to the institution of the state, an order is established that generates its authority by achieving a balance of governmental powers. This balance means that 'governmental power is not just a simple force but a rightful power capable of creating law'.[17] This concept of the institution is seen most explicitly in formally-established corporate bodies, but it extends beyond this to embrace all types of associations that are 'manifestations of communion' among the group members.[18] These institutions 'are born, live, and die juridically'.[19]

In constituted bodies, such as states, trades unions, and other incorporated associations, there exists an 'organized power' that is an expression of the 'directing idea' (*idée directrice*) of that body. These two concepts – 'directing idea' and 'organized power' – constitute the core of Hauriou's theory. The directing idea is an ideal manifestation of the tasks to be realized by that body. He is careful to explain that this is not the same as its function. 'The idea of the state', he says, 'far transcends the notion of the functions of the state'.[20] Its function is only that which has already been realized, whereas the directing idea contains an undetermined element intrinsic to the body. The second core concept is that 'the idea of the state has at its service an autonomous power of government that is imposed on the citizens themselves and in which they only participate'.[21] This organized power of government, which must conform to the principles of representation and separation of powers, exists in order to realize the directing idea. Governors may at times distort the task, but 'surely and progressively' they end up by 'submitting to its service'.[22] Constitutional mechanisms certainly assist but they 'would have been useless if they had not been supported by a public spirit imbued with the idea of the state'.[23] This point, Hauriou maintains, expresses the hegemony of the directing idea over the organized power.

14 Ibid. 98: 'Juridical rules are transactional limits imposed upon the claims of individual and institutional powers'.
15 Ibid. 99.
16 Ibid. 99.
17 Ibid. 105.
18 Ibid. 100.
19 Ibid. 100.
20 Ibid. 102.
21 Ibid. 104.
22 Ibid. 106.
23 Ibid.

Hauriou then asks: 'what laws of the state . . . precisely express the idea of the state?'[24] Since most legal rules impose limits, 'the highest forms under which the directing ideas of an institution tends to express itself subjectively are not properly juridical': they are primarily 'moral or intellectual'.[25] Nevertheless, they are capable of becoming juridical. They achieve this status as 'higher principles of law'.[26] Examples of these 'higher principles' include the declarations of rights produced during the American and French revolutions and that 'express the heart of the idea of the modern state'.[27] These higher principles, which are expressions of what he calls 'superlegality', are best grasped as expressions of a 'constituent power', a power that keeps the laws and formal constitution in tune with the evolving character of the directing idea.[28]

Hauriou's pioneering work on institutional theory has been interpreted in a variety of ways. In France, it has been regarded by some jurists as a philosophy that presents a modern re-interpretation of Thomist social thought.[29] But Hauriou himself did not accept this. Maintaining that his was a sociological positivist method, he claimed to be a faithful disciple of Comte.[30] Other assessments of his work accept that self-appraisal.[31] Irrespective of these ambiguities, Hauriou's work is of particular value in helping us assess the significance of Romano's study of the nature of the legal order. One reason is that, although Hauriou was undoubtedly the pioneering scholar of institutional theory, he himself recognized that Romano's was a remarkable (or noteworthy: *remarquable*) study that 'ran parallel' with his own.[32] But although he laid the intellectual groundwork for an institutional theory, Hauriou did not advance this so far as to develop a general institutional theory

---

24 Ibid. 114.
25 Ibid. 114.
26 Ibid. 114.
27 Ibid. 115.
28 Ibid. 120.
29 This is mainly because the next generation of institutional scholars, especially George Renard and Joseph Delos, gave institutional theory a distinctively Thomist interpretation. See G. Renard, *La théorie de l'institution: essai de l'ontologie juridique* (Paris: Sirey, 1930); J.T. Delos, 'La théorie de l'institution: la solution réaliste du problème de la personnalité morale et le droit à fondement objectif' (1931) 1 *Archives de philosophie du droit et de sociologie juridique* 97–153. For excerpts of their work see Broderick (ed.), above n.11, 163–213 (Renard) and 222–265 (Delos). See also O. Beaud, 'Hauriou et le droit naturelle' (1989) 8 *Revue d'histoire des facultés de droit* 123–138.
30 M. Hauriou, 'Le fondement de l'autorité publique' (1916) 33 *Revue de droit publique* 20–25: 'J'étais positiviste à la seconde pouvoir, à la façon d'Auguste Comte . . .' ['I was a positivist to the second power, in the style of Comte. . .'.]. Cited in C.B. Gray, *The Methodology of Maurice Hauriou* (Amsterdam: Rodopi, 2010), 9.
31 See, e.g., W. I. Jennings, 'The Institutional Theory' in Jennings (ed.), *Modern Theories of Law* (London: Oxford University Press, 1933), 68–85, at 69: 'I do not believe that Hauriou consciously adopted any Thomistic philosophy when he began to formulate the institutional theory.'
32 M. Hauriou, *Précis de droit constitutionnel*, p. 75: 'Un effort parallel le très remarquable est fait en Italie pour organiser la théorie de l'institution. Je citerai Santi Romano, *L'ordinamento giuridico*, 1917. . .'.

of law, and this is precisely what Romano sought to do. Romano's work stands as a systematic account of legal order from the perspective of institutional theory. And whatever doubts there may be about the orientation of Hauriou's theory, it is generally accepted that Romano presents a radically empirical account of legal order that contains no traces of Thomism or of natural law.[33] For this reason, a leading Italian political philosopher has claimed that Romano's work is 'the version [of institutional theory] that has most widely influenced contemporary legal and political thought'.[34]

IV.   Romano's institutional theory of law

Having developed its themes over the previous decade, in 1917 Santi Romano published *The Legal Order*.[35] The fact that Romano was a professor of public law is significant,[36] not least because, like Hauriou's, his thesis seems to have slowly gestated as he reflected on the rapid development of public law in its various forms (constitutional law, administrative law, municipal law, labour law, international law, etc.) before working through its implications for modern jurisprudence. Also like Hauriou, instead of imposing a clear hierarchical normative frame on his material in order to maintain the integrity of the 'legal system', Romano squarely faced the challenge presented by the emergence of special bodies of administrative law, recognizing in particular the dynamic role played by powers – rather than norms – in this development. *The Legal Order* represents the maturation of his thought in which Romano gives a concise and rigorous account of the implications for general jurisprudence.

The book is divided into two parts. The first is devoted to the phenomenon of legal order, but as he states at the beginning of Chapter II: 'From the concept of a legal order which I have offered in [Chapter I], we can deduce the corollary that there are as many legal orders as institutions' (§ 25). Consequently, in the second part he examines the issues raised by the plurality of normative orders. How the two parts relate has been the subject of debate but, before considering the book's overall achievement and significance, I summarize its salient features.

Romano explains that contemporary jurists assume that the essence of law is located in the norm, thereby defining law as normative order. In so doing they have systematically overlooked certain antecedent features of law with the result

---

33 Julius Stone, *Social Dimensions of Law and Justice* (London: Stevens, 1966), ch. 11.

34 Alexander Passerin d'Entrèves, *The Notion of the State: An Introduction to Political Theory* (Oxford: Clarendon Press, 1967), 127.

35 Romano initially divided the work into two parts that were published in two separate issues of the journal *Annali delle università toscane* in 1917 and 1918. The two were then published together in book form as: Santi Romano, *L'ordinamento giuridico* (Pisa: Mariotti, 1918).

36 Romano was appointed to his first chair at Modena in 1906 and in 1908 at Pisa. In 1901 he had already published *Principi di diritto amministrativo italiano* (Milan: Società editrice libraria, 1901).

that many legal problems remain 'obscure or unresolved' (§ 2). One reason for this oversight is their disregard for modern realities, especially the fact that public law has now grown to become the dominant part of the law. Despite private law being 'conditional' on public law (which 'constitutes its root and trunk, and is necessary to its safeguard'), legal theories are still presented in the image of private law (§ 2). A comprehensive definition, he argues, must take into account all parts of the law.

Romano's first contention is that a legal order cannot adequately be defined as a set of norms. A legal order must be seen as a unity unto itself. Although jurists pay lip-service to this idea, often referring to the legal order as a 'living whole' or as expressing the 'general will', this claim should not be seen as a metaphorical abstraction. Rather, the legal order is 'a concrete and effective unity' that must be differentiated from the distinct normative elements that comprise it (§ 3). Just as 'we cannot have a precise idea of the various limbs of the human being or of the wheels of a given machine unless we know in advance what a human being or that machine is', so too 'we cannot have an adequate concept of norms that are embodied in a legal order unless we provide in advance the unitary concept of it' (§ 3). Norms, Romano explains, are merely secondary phenomena that 'appertain to the essential traits of law almost by reflex' (§ 5). Consequently, a definition of law is not to be found in the norm but in 'that which informs it and gives it a certain shape' (§ 6). Law is 'the very entity that establishes that norm' (§ 7). It is, in essence, 'the impersonality of the power that elaborates and establishes the rule' (§ 7).

One great advantage of Romano's definition is that it incorporates contemporary phenomena into the idea of legal order. Jurists who define law as a set of norms frequently experience difficulties in including certain measures, such as those of an administrative character, within their concept of law. They therefore either exclude from their definition – because they are not sufficiently abstract or general – certain directives that evidently are part of the law, or they extend the meaning of the norm to such an extent that it strains common understanding. Similarly, normativists experience difficulties in incorporating the role of the sanction in their definitions of law. Some define law as a set of norms that include derivative rights of coercion, but Romano suggests that the sanction cannot be expressed as a norm: 'if one only concentrates on norms, one ends up denying that sanction is a feature of law' (§ 8). Far from 'being complementary or ancillary to the norms', sanctions 'form the base on which norms are constructed' (§ 8). The sanction exists as a more fundamental element than the norm, again suggesting that, rather than being normative order, law is a type of concrete order.

By exposing these limitations of normative legal positivism, Romano bring us to the core of his argument. His thesis rests on two basic claims. First, he maintains that law forms an *order* rather than a *system*, the latter conjuring a high degree of abstract integration that is one of the main causes of inaccuracy in its definition (§ 9). He contends, secondly, that this legal order is formed in a social context and only as a concrete unity: law is ordered existence and, before it can be expressed as norm, it is *organization*. These constitute the foundation of his claim that the concept that gives expression to any notion of legal order is that of institution (§ 10).

Some jurists invoke the idea of institution as a synonym for corporate legal personality. This, Romano argues, is mistaken: the claim would enable the concept of institution to be absorbed into the idea of normative order, and he is adamant that institution is an expression of concrete order. He recognizes the similarity of his thesis to that of Hauriou's broad concept of institution, noting in particular Hauriou's clear presentation of the concept as a juristic rather than a political or sociological entity. But he disagrees with Hauriou's account for three reasons: he rejects his claims that the concept of institution stands for a social organization that has reached a certain level of development, that an institution must have a constitutional and representative structure, and that law is a product of the institution. Romano suggests in particular that Hauriou 'was carried away with the idea of modelling his institutions on the broadest among them, that is, the state' (§ 11). It is not my intention here to evaluate the merits of that assessment, which in any case pre-date Hauriou's mature statement of institutional theory. Romano's criticisms have a particular value in offering clues to the nature and breadth of his ambition. The institution, he emphasizes, is not an object and, treated as a unity, 'the concept of institution and the concept of law . . . are absolutely identical' (§ 11).

For Romano, the most important characteristic of an institution is that it has 'a firm and permanent unity', that is, it retains its identity even as its membership, orientation and norms might change over time (§ 12). Consequently, all social bodies are institutions, even if they have only a relative autonomy. But he emphasizes that the institution 'is the prime, original and essential manifestation of law' and it 'exists and can be defined as such only inasmuch as it is created and preserved by the law' (§ 13). The corollary also holds: law is 'that which animates and holds together the various elements' that comprise the institution and which 'determines, fixes and preserves the structure of immaterial entities' (§ 15). Law and institution are not 'two phenomena standing in a given relation to one another, . . . it is the same phenomenon' (§ 15).

In the rest of Chapter I, Romano explains some implications of his institutional thesis. First, the problem that many jurists find in the relationship between state and law, that is, whether one is anterior to the other is easily resolved: if a state exists, there has to be a legal order. So the question of whether the state is a legal or an ethical entity makes little sense: it is like asking whether 'the human being is a living or a moral being' (§ 15). Similarly, state power is not 'a *de facto* power, a pre-legal attribute of the state itself' because the power of the state 'can never be extra- or pre-legal, but emerges with it and its order, which it always disciplines and regulates' (§ 21). Secondly, constitutional law is not a set of norms that regulate relationships within the state: rather, it 'encompasses the state in itself and for itself, in its elements, structure, [and] functions' (§ 24). Finally, Romano addresses the vexed question of whether or not international law is law. For him, the answer depends solely on the status of the international legal order as an institution, so that, for example, the question of whether the international community is a legal person is irrelevant. And the conclusion he arrives at is that, just as state law comes into being with the state, 'so does international law come into being with the community of states, which necessarily presupposes a legal order that constitutes and regulates it' (§ 17). International law is 'the immanent order of the community of states' and it is 'to be found in the institution to which this very community gives form' (§ 17).

Romano concludes Chapter I by emphasizing that the institution 'is not a rational requirement, an abstract principle, an ideal *quid*; it is a real, effective entity'. Though a reality, this entity is to be examined 'not from the point of view of the material forces that produce and sustain it, nor in relation to the environment where it develops and lives as a phenomenon intertwined with others, nor with regard to cause-effect relationships that affect it, and therefore, not sociologically, but in itself and for itself, inasmuch as it results from a legal order' (§ 24). This does not mean that norms are irrelevant; it is simply that 'norms that can be found in a particular positive law are nothing but elements of a broader, more complex order' (§ 24). Lawyers who focus on formal legal relationships often adopt a subjective conception of law, but legal order itself is institution and because it possesses 'an effective, concrete and objective existence' it constitutes 'objective law' (§ 18).

In Chapter II, Romano examines a range of practical issues arising from his institutional theory. These mainly come from his argument about the plurality of legal orders, viz, that there are as many legal orders as there are institutions. He notes that each state is 'an order completely distinct from the other states' and that the international community forms a distinct institution, though one which 'presupposes the various state orders' (§ 25). This is commonplace, but there are also legal orders that do not derive from state law. One needs think only of the law of the Church, 'which could hardly be considered as part of state law' (§§ 26, 29). 'In spiritual and disciplinary matters', he explains, 'the Church enjoys a normative power that certainly does not derive from the state' and the state, albeit within certain limits, recognizes the effects that the ecclesiastical order attributes to its own laws (§ 42). But there are many other similar institutions and it is only with the rise of the modern state and the extension of its role that the illusion has been nurtured that a unified legal order exists. In fact, says Romano, 'the state is nothing other than a species of the genus "law"'. (§ 26). Even though many entities that earlier were independent of the state have now become subsumed under its authority, 'the idea that the state system has become the only system in the legal world is to be most decidedly rejected' (§ 27).

Romano then directly confronts the claims of those who deny the proposition that there are as many legal orders as there are institutions. The concerns raised by those who object because it follows that criminal or immoral organizations must be given status as legal orders are given short shrift. This ethical argument, he suggests, can be defended only if one assumes 'the necessary and absolute dependence of positive law on morality' and that these are issues about which the jurist must be 'utterly indifferent' (§ 30). Romano finally examines the significance of the various types of institutions, drawing a distinction between original and derivative institutions and those that remain intermediate, or between those with particular, and hence limited, ends and those pursuing general, and hence potentially limitless, ends (§ 33).

Romano concludes by returning to the role of the state. He notes that with respect to complex entities 'such as the state, but certainly not only the state', a distinction should be made between their several institutions – such as the legislative body, governmental departments, other public agencies and so on – and the more general institution of the state. Based on this he distinguishes between general powers, founded on the order of the state considered as a whole, and special powers, founded upon the order of a state institution considered in itself. This, he concludes, might form the basis of a new theory 'of public law relationships and . . . the division of powers' (§ 48).

V.   Romano's uncertain legacy

Romano's institutional theory of law emerges from a specific intellectual milieu. It is to be situated within a framework of socio-legal thought that flourished in the late 19th and early 20th centuries and that remained open to the changes ushered in by modernity. The philosophical orientation of these social thinkers has already been outlined, but it should now be emphasized that this orientation was aligned to a progressive political outlook that not only embraced the coming of democracy, that is, the institutionalization of political and civil equality, but also viewed continuing progress as being achieved through incremental reforms rather than revolutionary action. Its empirical orientation is evident in the manner in which Hauriou and Romano distrust conceptualist legal thinking and present an account of law as it exists as a positive phenomenon in the modern world. But we see also a collectivist orientation in the way they highlight, and seek to integrate, an evolving sphere of administrative action within the legal order. Perhaps the most distinctive feature of institutional theory, however, is the hermeneutical method they adopt in conceiving of a legal order not as some abstract principle, but as an entity found in life itself.

Romano may have found common measure in the organic and pluralist conception of society that was shared not only with Hauriou and Duguit in France, but also with Gierke and Preuss in Germany, Ehrlich in Austria, Dewey and James in the US, and Green, Bosanquet, Figgis, Cole and Laski in Britain. But his singular achievement was to have turned this pluralist outlook into a systematic theory of law. Some have suggested that the relationship between the two parts of *The Legal Order* is ambiguous: is this a thesis on the plurality of legal orders in society or on the modern form of law as a concrete-order? But close study reveals this was for him a non-issue: he elaborates both themes equally and treats them as complementary. He was not unaware of the general problem: in a celebrated lecture in 1909 he attributed the crisis of the modern state to the growth in power of sectional interest groups with which the state was obliged to negotiate. He there recognized that the challenge for the idea of the state as the 'institution of institutions' is that of somehow being able to transcend these interests and realize the common good.[37] His lecture may not have provided clear indication of how the state might achieve that ambition, but it is evident that the Romano of *The Legal Order* regards this as a political question rather than a strictly legal issue, and therefore one that was not relevant to the juridical nature of his task in the latter work.

This political aspect cannot, however, be entirely avoided. If law is 'a concrete and effective unity' (§ 3) that constitutes an expression of impersonal power (§ 7), then, even though the state is simply a species of the genus 'law' (§ 26), the question of maintaining its efficacy to 'discipline and regulate' its field (§ 21), is a pressing juridical – and not solely political – question. It may not be a critical issue for jurisprudential inquiry into the nature of the genus, but it surely remains one for the predominant species of this genus: the legal order of the modern state. How the state relates to other institutional orders is a question that similarly confounded the political pluralists of the period. Their difficulties are vividly exemplified in the intellectual trajectory of Harold Laski, whose early pluralist studies sought to displace the state from its pivotal position,[38] but who later recognized the need to abandon this stance, moving on to a variant of Marxism that maintained that a more revolutionary shift, rather than gradual reform, was required.[39]

There is, I believe, an answer to this question of the relation of the state to other institutions, but before coming to it we might first note that the seeds sown by the institutional theories before the First World War found the interwar period infertile ground in which to flourish. The responses to the crisis of the state that Romano had so clearly identified in 1909 then met with a series of more radical responses, most dramatically in the political movements of fascism and communism. In these circumstances, Romano – in common with Laski, though for different reasons – felt obliged to downplay the pluralist aspects of his theory. In Romano's case this was because, after the establishment of fascism in Italy in 1925, pluralism was no longer considered an acceptable philosophy, and this general state of affairs was compounded personally when in 1928 he joined the

---

37 S. Romano, 'Lo stato moderno e la sua crisi' (1909): see M. Croce's essay in this book. A French translation is available as: S. Romano, 'L'État moderne et sa crise' (2014) 14 *Jus Politicum*: [http://juspoliticum.com/article/L-Etat-moderne-et-sa-crise-968.html].

38 H.J., *Studies in the Problem of Sovereignty* (New Haven: Yale University Press, 1917), id., *Authority in the Modern State* (New Haven: Yale University Press, 1919); id. *The Foundations of Sovereignty and other essays* (New York: Harcourt Brace, 1921).

39 H.J. Laski, *The State in Theory and Practice* (London: George Allen and Unwin, 1935); id., *Law and Justice in Soviet Russia* (London: Hogarth Press, 1935).

Fascist party and accepted Mussolini's offer of appointment as President of the Italian Administrative Court.

During the interwar period, the most prominent German advocate of institutionalism was Carl Schmitt, who in 1933 had joined the Nazi Party. In his 1934 book, *On the Three Types of Juristic Thought*, Schmitt explained that all legal theories emphasize one of three foundational elements of law: norm, decision, or concrete-order. Although Schmitt had vigorously promoted a decisionist theory during the 1920s, in his 1934 work he shifted towards an institutionalist approach, a re-orientation for which the influences of Hauriou and Romano were explicitly acknowledged.[40] Nevertheless, Schmitt underplayed the pluralist dimensions of Romano's work, which is not surprising since his aim was to promote the idea of the state as the 'institution of institutions' and to subject the plurality of normative ordering to the ultimate authority of the state.[41] Only by establishing a stable institutional structure founded on the primacy of the state, he argued, could political unity be maintained. And for Schmitt, this led to the disastrous argument that such unity requires the formation of an ethnically homogeneous people at one with a leadership imbued with the 'concrete, substantive thinking of the National-Socialist Movement'.[42]

Institutionalism was slow to revive following its neglect and misrepresentation in the turbulent interwar period. When it was ostensibly restored in European legal thought, it took the form of the so-called 'neo-institutionalism' of Ota Weinberger and Neil MacCormick. This was announced in their joint work of 1986, *An Institutional Theory of Law: New Approaches to Legal Positivism*.[43] But their work has precious little in common with the institutional theories of Hauriou and Romano and did not contain even a single reference to any work of the two earlier scholars.[44] Neo-institutionalism does not engage with the philosophical basis of institutional

---

40 C. Schmitt, *On the Three Types of Juristic Thought* [1934], trans. JW Bendersky (Westport, Conn.: Praeger, 2004), esp. 56–57 (on Romano) 86–88 (on Hauriou and Romano). In the preface to the 2nd edition of *Political Theology* in 1933, Schmitt noted that he had arrived at institutionalism as a result of studying Hauriou's work: C Schmitt, *Political Theology: Four Chapters on the Concept of Sovereignty* trans. G. Schwab. (Chicago: University of Chicago Press, 2005), 2–3.

41 Schmitt, *Three Types*, ibid. 88: 'the state itself is no longer a norm or a system of norms, nor a pure sovereign decision, but the institution of institutions, in whose order numerous other, in themselves autonomous, institutions find their protection and their order'. For analysis see: M Croce and A Salvatore, *The Legal Theory of Carl Schmitt* (Abingdon: Routledge, 2013), ch. 7.

42 C. Schmitt, *State, Movement, People: The Triadic Structure of Political Unity* [1933] S Draghici trans. (Corvallis, Oregon: Plutarch Press, 2001), 47.

43 O. Weinberger and N. MacCormick, *An Institutional Theory of Law: New Approaches to Legal Positivism* (Dordrecht: Reidel, 1986).

44 O. Weinberger's subsequent work, *Law, Institution and Legal Politics: Fundamental Problems of Legal Theory and Social Philosophy* (Dordrecht: Kluwer, 1991) does make some reference, but he explains that the new work is best described as 'institutional legal positivism' and emphasizes that 'our conception is not based on the sociological theory of institutions, nor is it in terms of the history of ideas an offspring of Hauriou's theory of law'. But MacCormick's mature statement of the theory

theory as an expression of lived experience; rather, it reinforces a clear division between is and ought, converts institutions into 'social facts', and confuses institutions and legal institutions.[45] It is as an attempt by orthodox legal positivism to colonize the field of institutionalism.

VI. Restoring Romano

Is it the case, as La Torre suggests, that there has been 'a steady exhaustion of the "driving force" of [Romano's] theory'?[46] And if so, is there any prospect of its restoration? What seems clear is that there can be no restoration by integrating Romano's thought into the intellectual framework of legal positivism. The distinctiveness of his approach to institutionalism, in common with the methods of Hauriou and Schmitt, is that its philosophical basis depends not only on differentiating between the human and the natural sciences but also on grasping human life as 'lived experience'. Institutionalism is sceptical both of the rationalist's conceptualism and the empiricist's 'social facts': it rests its claims on the belief that social life is intrinsically relational and that its meaning is embedded in a specific culture that can be conveyed only through 'concrete order' thinking. And if such an approach wins little favour within contemporary jurisprudence, this might reveal more about the rationalist and instrumentalist proclivities of legal thinking than about the realities of the regimes under which we live. But the question remains: where do we find contemporary resonances?

They certainly do exist, but are not easily recognized. They are not easily recognized because they no longer fall under the rubric of institutionalism. Consider by way of example Robert Cover's highly-influential study '.Nomos and Narrative'.[47] In this paper, Cover argues that law is 'not merely a system of rules to be observed, but a world in which we live':[48] the rules and institutions of law are merely second-order phenomena forming only a small part of the normative world of the *nomos*.

---

again makes no reference to Hauriou or Romano: N. MacCormick, *Institutions of Law: An Essay in Legal Theory* (Oxford: Oxford University Press, 2007).

45 Even a disciple of neo-institutionalism, one who believes that there has been a 'steady exhaustion' of the institutional theories of Hauriou and Romano and that we are 'indebted to the work of Neil MacCormick and Ota Weinberger for reopening discussion of institutionalism in the context of the theory of law', recognizes that a 'confusion of terms [between 'institution' and 'legal institution'] is . . . present in the neo-institutionalist authors': M. La Torre, *Law as Institution* (Dordrecht: Springer, 2010), 98, 104.

46 La Torre, ibid. 98.

47 R. M. Cover, 'Foreword: *Nomos* and Narrative' (1983–84) 97 *Harvard Law Rev.* 4–68. According to Google Scholar citations, this article has been cited over 3,000 times (3,267 at November 2016). It appears at number 16 in the 'most-cited law review articles of all-time': see F.R. Schapiro and M. Pearse, 'The Most-Cited Law Review Articles of All Time' (2012) 110 *Michigan Law Rev.* 1483–1520.

48 Cover, ibid. 5.

This *nomos*, he suggests, 'is as much "our world" as is the physical universe' and 'our apprehension of the structure of the normative world is no less fundamental than our apprehension of the structure of the physical world'.[49] *Nomos* signifies a form of civilization. It generates 'paradigms for dedication, acquiescence, contradiction and resistance' and is held together 'by the force of interpretive commitments' that are mediated by narrative schemes – languages and myths – that 'build relations between the normative and the material universe, between the constraints of reality and the demands of an ethic' and that 'integrate . . . the "is" and the "ought".'[50] What Cover here calls a *nomos* is precisely the concept of institution that Hauriou and Romano had elaborated in considerable detail over half a century earlier.[51]

Like the early institutionalists, Cover maintains that although *nomos* emerges through a collective process, the order it creates is not primarily attributable to a 'state'.[52] Like the early institutionalists, he recognizes that *nomos* is a 'jurisgenerative' – that is, a 'world-creating' – phenomenon. Further, that since a multiplicity of worlds – that is, institutions or legal orders – are created that are 'subject to no formal hierarchical ordering', there is 'a radical dichotomy between the social organization of law as power and the organization of law as meaning'.[53] Like the early institutionalists, he recognizes the normative power of the factual, such that utopian movements that engender no social traction 'may be movements, but they are no longer movements of the law'.[54] When Cover states that the problem for the judiciary (of a state) arises because of the proliferation of legal meaning and that its rulings are 'jurispathic',[55] he echoes Hauriou's claim that the legal rule is a product not of action but of reaction. When he states that 'each "community of interpretation" that has achieved "law" has its own *nomos*',[56] he is, in essence, restating Romano's claim about the plurality of legal orders. When he says that 'for every constitution there is an epic' to be understood through 'the narratives that give it meaning',[57] he is giving voice to Hauriou's observation that the highest forms of expressing the 'directing idea' are the 'higher principles' of 'superlegality'. Cover may never have read their work and may have believed in

---

49 Ibid.
50 Ibid. 6, 7, 9, 10.
51 This is made even more explicit in Schmitt's post-war work: see C. Schmitt, *The Nomos of the Earth in the International Law of the Jus Publicum Europaeum* [1950] G.L. Ulmen trans (New York, Telos Press Publishing, 2003). For analysis see: M. Loughlin, 'Nomos' in D. Dyzenhaus and T. Poole (eds), *Law, Liberty and State: Oakeshott, Hayek and Schmitt on the Rule of Law* (Cambridge: Cambridge University Press, 2015), ch. 4.
52 Cover, above n.47, 11.
53 Ibid. 11–12, 17, 18.
54 Ibid. 39.
55 Ibid. 40.
56 Ibid. 42.
57 Ibid. 4–5.

the originality of his thesis, but he writes entirely within the frame of Hauriou and Romano's institutionalism. Romano's ideas evidently live on.

There is, however, one major point of disagreement between Cover and Romano, and that is over scholarly method. Romano deploys a rigorous empirical method to specify the character of the modern phenomenon of law. This leads him to accept that the law of the state is simply 'a species of the genus "law"' and to maintain a strict agnosticism over the relationship of the state's law to other legal orders in society. Cover, by contrast, presents a radical ideological argument: that the modern state assumes an entirely bureaucratic – what he calls 'jurispathic' – form. Judges 'are people of violence' who 'characteristically do not create law, but kill it'[58] and he concludes by claiming that 'we ought to stop circumscribing the *nomos*; we ought to invite new worlds'.[59] This is not only radically pluralist and ultimately anarchic, it is also incoherent.[60] If his position is that officials of the state's legal order occupy a jurispathic office then, as Hauriou and Romano clearly grasped, logically this claim is not unique to the institution of the state: it can be made of all organized normative orders. And if, as Cover implies, no agency can legitimately perform a mediatory or regulatory role with respect to the plurality of legal orders, then how – except by force – are conflicts between these orders to be resolved?

Cover's argument once again exposes the weakness of the ideologically-driven pluralist claim. But it also impels us to confront the question of how to specify the role of the state in institutional theory. Hauriou and Romano were both able to isolate and identify the key point, which is that states are founded not on violence but on power. Whatever violence may have been involved in the foundation of the state, the authority of the norm is a function of the power that any order is able to generate. But neither writer fully develops or explains the significance of this

---

58 Ibid. 53. This argument is reinforced in his article 'Violence and the Word' (1985–86) 95 *Yale Law J.* 1601–1629, the thesis of which is that: 'Legal interpretation [sc. acts of the state's judiciary] takes place in a field of pain and death. This is true in several senses. Legal interpretive acts signal and occasion the imposition of violence upon others: A judge articulates her understanding of a text, and as a result, somebody loses his freedom, his property, his children, even his life. Interpretations in law also constitute justifications for violence which has already occurred or which is about to occur. When interpreters have finished their work, they frequently leave behind victims whose lives have been torn apart by these organized, social practices of violence. Neither legal interpretation nor the violence it occasions may be properly understood apart from one another.' (at 1629).

59 *Nomos*, ibid. 68.

60 Cover himself glimpses the incoherence of his argument by equivocating on the violence of the judicial office and stating that 'judges are also people of peace' who 'assert a regulative function that permits a life of law rather than violence' (ibid. 53). Quite where this leaves his thesis is anyone's guess.

claim. They accept that orders build authority by virtue of acceptance of their subjects, but they do not examine what is special about political power. This rests, I suggest, on a vital distinction being made between two concepts of power: *potestas*, the power generated by being-in-common and experienced as 'power to', and *potentia*, the ability to achieve intended effects, and experienced as 'power over'. Institutions evolve and maintain their world-building capacity only through the dialectical interplay of *potestas* and *potentia*.[61]

Potestas is the power created by drawing people together in a common undertaking. Its originating source is often traceable to some founding moment in which a multitude begins to conceive itself as constituting a collective singular, a 'we', a movement, a people. Although that foundation is invariably shrouded in myth and legend, the institution generally builds its power through the augmentation of these founding myths. *Potestas* is, then, a type of imaginative power that produces some symbolic representation of the group existing in common association. Cover recognizes this when he refers to the role of 'narrative'. But he does not appear to recognize that it is only by the generation of *potestas* that officers of an institution are able to use their *potentia* ('power over') to control and regulate conflict, to maintain order, and to promote the collective aims of the institution. Institution-building – world-building, legal-order creation – involves a ceaseless dialectic of *potestas* and *potentia*, that is, between the juris-generative and the juris-pathic.

An institution's power in the world rests primarily on the scale of its membership, the resources at its disposal, and, crucially, on the bonds of allegiance of the membership to the collective aims of that institution. If we widen Romano's empirical method of observing the working of institutions in the world, we might identify the existence of a plurality of institutions (or nomoi, or legal orders), examine their interaction, and draw conclusions about their relative authority in society. Some ideological pluralists today seem to believe that, because a multiplicity of orders exist in the world, they must be worthy of equal respect or be assumed to carry equal authority.[62] But this is a normativist fallacy, one that denies the most basic of Romano's claims about the nature of institutions as concrete-orders. Institutions range in aim and scale, from those formed for singular and limited purposes to religious bodies that believe they hold the key to the meaning of life. But as social life is presently constituted, it is idle to deny that, notwithstanding the growing influence of international or transnational institutions,

---

61 See M. Loughlin, *Foundations of Public Law* (Oxford: Oxford University Press, 2010), esp. ch. 6. For a concise account see M. Loughlin, 'Political Jurisprudence' (2016) 16 *Jus Politicum: Revue de Droit Politique*, s.6: http://juspoliticum.com/article/Political-Jurisprudence-1105.html.

62 See M. Loughlin, 'Constitutional Pluralism: An Oxymoron' (2014) 3 *Global Constitutionalism* 9–30.

the rise of religious movements with worldly aims, and the weakening of ties of nationality, the legal orders of nation-states still constitute the primary form of institutional world-building in contemporary life.[63]

Martin Loughlin

63 Another polemicist, one who in the 1930s sought to bolster the absolute authority of the state, in later life felt able to make the alternative though equally bold claim: see C. Schmitt, *Der Begriff des Politischen*, foreword to 1963 edition at 10: 'Until recently, Europeans lived in an epoch whose legal concepts were completely dominated by the state and which assumed the state as a model of political unity. The epoch of the state is now coming to an end. Over it, no more needs to be said. With it the whole superstructure of state-related concepts, which erected a Eurocentric science of state and international law that lasted 400 years, comes to an end. The state as a model of political unity, as the bearer of the most astounding of all monopolies, namely the monopoly of political decision, this masterstroke of European form and occidental Rationalism has been dethroned. But its concepts have been retained and have even become *classical* concepts.' Rather than philosophical or conceptual assertion, however, we might more sensibly follow Romano and examine carefully the empirical evidence.

Translator's note

As is often the case with continental authors, it has at times proved difficult to translate Romano's thoughts with surgical precision. As a consequence, wherever possible, I have divided long paragraphs and sentences, without prejudicing the message he wanted to convey.

It is imperative to say a word about the title of the book. The translation of the original *L'ordinamento giuridico* with *The Legal Order* can be misguiding. For 'legal' is an equivocal term when associated to an author who wrote and worked in a context that has always fed off a permanent tension between *ius* and *lex*.[64] The English equivalent of *giuridico* is *juridical*, which doubtless relates to the way law is produced and administrated, and yet fails to capture the specifically legal nature of the order that Romano strongly emphasizes. At the same time, in his jargon *giuridico* is something broader than a body of laws or the activity of legal officials, as it denotes a process of self-organization, regardless of the degree of formalization and specialization. On the contrary, *order* is an appropriate translation for *ordinamento*, provided that it is not understood as synonymous with *system*. *Order* conjures up an ordering force that emanates from a normative entity's establishing itself as a normative entity. Therefore, the order hardly derives from the systematization of a set of norms and procedures, while this set is nothing other than a fallible and revisable verbalization of the ordering force, which can never be encapsulated in a system of written norms and procedures. *L'ordinamento giuridico* signifies the innate 'legality' of an entity's self-organizing practice, which characterizes all organized social bodies, from small-scale groups to large-scale political formations.

---

64 On the foundational tension between *ius* and *lex* in Roman law see A. Schiavone, *The Invention of Law in the West* (Cambridge, MA: Harvard University Press, 2012). On later developments see P. Grossi, *A History of European Law* (Malden, MA: Wiley-Blackwell, 2010). See also C.H. McIlwain, *Constitutionalism. Ancient and Modern* (Ithaca, N.Y. Cornell University Press, 1947), which nicely brings out the key dialectic between *jurisdictio* and *gubernaculum*.

Preface

The present work, which I wrote with the intention of producing other texts in the general theory of law, is thoroughly self-standing, and first appeared in two issues of the *Annali delle università toscane* [*Annals of Tuscan Universities*] in 1917 and 1918, and simultaneously in a volume dated 1918, published in Pisa.[65]

I thought it was important in this second edition, which sees the light when the first edition has been out of stock for years, to reproduce the original text without any modifications. In the footnotes I have added some text between square brackets as well as new footnotes – again between square brackets in order that they may be distinguishable from the others – to take issue with the subsequent literature on the various topics I had tackled and, quite soberly, with the most important criticisms that have been made. But I have made no mention of a particular literature and particular criticisms that conspicuously lack scientific import and show utter misunderstanding of the fundamental problems of the general theory of law.

I hope that now that the book is easy to read there will be not many people who speak of it without knowing it directly, as has often occurred, and, because of this, fall into serious misunderstandings.

S.R.

Rome, November 1945

---

65 Translator's note: The 1917 edition has a subtitle, which is not present in the 1946 edition: 'Studies on the concept, the sources and the characteristics of law. Part I'. I should also like to note that in the 1917 edition Romano accounts for the 'unfinished' nature of his book, as he writes: 'I am now publishing the first two chapters of an unfinished work ("The concept of a legal order" and "The plurality of legal orders and their relations") that deals with general legal theories, and in particular the concept, the sources and the characteristics of law. Therefore, these studies inaugurate the actualization of a much broader programme. This explains why I do not even mention some developments that, while useful in themselves, could have helped confirm and further demonstrate the principles and the view I build on. I will attend to these developments in the subsequent parts.'

Chapter 1

§ 1. All the definitions of law that have been advanced so far have, without exception, a common element, that is to say, the *genus proximum* to which that concept is reduced.[1] Specifically, they agree that the law is a rule of conduct,[2] although they to a greater or lesser extent disagree when it comes to defining the *differentia specifica* by which the legal norm[3] should be distinguished from the others.

The first and most important goal of the present work is to demonstrate that this way of defining law, if not mistaken in a certain sense and for certain purposes, is inadequate and insufficient if considered in itself and for itself. Consequently, it is to be integrated with other elements that are usually overlooked and that, instead, appear more essential and characterizing. That the law also manifests itself as

---

1 Translator's note: I have omitted the aside 'in an objective sense', which in the original Italian text follows '[a]ll the definitions of law'. This locution was meant to distinguish the Italian term *diritto* as law from the term *diritto* as right: while the former denotes the law as a legal order, and is thus qualified as having 'an objective sense', the latter denotes a right, and is thus qualified as having 'a subjective sense'. However, thanks to the Old English etymon of 'law' and the Proto-Germanic etymon of 'right', the English text does not engender any confusion and therefore the aside 'in an objective sense' is superfluous. Therefore, to improve readability, it will be omitted also in the rest of the present translation. The same goes for 'in a subjective sense', which, as I explained, designates *diritto* as 'right'.

2 Recently this point of view has, so to say, been taken to its extreme consequences by many in many respects. In addition to Duguit's (1901: 10 ff.) peculiar work, were all aspects of the legal phenomenon flow into, and are entirely subsumed under, the 'règle de droit', see also Kelsen, 1911, whose very title betrays its intents. [In the most recent literature, which I will refer to later on, many have reacted against this view in many ways.]

3 I will use the word 'norm' and the word 'rule' indistinctly. However, to avoid misunderstandings, it is useful to point out that when in the German literature scholars debate the question of whether or not law is only comprised of norms (see e.g. Thon, 1878; Bierling, 1894; Windscheid and Kipp, 1906; Enneccerus, 1911) the word 'Norm' does not take the meaning of 'rule', as I understand it here, but the meaning of 'command' or 'prohibition', or rather, 'imperative'. This has to do with the issue of the so-called law's imperative character, with which I am not concerned here. In Italy this terminology is adopted by Brunetti, 1913, § 5 ff. As regards law as a rule, Jellinek (1914: 332) comments: 'There is no disagreement about this, that the law consists in a sum of rules for human action' [translator's translation from German].

a norm and that it has to be considered also under this guise; that this point of view is most often, and especially for the sake of the common practice, not only necessary but sufficient; these are reasons that, along with others, explain why in the abstract definition we fail to go beyond the category of norms. But, naturally, this does not exclude that it could and should be overcome by foregrounding some other more fundamental features of law that are antecedent both as to the logical requirements of the concept and as to the correct evaluation of the reality in which the law materializes.

§ 2. The soundest and most convincing proof of these claims will, of course, be provided in this overall work, insofar as, by doing so, I will be able to clarify or unravel a host of problems related to the various branches of law that still remain obscure or unresolved. But meanwhile it is worth providing evidence, as well as some indirect hints, of the inadequacy of the conventional definitions.

Among them, I would like to mention the following ones.

First, the fact that many claim and acknowledge that the concept of law is not thoroughly clear to us.[4] This impression is not merely due to the neither numerous nor serious disagreements that surface in the literature. While authors by and large concur on the idea of reducing the law to the category of norms,[5] they then distinguish – through various formulae that more often than not are only apparently different – legal norms from other norms. Rather, this impression is triggered by the intuition, though vague and indistinct, that the whole problem is not opportunely framed, and that a convincing solution cannot be found unless its terms are changed.

Second, it is a revealing symptom that, while an exact definition of law is believed to be necessary not only to those more abstract disciplines, such as philosophy and the general theory of law, but also to specific legal disciplines, the conventional definition is of little or no use to the latter.

Indeed, in determining the principles of public law and private law, but especially of the former, we have reached such an extent of coordination and subordination of the one to the other that they appear to derive directly and indirectly from the general conception of law and to vary, at least in terms of position and perspective, as the general conception does. The most serious disagreements we find in their determination clearly gesture towards the key and fundamental point that is to be tackled. Those who are familiar with the main problems, for example,

---

4   Even today, as Radbruch (1914: 30) notes [this does not apply to the 3rd edition (1932) published with the title *Rechtsphilosophie*], Kant's mocking words are well-placed: 'Jurists are still searching for a definition of their concept of law' [translator's translation from German].

5   I leave aside all those very particular, and yet relevant, points of view that give up 'the hope to identify the *quid proprium* of law, its specific aspect, or the definition that most philosophers care so much about'. See also [among others] Maggiore, 1916: 59 ff. [but see also Maggiore's other works that I will quote later on].

of international law, or constitutional law, or even ecclesiastical law, are aware that, more often than not, the discussion over these problems on the part of those who solve them differently turns out to be useless, even impossible, because there is no firm point of departure from which the discussion can take off. And doubtless, as has been sometimes noted,[6] this point of departure is the very same definition of law: 'the one on which they build, whether implicitly or explicitly, can well be agreed upon, but falls short of its goal, as it only contains irrelevant and undifferentiated elements'.

Furthermore, it is particularly important to identify the likely origin of current definitions of law. These have been propounded either by the discipline of private law, which has then imposed them on the others, or from points of view that have failed to overcome that of this discipline. These definitions, in fact, appear more apposite to private law than they are to other fields. Even within this field, as we will see, some questions would significantly benefit from drawing on a more complete concept of law; but there is no denying that, for most of its principles and problems, there is no need to portray the law other than as norm. But this is not the case with some branches of public law. It is known that this is not the sole example of the detrimental consequences engendered by the fact that many general concepts that are common to public law and private law have been considered unilaterally by the science of private law, while the science of public law either did not exist or was at a lower developmental stage. Consequently, these general concepts had to be revisited, corrected and completed by taking into account a host of new elements. Those who are acquainted with such a demanding but key process of integration and modification of concepts – which in the past were exclusively private law ones – undertaken by modern public lawyers, will readily understand the need that an analogous process be carried out for the definition of law itself, which, it is worth repeating, public law and philosophy of law have blindly borrowed from private law.

On the contrary, in order to provide this definition, we need to take into account what is true – and it is a lot – of the old, but also of the recent claim that the law, in its culminating and virtually, as it were, most essential part, is primarily public. I cannot agree with the very modern view that, by pushing this truth to the extreme, jettisons the distinction between public law and private law.[7] But the latter is undoubtedly a mere specification of the former, one of its forms and trajectories, one of its ramifications. Not only is private law conditional upon public law, which constitutes its root and trunk, and is necessary to its safeguard, but it is also constantly dominated by public law, albeit sometimes silently.[8] If this is the

6 For international law, see Anzilotti, 1913: 567; for ecclesiastical law, see Del Giudice: 20 ff.
7 See in particular Weyr, 1908: 529 ff.; Kelsen, 1911: X, 268 ff.; Wey, 1913: 183; Laun, 1913: 397 ff.; Kelsen, 1913: 55 ff.; Weyr, 1914: 439 ff.
8 Cf. Petrone's (1910: 134 ff.) observations, with which I disagree, in that they hinge on a profoundly state-centred conception of law. Similarly, see also Coviello (1915) [4th edn. 1929]. Also in the

case, we can evince the consequence that the elements of the general concept of law should be drawn more from public law than from private law. This means that we need to adopt an opposite approach to the one that has so far prevailed. Yet we should not go so far as to forge a definition of law that, drawn from an exclusive consideration of public law, runs the risk of being useless to private law, and thus replicating in reverse the difficulties I am now complaining about. In other words, a true, complete definition of law in general has to take into account elements that have hitherto been, so to say, overlooked. It also has to pursue the aim, not only in theory but also in practice, of being useful to all special branches of law, if it is true that, although not unified in all its subdivisions, law can nonetheless be reduced to a unified concept.

To further prove and complement what I have noted so far, I should like to add that jurists have usually constructed a notion of law that scarcely goes beyond the law that is applied, or is otherwise considered, in court.[9] Now, from the judge's point of view, it is natural to regard law as nothing other than a rule, or even a rule for decision. And given that even today the most part – which might actually be the fundamental part – of public law lacks judicial enforcement, which used to be almost entirely restricted to private law, this explains why the law has been primarily configured by keeping in mind private law norms for dispute resolution.

§ 3. There are more direct and substantial arguments that attest to the need to revise the concept of law.

Often the inaccuracies besetting the definition of very abstract ideas are caused and perpetuated by the indeterminacy of the words that correspond to them, by the poverty of language, which lacks distinct terms to distinguish them from similar words. Therefore, arguably also because of that, when one avers that the law is a norm of conduct, one neglects that the word 'law' is actually used in various senses. While such a difference in the use should be emphasised, it often goes unnoticed.

A first meaning denotes law as one or more norms – a law, a custom, a code, and so on – by considering each distinct norm or grouping them together, whether in light of their shared object, or their source, or the document that contains them, or other more or less extrinsic and particular criteria. In this case, the conventional definition appears thoroughly correct.

---

doctrine of the past claims that set out from the same point of view can be found. For example, Rossi affirmed that civil law is a segment originating from within constitutional law. On the contrary, the opposite view (adumbrated by many writers, sometimes used in the context of special arguments, and explicitly formulated by Ravà (1911: 102)) that only private law is genuine law, while public law relationships are not intrinsically legal, cannot be explained other than by keeping in mind what I have argued so far: the widespread definition of law is mainly formulated with reference to private law; and thus, in a way, expunges public law from its conceptual sphere. Therefore, this is a view that confirms the need to revise this definition from a public law vantage point.

9   One should bear in mind Maitland's contention that writing the history of English actions would amount to writing the history of English Law. Cf. Ehrlich's (1913: 8 ff.) observations.

Yet, often by law one means something that is not only more comprehensive, but also substantially different. This happens when one focuses on the whole legal order of an entity: for example, when one speaks of Italian or French law, of the law of the Church, etc., so as to embrace them in their entirety. In this case, in order for the common definition to obtain, it needs to resort to an expedient: that of conceiving each of these orders as a whole or as a complex of norms. However, I believe this is a makeshift at odds with the laws of logic governing definitory clauses and, because of this, is far from capturing reality.

In effect it is clear that, to define a whole legal order, one cannot only consider its distinct parts or those that are believed to be such, that is to say, the norms that the order comprises, and then claim that the order is the collection of these parts; rather, one needs to pinpoint the characterizing feature, the nature of this collection or this whole. This might not be necessary only if one reckons that a legal order is nothing but an arithmetic sum of various norms, just like a law, a regulation, a code – indeed viewed from a material and extrinsic standpoint – are nothing but a sequence of determinate articles that can be aggregated. If, on the contrary, one recognizes that, as is the case, a legal order in the sense mentioned above is not a sum of parts but a unity in itself – and a unity, it is worth stressing, not artificial or obtained through a process of abstraction, but a concrete and effective unity – one has also to recognize that it is something different from the distinct material elements that comprise it. Rather, we should acknowledge that we cannot have an adequate concept of norms that are embodied in a legal order unless we provide in advance the unitary concept of it. In much the same way, we cannot have a precise idea of the various limbs of the human being or of the wheels of a given machine unless we know in advance what a human being or that machine is.

§ 4. The need to consider a legal order as a unity, in the sense I mentioned above, has been emphasized many a time;[10] it has even become a sort of commonplace in the formulation of theories concerning the interpretation of laws. Yet surprisingly its logical consequences for the definition of law have never been unpacked and pushed to their logical consequences. For this reason, importantly, it remains little more than a claim, and often a mere hunch, a vague, nebulous and almost unfathomable idea, even within these very theories of interpretation that construct their fundamental principles upon it. These theories do not limit themselves to pointing out that the legal order is a 'system' of norms logically tied to each other, despite the fact that it takes shape on a piecemeal basis and is affected by imperfections. This might be explained in a simple manner with recourse to the intent of legislative bodies. These bodies not only know that, once a law is enacted, it connects with existing laws, as they also count on this

---

10 See among others Perozzi, 1912: 13 ff. See also Redenti, 1916: 5. [See recently Giannini, 1939: 111, and the authors mentioned therein, and also Romano, 1945: ch. 6, § 7.]

sort of amalgam that falls under the scope of interpretation.[11] But scholars often go beyond this concept, not only with a view to making it more colourful or to representing it with more vivid images but in order to hint at another, substantively different concept. In this way, for example, some speak of will, authority, of a *mens*, of an inner force of the legal order, separate from that of distinct norms, and also independent from the will of the legislator that laid them down; some maintain that the order itself constitutes a 'living whole', an 'organism', which has a 'typical power, though latent, to expand and to adapt itself', which permits making the analogy.[12] And it is known that, for the champions of the so-called evolutionary interpretation, the legal order's autonomous will is as amenable to change, with no need to incorporate new norms, as the social environment in which it is applied changes.

Now, leaving aside exaggerations that are so frequent with respect to this subject matter, but that are significant all the same, those concepts that, as I pointed out, have become commonplaces, can hardly be considered subtle artifices or cabals of the legists, inclined to place up in the air and to shroud in mystery the foundations of their interpretive undertaking. Rather, these are precious insights, still needing to be demonstrated, into the true conclusion that one cannot appreciate the nature of a legal order and grasp it as a whole if one's focus is not on its unity, but on the various norms comprising it. For the *quid* constituting its unity is something different and, at least to some extent, independent from the latter. Failure to cast light on such a unity, so conceived, at the same time explains the inexact meaning that is commonly attributed to the principle of so-called 'logical expansion' of distinct norms, as well as the claims, just as untenable, made by those who believe this principle can be dismantled and by doing so dispose of the part of truth it retains.[13]

§ 5. On the other hand, I think we could and should go farther. I have so far argued that the definition of law cannot coincide with the definition of the norms it comprises, even in the hypothesis that no elements could be found other than norms. It is my claim that this hypothesis, which appears to be an agreed-upon presupposition of all definitions of law, conflicts with reality. Therefore, these definitions, because of the reasons I mentioned, are untrue, or rather, logically incorrect. Not only do they leave what they are supposed to explain undetermined; they also exhibit the much more serious flaw whereby they proceed from an outright erroneous postulate.

This claim can be justified in many ways.

First of all, it is not pointless to rely on the widespread experience, or better, on the meaning that the expression 'legal order' spontaneously conjures up. When, in this sense, one speaks of, say, Italian law or French law, hardly ever does one think

---

11 On this point see Tuhr, 1910: 37 ff., and xi.
12 See Coviello, 1925: § 28; Miceli, 1914: § 135. After all, I might provide a variety of references on the same wavelength.
13 See e.g. Stampe, 1905: x; Donati, 1910: *passim*, and especially 126 ff.

only of a set of rules or invoke the image of that series of volumes comprising official statute- and decree-books. What jurists think of, and *a fortiori* non-jurists – who have no knowledge of the definitions of law I have spoken of – is something more lively and animated. It is, in the first place, the complex and multi-faceted organization of the Italian and French states, the numerous mechanisms and gears, the links between authorities and forces, that produce, modify, enforce, guarantee legal norms, but cannot be identified with them. In other words, the legal order, taken as a whole, is an entity that partly moves according to the norms, but most of all moves the norms like pawns on a chessboard – norms that therefore represent the object as well as the means of its activity, more than an element of its structure.[14] In some respect, it can be rightly said that norms appertain to the essential traits of law almost by reflex. For they, or at least some of them, can vary without any change being effected on those traits, and most often the substitution of particular norms for others is the effect rather than the cause of a substantial modification of the order. But for the time being it is pointless to anticipate the justification of this concept, on which I will return to detail its consequences.

§ 6. Meanwhile it might be useful to remain in a more concrete and less elevated domain, commencing from some arguments that display the various attempts at differentiating legal norms from other, more or less similar norms. One could hardly say that these attempts have generated satisfying results. This might lead us to suppose that a flaw besets the way in which the problem has been commonly framed. This flaw seems to be the following. By setting out from the postulate that law is nothing but norm, scholars have tried to pin down the specific character or characteristics of the legal norm; and yet this inquiry was not conducive to the notion of law, precisely because law cannot be always and in its entirety reduced to norms. As a consequence, scholars have tried to solve a problem, whose scope is wider, while believing that it is equivalent to another, narrower problem. Some, then, believed that a series of makeshifts and expedients could shed some light on this thesis. In effect, the solutions advanced so far, more coherent in their seeming variety than one might think, have a common element, which is to say, without being aware and without noticing it, they search for the distinguishing characteristics of the legal norm in elements that are alien to the concept of norm. In this way, they contradict the postulate they build on, and, however unwittingly, affirm that this concept is not adequate to the concept of law.

It is not pointless to examine from this perspective the common claim that the law is different from other norms above all on account of its 'formal' characteristics. This very expression should make us think, for it evidently hints at something that falls outside the legal norm and represents its shell or extrinsic aspect. In this way, we are still left questioning why the law should be defined with reference to this

---

14 [This observation is endorsed by Schmitt, 1934: 24].

guise, rather than to the substance of the norms that comprise the law. Rigorously, we should conclude that the law is not the norm: it is that which informs it and gives it a certain shape. But I do not want to insist on this type of considerations, not least because the word 'form' is one of those words that can be interpreted in many ways[15] (see § 14). Instead, let us see what these so-called formal characteristics are.

We can disregard some of them, either because not everyone agrees they are formal characters, or because, elsewhere in my studies, I should examine them in more detail. It will be sufficient to dwell on two characteristics that, although they are not always understood in the same way, are almost unanimously agreed upon. These are commonly labelled as the objectivity of the norm and the legal sanction.

§ 7. Based on the former of these characteristics, it is stated that law is composed of norms, which are detached from the consciousness of those who ought to comply with them, and have acquired their own autonomous existence. This is not to deny that the law is deeply rooted in that conscience, that it is projected in its intimate core and it is not a shining reflection of it; but the law transcends, exceeds and conflicts with it. Generally, individuals recognize one another as associates, and are spontaneously inclined to collaborate and to respect each other's liberties; and yet, since disagreements and disputes can always occur, a higher conscience has to step in, one that might be able to reflect and represent the unification of them. This conscience, that embodies the reasons for the coexistence and the system through which individuals join together, that serves as a mediator, that calls for a relationship of the parties with each other as well as with the whole, that is something of the incarnation of a social *self*, of the typical, abstract, objective *socius* – this all is the law. From this derives the so-called formal position of law, which is defined as the domain of objectivity.[16]

Nonetheless, this logically implies the following principle: law is not, or is not only, the norm that in this way is established but the very entity that establishes

---

15 See Del Vecchio, 1905: 173. [Indeed, when Del Vecchio (1921a: 6) objects that the formal characters of law amount to its essential characters because *forma dat esse rei*, he is perfectly right; but he is using the word 'form' in a philosophical sense that is not exactly the one I am referring to.]

16 See Petrone, 1910 and Petrone, 1897: 367 ff. See also Miceli, 1906: 197 ff.; Miceli, 1914: § 54. Croce (1915: pp. 323 ff.), in keeping with his thesis that the law can be reduced to the economy, places social norms and self-ascribed norms under the same category. By doing so, he intends to efface the formal elements of law, given by objectivity and sanction, as they represent empirical concepts that cannot be of any use to philosophers. I cannot scrutinize Croce's theory in this context; I would just like to point out that, by denying from an exclusively philosophical viewpoint the autonomy of the concept of law, which he displaces in a broader category, this view cannot provide any basis for those who aim to affirm the existence and autonomy of that concept, although in an empirical sense. In other words, whatever the philosophical value of that view, it does not have, and does not aim to have, any for genuine legal science, which can hardly give up constructing a concept of law without denying itself. On the 'intimacy' of all authorities and all laws, which are claimed to be present 'even in the *foro interno* of the person whom is deemed individual', see also Gentile, 1916: 39 ff.; 47 ff.

that norm.[17] The objectifying process giving rise to the legal phenomenon does not commence with the production of a rule, but in a prior phase: norms are nothing but a manifestation, one of law's multiple manifestations, a device to impose the power of that social *self* I spoke of. I can see no reason why the latter should be a term *a quo* of the law.[18] This is the law itself, and the norm is nothing but its voice, or better, one of its voices, one of the ways in which it operates and achieves its end. Its existence and structure, representing the acme of the element of objectivity that is claimed to be proper to and characteristic of the law, are to be located within the law's boundaries. The objectivity of norms is but a much weaker and sometimes quite pale reflection of the objectivity of such an entity; it could not even be defined without the latter. The norm is not objective only because it is written or otherwise exactly formulated; if this were the case, then we could not distinguish it from many other norms that are amenable to such an extrinsic formulation, on top of the fact that at times some legal norms, e.g. customs, lack this kind of precision. The characteristic of objectivity is one that is anchored to the impersonality of the power that elaborates and establishes the rule, to the fact that this power is something that transcends and raises individuals: it is the law itself. If we neglect this concept, the so-called characteristics of objectivity either do not mean anything at all, or, worse, entail errors.

This is so true that, as is abundantly known, there are examples of legal orders – that not only can be imagined in the abstract but that existed in history, where neither written nor unwritten norms, in the proper sense of the word, were available. It has been repeatedly said that it is possible to conceive of an order that leaves no room for the figure of the legislator, but only for that of the judge. The claim that, as judges settle an actual dispute they also issue the norm that governs their judicial practice, is but an expedient insinuated by our modern mind-set. On the contrary, the truth is that judicial practice can be determined by the so-called justice of the single case, by equity or other elements, which is something quite different than the proper legal norm, while the latter, by its own nature, concerns a series or set of actions and is therefore abstract and general. If this is the case, then the legal element in the hypothesis I am alluding to is to be found not in the norm, which is lacking, but in the power, in the official who expresses that objective social conscience with different means than those that are typical of more complex and evolved orders.

After all, those who champion the burgeoning view that law is not only comprised of having the quality of generality, but also of individual and concrete

---

17 In this light, the theory that ties the bindingness of law to the associates' recognition has pointed out that this recognition does not so much refer to the norm as such, as to the authority from which it arises. See Anzilotti, 1912: 27.

18 Particular objections to this view, that I believe to be correct, have been advanced from another perspective, which I will deal with later on; see Petrone, 1910: 140 ff., and others whom I will mention below.

precepts, have also to admit either that those are to be considered as norms, or that the law contains elements other than norms. Now, it seems doubtless to me that a norm is a norm as long as it is general and abstract, and attempts to stretch this concept in order for it to cover measures or, better, certain special measures, are vain and specious. In fact, the famous constitutional law issue of whether the so-called material law has to be general is for this reason frequently framed incorrectly. The postulate, which I believe to be erroneous, is advanced that the law in a proper or substantive sense does not contain legal norms; at this point, one is caught in the insoluble dilemma of whether one should refute the legal character of some measures that evidently form part of the law, or if one by norm should mean what, no less evidently, is not norm.[19]

In sum, one always winds up in the same place. The so-called objectivity of the legal order cannot be confined and limited to legal norms. It refers to them and gets reflected in them, but takes place in a context that is logically and materially anterior to the norms and, at times, even often, takes on elements that cannot be identified and confused with those that are relative to the position of the norms. Which is to say that norms are, or can be, part of a legal order, but are far from exhausting it.

§ 8. The other so-called formal element of law – the sanction – which some believe is the sole formal element, elicits similar considerations.[20] It is pointless to mention the many questions about what we should mean by sanction and, as a consequence, to determine whether or not it is necessary to replace this word with some other word that might best account for this concept. If it is possible to speak of an irrefutable bindingness of the law, if it is a coaction or coercion, as some prefer to say; if, on the contrary, it is sufficient, as I believe it is, a simple guarantee, whether direct or indirect, immediate or mediated, pre-emptive or repressive, certain or merely probable, and thus uncertain, provided that it is, in a sense, pre-ordered and organized within the framework itself of the legal order. What I intend to emphasize is that, when one says that the law is a norm backed by sanction, however one may understand it, in no way – although many seem to think otherwise – can this mean that the law is a norm accompanied by another norm threatening sanction. If this were the case, then we should necessarily conclude that the latter is not a necessary and essential feature of law. This conclusion has in fact been reached by those who have pondered all the logical consequences of that premise. In substance, they reasoned as follows. According to the dominant view, a precept can be said to be legal only when it is accompanied by another norm that, by granting a right of coercion, is able to protect the right created by the former. Formally, these different precepts can be coupled, but essentially are to be regarded as uncoupled. They bring about two rights, of which the one

19 [For a more accurate and partly different formulation of these concepts, see Romano, 1945: ch. 7, § 2, fn. 2 and 3; ch. 11, § 5, fn. 1; ch. 22, § 1, fn. 10.]
20 See especially Jhering, 1897: 435 ff.

is primary or principal, while the other secondary and ancillary; hence, they do not stem from the same norm.[21] At the same time, for the second precept to be deemed legal, it should be accompanied by a third one, and the third by a fourth one, and so on and so forth; in this way, we necessarily come to a point where this precept is not available at all, and we are left with a norm without sanction.[22] In truth, this line of reasoning, which is right *in se*, and has been used to deny sanction being a necessary feature of law, in my opinion simply demonstrates that its premise is groundless, and hence can well be utilized. Indeed, it is my opinion that the sanction can be neither contained nor threatened by any specific norm: it can be immanent and latent in the mechanisms, in the organic apparatus of the legal order taken as a whole, it can be a force operating indirectly, a practical guarantee that does not give rise to any subjective right, and thus to any norm from which this law emerges, a constraint that is inborn in, and necessary to, social power. Put otherwise, one's saying that the sanction is a feature of law implies saying, whether intentionally or not, that the law comprises elements other than legal norms, and that these are bound up with, or even hung up on, other elements from which their force derives. In this way, the sanction or, rather, those other elements, far from being complementary or ancillary to the norms, actually pre-exists them: they form the base on which norms are constructed, their root, and, while defining law, it is necessary to take them into account ahead of the norms.[23] As I have pointed out, if one only concentrates on norms, one ends up denying sanction being a feature of law; and it is of no help to stop midway, as has sometimes happened, by including this element but at the same time attributing an extra-legal character to it. Indeed, it would be illogical to search for an essential feature of law outside the law, and therefore this claim necessarily merges with the other claim that crosses the sanction off the features of law.[24] Nonetheless, it is significant, in that it makes it clear that if law, as the conventional view has it, is norm, then the sanction cannot be considered as law, and yet it must be accommodated in some sort of way (see § 22).

§ 9. Having so far deployed the thesis as a critique of the prevailing theories, I will now vindicate it through more constructive arguments. Some of the difficulties in accepting this thesis are created by the over-literal sense that is attached to the expression 'legal order'. In fact, it conjures up the idea of rule and norm in such a way that it is hard to imagine an order that cannot be entirely reduced to that idea. Still, it is evident that this difficulty is not substantial, but has an extrinsic origin, almost exclusively linguistic: as I noted above, it is one of those difficulties generated by the indeterminacy and poverty of language, which in turn are the root causes

---

21 On this point, see on the same wavelength Anzilotti, 1902a: 61, and the authors cited there.
22 Triepel, 1899: 103 ff.
23 [Among those who at present embrace these concepts, see Ago, 1943: 24 ff.]
24 I will come back to this claim (Marinoni, 1914: 35 ff.) in § 22.

of the inaccuracies in the definitions of highly abstract concepts. To overcome this difficulty, it would suffice to substitute the word 'order' for some other word that does not evoke – because of our mental habits – the idea of norm so forcefully, but at the same time does not cut it out – as this would be just as mistaken.

§ 10. In my opinion, the concept of law must encompass the following essential features:

a.   First, it must be traced back to the concept of society. This in two recipro-cal senses that complete one another. What remains in the purely individual sphere, and fails to overstep the individual's life as such, is not law (*ubi ius ibi societas*).[25] Moreover, there is no society, in the proper sense of the word, unless the legal phenomenon manifests itself within it (*ubi societas ibi ius*). Neverthe-less, this latter claim presupposes a concept of society that I need to bring to the foreground. By society I do not mean a simple relationship between individuals, such as e.g. friendship, where no legal elements are to be found.[26] Rather, society is an entity constituting a concrete unity, though formally and extrinsically – one that is distinguished from the individuals who comprise it. And this has to be an effectively constituted unity. To give another example, a class or a group of people that is not organized as such, but is only deter-mined by mere affinities between people themselves, is not society proper. I will return to this point later on.

b.   Secondly, the concept of law must encompass the idea of social order. This is necessary to eliminate all of the elements that can be reduced to mere arbi-trariness [*arbitrio*] or material (viz., not ordered) force. After all, this principle is but one aspect of the preceding one; it indeed has to be understood as a pure corollary of the latter. Any manifestation of law, by dint of being social, is ordered as far as its population is concerned.[27]

---

25 On Croce's (1915: 323) view, see what I said earlier (fn. 16). Rosmini (1841: 146–147) also expunged 'from the notion of law in general not just the concept of society, but even that of a *real* coexistence', but he meant to say he believed a 'possible coexistence' was sufficient for individuals to consider themselves 'in a hypothetical relation with possible counterparts'. [After all, it is known that the contention that the law is not bound up with any form of society re-emerges continuously, even in the most recent literature. Yet, no matter how one assesses it from a philosophical view-point, this conception entails a notion of law that is not the positive law from which the jurist has to set out.]

26 The fact that in relationships such as friendship the element of authority is also present as it stems from esteem, intimate recognition, etc. (Gentile, 1916: 47 ff.) naturally does not prevent distin-guishing such a broadly conceived society from the other strictly conceived societies in which the legal phenomenon is produced.

27 Evidently I am not bringing up the question that is often brought up within philosophy of the general relation between law and force; nor am I dealing with that particular aspect of the prob-lem – which is subordinate to the broader issue of the morality of law – concerning the relations between so-called just law and the unjust law that is however coercively enforced.

c.   The social order that the law brings about is not the one produced by the presence, however obtained, of norms governing social relationships. Such a social order does not exclude these norms, and indeed it uses and includes them under its scope; but at the same time, it oversteps and surpasses them. This means that the law, before it is norm, before it concerns a simple relationship or set of social relationships, is an organization, a structure, a position of the very society in which it develops and that this very law constitutes as a unity, as an entity in its own right. This is also a corollary of what I observed above when I clarified and delimited the type of society where the legal phenomenon arises.

If this is the case, the concept I believe to be necessary and sufficient to provide an accurate account of the concept of law – as a legal order taken as a whole and as a unity – is that of institution. Any legal order is an institution, and vice versa, any institution is a legal order: the equation between the two concepts is necessary and absolute.

Thus, I believe the expression 'law' can have a twofold meaning. It can denote:

a.   A complete and unified order, that is, an institution;
b.   A precept or a complex of precepts (whether they are norms or specific measures), gathered and assorted in various ways, that I label 'institutional' in order to distinguish them from non-legal ones; doing so enables the connection they have with the overall order or, rather, with the institution of which they are components to be highlighted. This connection is necessary and sufficient to attribute a legal character to them.

I will need to elaborate on this latter point elsewhere in my work. For now, I intend to focus on the former aspect of law in order to emphasize both the convergence and the divergence between my conception of law and the prevailing ones. To commence, I first need to clarify in more detail the meaning I attribute to the word institution, which lends itself to many interpretations.

§ 11. Indeed, it should be noted that in a language that may be defined not so much vernacular as extra-legal, people commonly speak of institutions in a very broad sense, one that comes close to the way I use it. Moreover, there are common expressions such as 'political institutions', 'religious institutions' and the like. On the contrary, in legal parlance we draw on quite a narrow concept of institution, and it was not until recently that we have little by little expanded and reappraised this concept, although we still fail to use it comprehensively.

Until recently, in the eyes of jurists the institution was nothing but a species of the genus legal persons. Of late it has been used to denote those institutions that are to be distinguished from corporations. The relative concept, therefore, has only featured in the theory of moral subjects of law. Since this theory was developed in the field of private law, the idea of institution, at least in part, has been of no use to the field that most needed it, that is, the field of public law. To a limited extent, this was mitigated by the longstanding tendency to consider moral entities as entities of public interest. Despite this, the fact remains that the institution has always been thought of as neither more nor less than a legal person. It is necessary to point out, though, that I will not take up this concept in this sense and within this sphere.

In recent times, however, French and German scholars have begun to widen this concept with a view to taking it out of the sphere where it developed: in the German doctrine, sneakily, occasionally, and for the most part mistakenly, with regard to legal persons; in the French doctrine, with more autonomous developments, with regard to both public law themes and some private law ones, but not always with a rigorous and accurate approach.

In this sense, I would like to recall the theory[28] that identifies the base of legal persons with an organization, and thus depicts this latter concept as anterior to the concept of legal person. On this account, the organization or institution (*Einrichtung*) is not a natural entity with a life of its own; as it is an entity serving as a means to a social end, an entity that is considered as a legal subject. But what this organization, this new social dimension, should be like is left unquestioned. It is even stated that, as it is an elementary concept, it is not amenable to further scrutiny.[29] Anyway, let me stress again that in the German doctrine this concept is used to clarify that of legal person. For present purposes, then, it is of indirect importance. I can sum it up by saying that in the legal world there are entities (no matter if and how they are understood as endowed with legal personality) that are not proper natural bodies, as the so-called organistic theory suggested; instead, they are simple institutions, that is, organizations made up of more persons (corporations) or other elements (foundations).[30]

German administrative law has established the figure of public institute (*Anstalt*). This is not a legal person, but an ensemble, a unity of material and personal means in the hands of public administrative bodies, which are designed to serve permanently a certain public interest: the army, a school, an observatory, an academy, the mail service, etc.[31]

In France, in many of his texts and later modifications,[32] Hauriou has delineated a broader concept of institution. He claims that the institution is, for all the branches of public law, a general category apt to explain a host of principles. It then lends itself to remarkable applications.

---

28 See Ferrara, 1915: 315 ff. [and more recently Ferrara, 1938: 27 ff.].

29 Behrend, 1905: 312 ff. It is worth noting that Behrend confines the figure of legal personality to the field of private law, and therefore the institutions he talks about do not encompass public ones, which I believe to be the most typical.

30 For this juxtaposition between organism and organization, see Enneccerus, 1911: § 96 (231, Part I).

31 See in particular Mayer, 1917: II, 51; Fleiner, 1913: § 18.

32 The latest formulation of his own theory Hauriou has proposed, to which I will refer, is contained in Hauriou, 1916: 41 ff. [Subsequently Hauriou returned to this issue in many of his writings: in later editions of the book I just mentioned and in Hauriou, 1925 and 1929. On Hauriou's theory see Leontovitsch, 1937 and 1941: 85 ff.].

According to Hauriou, the institution is a social organization, that is 'every permanent organization through which, within a determined social group, organs endowed with ruling power serve the aims that concern that group through an activity coordinated with the whole of it' [translator's translation from French]. Indeed, we should distinguish between two types of institution. Some belong to the category of inert things (e.g. a piece of land, which is considered in its own right in the real estate registry, a country road, etc.), while others form social bodies, that is, corporatist institutions. While both the former and the latter are social individualities, only corporatist institutions are to be considered as figures in their own right within the legal system. For, unlike the others, they are endowed with autonomy. This means that every such institution is a genuine social reality, a bordered entity, separate from its members, which has its own personality, or at least, is eligible for personification. Hence, it can be considered in two respects. First, from the viewpoint of its relational life, which brings out its subjective individuality, its quality as a legal person. Second, from the viewpoint of its inner life, which makes it an objective individuality. This latter aspect, which coincides with its autonomy, implies that the corporatist institution is a primary source of law, in that it spontaneously generates the three forms of law: regulative, customary and statutory.

This is the fundamental core of Hauriou's view, whose developments I will discuss here only as long as it will be necessary to justify a few quick critical remarks on which I intend to dwell.

The French jurist's main virtue is, in my opinion, that he suggested subsuming the general concept of institution – of which we had just a few, quite feeble traces in the terminology – under the legal world, rather than under political and sociological speculation.[33] In addition, he opportunely decoupled the concept of institution from legal personality, which might overlap with it as the appropriate circumstances arise, but might also fail to do so. Perhaps such a distinction was clearer in earlier formulations of Hauriou's theory, but even today his elaborations on the institution, considered in an objective sense, are remarkable.

However, it seems that the figure of the institution can be delineated more thoroughly and at the same time more precisely, and, in addition, that its essence, its basic mark, can be portrayed differently.

I will discuss my own thinking in more detail in the subsequent sections, but I would like to point out here that which I see as unjustified, that is, the criterion whereby Hauriou has restricted the concept of institution to one kind of social organization

---

33 This observation applies to the modern doctrine, which I have considered, and not to the more ancient one, which, as far as this issue is concerned, exhibits nuances that today get mistakenly unnoticed. For example, one might think of Hobbes's (*Leviathan*: ch. 22) analysis of 'systemata', and Pufendorf's (*De jure naturae et gentium*, I: ch. I) analysis of 'entia moralia'. Unlike physical entities that come about through *creatio*, these entities arise through *impositio* (word which the French translator, Berbeyrac, renders with *institution*). However, it has to be noted that Pufendorf's *entia moralia* only those 'ad analogiam substantiarum concepta' can be likened to institutions in the way I conceive of them.

apt to reach a certain level of development and perfection. In addition to those institutions that he qualifies as corporatist, there are others that should equally be accommodated in the system of law; namely, institutions that have an existence of their own, independent of the existence of particular individuals, and that are endowed with a more or less wide autonomy. By the same token, I cannot agree on the idea that institutions only are organized entities with a constitutional and representative structure; whose members enjoy a liberty which I cannot see how we can qualify. . . political, when it comes, for example, to shareholders in a corporation; that have decentred and separated powers; that adhere to the principle of publicity; and that, finally, have a constitutional status. This is evidence that Hauriou was carried away with the idea of modelling his institutions on the broadest among them, that is, the state, even the modern state, while it behoved him to delineate a very general figure, whose contingent characteristics can vary, and actually vary indefinitely.

Moreover – and this relates to my own view, which I already mentioned, and that I will need to demonstrate constructively – I do not believe that the institution is a source of law and that, therefore, law is an effect, a product of the former. Rather, I believe that the concept of institution and the concept of a legal order, considered as a unity and as a whole, are absolutely identical. But this conclusion could not be reached before we overcame the traditional view that thinks of law only as a norm or complex of norms.

On the contrary, Hauriou maintains that it 'approximates' an ensemble of things; more, 'it is just a particular kind of thing; in truth, it is both an active thing and a type of mechanism' [translator's translation from French]. Apart from the fact that this sentence raises a few uncertainties and doubts, I would like to note that most probably this conception has been elaborated on by exclusion rather than by direct arguments. We rightly denied the institution the status of a legal person because, even when it is endowed with personality, it is but the base for the latter and thus something that is anterior to it. Nobody thought it should be identified with the overall legal order; the idea then came up spontaneously, not to say necessarily, of listing it among things. Now it is true that the label 'res publica', by which the Romans designated their state, that is, the most important institution, might support this view. Yet, it is evident that, if the word 'thing' is taken in its specific legal meaning, it can hardly render the concept of institution, for it even annihilates it as a self-standing category. If it is taken in a broader sense, then it fails to explain the concept itself, because we still need to determine what this sense should be. In reality, Hauriou wanted to bring to light the institution's objective character, but this character does not imply that the institution is to be considered as an object, a *res*. Indeed the institution is an objective legal order.[34]

---

34 [Subsequently, the French doctrine has elaborated on other concepts of institution, different from Hauriou's as well as from my concept, and anyway from viewpoints that exceed legal inquiry. See Renard, 1930; Delos, 1931; Gurvitch, 1932, 1935. On these authors see, among others, Bobbio, 1936. See also Desqueyrat, 1935.]

§ 12. By institution I mean any entity or social body. This pithy and simple definition has to be followed by a longer comment.

1. The entity I am talking about must possess an objective and concrete existence, and its individuality, however immaterial, must be outward and visible.[35] It is to emphasize this character that I also called it social 'body'. This implies that I use the word institution in its proper meaning, not in the other, quite frequent but merely figurative sense. Accordingly, when in the language of everyday life we speak of e.g. the institution of the press, or in legal parlance of the institution, or, more often, of the institution [*istituto*] of donation, of trade, etc., we do not mean to refer to an actual social entity, but, in the first case, to the concomitant manifestation of particular, disjointed and often divergent forces, and, in the second case, to the various relationships or distinct norms that are conceptually glued together because of the common shape of their typical characters.[36]

35 [It is not always easy to determine when we are faced with an institution that possesses the characteristics I delineated in the text. There are borderline cases: for example, when we are faced with very rudimentary organizations such as, for example, people standing in queue at a bank counter or waiting to enter a club, or those less embryonic organizations but 'at a diffuse state', which ideally put together compliance with customs or other shared rules, games and sports lovers, and the so-called chivalry, those who obey particular worldly customs, etc. On these institutions, see Cesarini Sforza, 1929: 25 ff., 1933 (see the authors mentioned there: Perreau, Huguet, etc.); Calamandrei, 1929: 145 ff., 1934. In any case, however large the criteria may be for identifying the features of institution in very simple and scarcely developed forms of society, I do not think we can go so far as to say that the legal phenomenon can be found in 'all states of human coexistence', as Orlando (1926b; 1940: 223 ff.) believes.]

36 Yet, sometimes scholars have advanced a concept of the legal institution that would seem at odds with its character of pure and simple abstraction, unless we suppose that the expressions they use are meant to be graphic images of this very same concept. See e.g. Jhering's (1895: 10) observations in the programme with which he commenced the publication of his *Jahrbücher für die Dogmatik des bürgerlichen Rechts*, which while they seem to go too far as to the legal institution [*istituto*], are appropriate to my institution [*istituzione*]: 'The entirety of law now no longer appears as a system of sentences, thoughts, but rather as the embodiment of juridical existences, as they were, living beings, subservient spirits. We want to maintain the idea of the juridical body, since it is the least complicated and most natural' [translator's translation from German]'. It is apparent that Jhering intuited those essential traits of law that I endeavoured to illuminate, although he looked out for them where they could not be found. [Other scholars, on the contrary, either do not distinguish or confuse the two notions of institution, that is, *istituto* and *istituzione* (in the sense of social body). This is what some of the French authors mentioned in fn. 35 do. When Croce (1945: 133) speaks of *istituti*, he gives this word 'a very broad sense, or rather, one that encompasses all practical conducts of individual and human societies, from the most intimate feelings to the most visible modes of life' – this naturally does not interest the jurist. He then speaks of *istituzioni* in a literal sense: '[. . .] the family, the state, trade, industry, the army, and so on', and gives the word 'istituzione' a much broader meaning than that of entity and social body, which, among the examples he gives, refers only to the family and the state. Although he remains within the scope of the law, Orestano (1941: 103, 143) evidently confuses the two concepts, which prevents him from correctly assessing my theory.]

2. In addition, my claim is that an institution is a social entity or body, in the sense that it is a manifestation of the social, not purely individual, nature of human beings. This does not mean that the base of an institution cannot be but human beings connected to each other. Such a connection gives rise to a particular form of institution. For some of them are actually comprised, among other elements, of more individuals, who may coexist or succeed each other, bound together by their common or contiguous interests, or by a goal, a mission they pursue. But there are institutions with a different base that are composed of an array of means, whether material or immaterial, personal or real, patrimonial or with an ideal nature. These are designed to permanently serve a determinate purpose, not to the advantage of the members of these very institutions, but of non-members, who are but the addressees. In this case, like all institutions, these go to the advantage of human beings, are administered and governed by human beings, and yet they are not composed of human beings. After all, broadly speaking, and leaving aside controversial aspects that are not relevant to the present discussion, as far as these concepts are concerned we can refer to their developments in the context of the theory of legal persons. The distinction this theory has advanced between corporations and foundations or strictly speaking institutions, as well as the subdivisions of these two fundamental categories, are also applicable to institutions without personality. This latter quality requires an entity to have a specific structure, but not the one that is mentioned when the above categories are outlined. For these categories can be referred to as legal persons only as long as these are a species of a broader genus, that is, the genus 'institutions'.

3. The institution is a bordered entity, which can be considered in itself and for itself precisely because it has an individuality of its own. This does not mean that it cannot connect with other entities, other institutions, so as for it to be more or less integral part of them from another vantage point. Accordingly, along with simple institutions, there are a great many institutions that can be described as complex – institutions of institutions. For example, while the state is itself an institution, it is encompassed by the broader institution of the international community, while other institutions can be distinguished inside it. Such are sub-state public bodies, municipalities, provinces, its various agencies understood as departments; in the modern state, the so-called legislative, judicial and administrative powers, as unities constituted by departments connected with each other; institutions delineated in particular within administrative law, such as schools, academies, establishments of various types; and so on. Each institution's autonomy does not have to be absolute, but can merely be relative, as its conception only results from certain points of view, which can vary. There are institutions that affirm themselves as perfect, self-sufficient, at least basically, that have the means to attain their own goals. There are imperfect or less perfect institutions that hinge on other institutions in many ways. While they might simply coordinate with the latter, sometimes there are higher entities that encompass and subordinate the former. This

subordination can take different shapes, depending on whether or not there are institutions that are more or less an integral part of them (as is the case with state departments or institutions), or else as just protected or safeguarded (as is the case with so-called private entities). Finally, there are institutions that affirm themselves by assuming an antithetical position to the others, which in their turn can deem the former to be unlawful, as is the case with entities pursuing goals in conflict with state law, or schismatic churches in the eyes of the church they left. These potential aspects of institutions will be treated later on in more detail. For now, it suffices to mention them systematically, also with a view to foregrounding the width of the concept of institution I have advanced.

4. The institution is a firm and permanent unity. In other words, its identity does not get lost, at least always and necessarily, as its distinct elements vary, as well as its members, patrimony, means, interests, addressees, norms, and so on. It can regenerate itself but continue to be itself without losing its own individuality. Here lies the possibility of considering it as a self-standing body, so as not to identify it with that which might be necessary to give it life but, at the same time, by giving it life, merges with it.[37]

§ 13. I have so far pinpointed the essential traits of the institution, that is, those that allow investigating its essence, while I passed over others that will be examined later. What is this essence like?

So far I have deliberately eschewed a word, one that might seem necessary and sufficient to clarify the nature of the institution, to wit, 'organization'. Indeed, there is no doubt that the institution is a social organization. As I illustrated, by doing so some have tried to define those institutions that are legal persons, claiming that such a basic and elementary concept cannot be analyzed further. However, apart from the understandable diffidence engendered by such a clichéd term, that is often used to cover up that which one fails to explain or clarify, I would like to stress (and this is crucial) that the concept of organization cannot be of any help to jurists unless it is turned into a legal concept. To this end, paraphrasing or alluding to it through words with an identical or similar meaning is not enough. Insofar as one speaks of 'corpus mysticum', structure or edifice or social system, or even mechanism to differentiate the organization from a natural organism, the terminology in use might well be correct, it might well serve to make the idea imaginative and

---

37 [My concept of institution has often been charged with indeterminacy: among others, see Orlando, 1929: 250; and recently Gueli, 1942: 12 ff., fn. 7. I cannot make sense of this criticism, which many reiterate mechanically. To define the institution, it would have sufficed to say that it is a social entity or body. For I could have omitted the other specifications that I added, in that jurists cannot do without the concept of social entity or body, as it is a fundamental and, at the same time, elementary concept, without which we fail to understand others that presuppose it. Among them, for example, the concept of family, 'de facto entity', legal person, at least the shapes legal persons take within modern law. The more one tries to clarify certain elementary concepts, the more one makes them more obscure.]

plastic, but it is not legal. Therefore, it might help jurists but it does not discharge them from the duty to replace it with another word, one that has both the form and the substance that are needed to draw this concept in their own realm, which is not that of sociology.[38]

The solution to this problem, it seems to me, is the one I put forward: the institution is a legal order, a self-standing, more or less complete sphere of law. The essential characters of law, which I singled out above (§ 10), coincide with the institution's. Without doubt, the institution is an order. The words organization, system, structure, edifice, etc., used to qualify the institution, are indeed meant to put emphasis on this concept; the etymological meaning of the word 'state', which nowadays designates the most important institution, while in the past it was also used to designate other public entities (especially the Communes), is no different. That such an order is always and necessarily legal can be attested by noting that the characterizing purpose of law is that of social organization.[39] The law does

38 [These observations and the subsequent ones have been overlooked, or even misinterpreted, by those who contended that my inquiry is not jurisprudential, but pre-jurisprudential, and thus socio-logical, that it fails to identify the difference between the fact of social order and the legal order that it brings about, and so on (see Bonucci, 1920: 97 ff.; Bobbio, 1936: 35–36; Capograssi, 1939: 6 ff.; Ziccardi, 1943: 72; and others). Some of these criticisms have been deftly rejected by Orlando (1940a: 17 ff.). He argued that 'these criticisms turn out to be the highest praise, as they attest to what I claim represents an incomparable virtue of Romano's treatise, to wit, that it is a perfect type of inquiry apposite to general public law'. On my part, I would like to add that it was my aim to include in the legal world a fact of social order that was generally believed to be anterior to the law; to this end, I tried to demonstrate that this mistake is the source of most faults and incongruities of conventional definitions of law, especially as these definitions are all, to different degrees, forced to employ non-legal elements or concepts. The criticisms to my conception of law mentioned above, in reality, should be levelled against the other conceptions. Moreover, whatever the assessment of my conception, one should at least acknowledge that I tried to provide a jurisprudential definition of law. It would have been impossible to achieve this result unless I had reduced the legal phenom-enon to the social-institutional phenomenon, and the latter, in its turn, to the legal phenomenon, so as to identify the former with the latter. This entails no vicious circle, tautology or *petitio principii*. For it just proves the complete autonomy of the concept of law and its capacity to contain and encompass itself. Indeed, Orlando (1926a, 249) averred that, as far as my conception is concerned, it cannot be said 'that it is the order that generates the institution or the institution that generates the order. In a sense, either concept becomes the generator and the generated, the one vis-à-vis the other'. Also Messineo (1943, I, fn. 10), although he places emphasis on the normative aspect of the concept of law, points out that the norm and the institution come about *uno actu* and are in a relationship of 'mutual implication': the institution is such insofar as it establishes norms, while the norm gets its force from the institution. That is right: this is the theorem or the series of theorems that I set out to prove, and this intent is the leitmotif of my overall work.]

39 Filomusi Guelfi, 1917: § 13. Among those who contributed to bringing this character of law to sur-face I should mention Gierke, who arguably devoted all his oeuvre to substantiating this thesis. Just as important might be the distinction made by some authors, in a narrower sphere and from dif-ferent viewpoints, between normative and constructive laws (Duguit, 1901: 551 ff.; Duguit, 1913: 77 ff. [similarly Duguit, 1927: I, 172 ff.]) and between legal norms for decision and legal norms for organization (Ehrlich, 1913, and other, preceding texts).

not simply consecrate the principle of the coexistence of individuals, but above all takes it upon itself to overcome the weakness and limitedness of their forces, to exceed their feebleness, to perpetuate particular goals beyond their natural life, by creating social entities that are more powerful and durable than individuals. Such entities establish a synthesis, a syncretism in which the individual gets caught. It not only regulates the individuals' activity, but also their position, at times superior and at other times inferior to the others'; things and energies are instrumental in permanent and general ends, and all this with a set of guarantees, powers, subjections, liberties, checks, which systematize and unify an array of scattered elements. This means that the institution, as I understand it here, is the prime, original and essential manifestation of law. The law cannot develop but into an institution, and the institution exists and can be defined as such only inasmuch as it is created and preserved by the law.

§ 14. Evidence for this can be obtained by observing that, within the institution, there are certainly manifest and active forces other than the law, but these are, and cannot but be, merely individual or in any case unorganized forces. Every force that is actually social and thus is organized, for this very reason, morphs into law. If this institution, as sometimes happens, turns against another institution, this can provide the grounds for denying its legal character, or even for considering it as anti-legal in the eyes of the institution, or better, the order that the former challenges and against which it operates as an upsetting and anti-social force. Nevertheless, it is a legal order when we leave out of consideration this relationship and this standpoint to focus on the institution in itself as long as it sways and governs its own elements. As I noted, a revolutionary society or a gang are not law for the state they aim to wipe out or whose laws they infringe; likewise, a schismatic sect is declared to be outlaw by the Church. But this does not exclude the fact that in these cases we are presented with institutions, organizations, orders, which, taken in isolation and in their own right, are legal. On the contrary, something is not legal if and only if it is not organized.

I will come back to this issue from another vantage point. For now, it suffices to emphasize that this is the crucial truth contained in the quite widespread view that the law is nothing but 'form', and that its material contents are irrelevant to it and its concept. There are no elements, forces or social norms that are necessarily and absolutely antithetical to the law, or even just distinct from it. The antithesis, or at least the opposition to the law is present only in that which is irretrievably antisocial, or rather, individual by nature. All that lacks this characteristic might stay outside the law, until it is placed within an institution, until it gets shaped within its form, that is, within the structure, the regime of the latter.

This is why it is altogether pointless to try, as many do, to pin down the characters that distinguish law from religion, morality, customs, so-called conventions, economy, technical rules, etc. Each of these manifestations of the human spirit can in whole or in part be incorporated in the legal domain and give content to the latter, every time it falls within the scope of an institution. The celebrated contention that the law represents the ethical *minimum*[40] is partly true and partly seriously mistaken. The law not only represents an amount of morality, but also of economy, customs, technique, etc. And this amount, which cannot be circumscribed and measured *a priori*, might not be a *minimum*. As far as modern states are concerned, it might generally be true that only the fundamental and essential principles of ethics are organized and thus made legal by their orders. However, this could not apply to other states that undertook and will undertake a broader and more demanding moral mission; let alone to other institutions whose objective, perhaps the only one, is this moral mission. By the same token, we can imagine a socialist state that centralizes and organizes most economic manifestations. In this regard, the law of the Church is highly significant, as many ethical and religious principles have acquired a legal character, along with principles of pure liturgy. What is more, it is a long-standing and common view that the system of ecclesiastical law also encompasses the precepts concerning *in foro interno* conduct either, as some believe, when it is connected to external conduct, or in general, as others believe, even when there is no connection of sort,[41] given that the institution is provided with agencies that preside over the observance of these precepts. This does not make sense at all in the eyes of those whose concept of law is modelled on state law; and yet, it is a state of things that is to be accounted for in the light of the principles I am advocating. By the same token, the claim many scholars make that the law of primitive societies merges with customs and religion is seriously misguided. There is no confusion or undifferentiation of elements that by nature should be kept separate; rather, in those societies the law – which is to be considered as pure as the law of more advanced societies – is composed of a rich variety of principles drawing from customs and religious creed. Even today, English law, which nobody would ever deem underdeveloped, considers as 'law'[42] not only statutory law but also any rules (regardless of their origin and contents) applied and enforced by courts.

§ 15. If law only can materialize and take shape within the institution, and if, conversely, all that is socially organized and is subsumed under the institution as one of its elements takes on a legal character, we obtain the following corollary: the law is the vital principle of any institution, that which animates and holds together the various elements that compose it, which determines, fixes and preserves the structure of immaterial entities. In its turn, the institution is always a legal regime. While in a way it is not incorrect to think of the institution as the body, the frame, the limbs of law, the law is as inseparable from the institution, either materially or conceptually, as life from the living body. They are

---

40 Jellinek, 1908: 45 ff.
41 On this point see Wernz, 1905: fn 98 [; Wernz, 1938: 148, 150 ff.]; Sebastianelli, 1905, fn. 50.
42 Translator's note: English term present in the original Italian text.

not two phenomena standing in a given relation to one another, or that follow one another; instead, it is the same phenomenon.[43]

In this light, many problems that are often brought up appear straightforwardly incongruous. For one thing, the problem of whether the law is anterior to the state or the other way around; slightly different is the problem of whether there is law not before, but outside the state, or rather, if genuine law is only state law. From my point of view, it is easy to reply that, if there is a state, there has to be a legal order at the same time, that is, the state regime; likewise, if there is such a regime, there has to be a state.[44]

Analogously I believe the question of whether the state is essentially a legal or ethical entity is unwarranted, or at least ill-placed.[45] Ethics might well be the fundamental, albeit hardly the only, objective of the state – if one can ever attach to the state an *a priori* objective that is valid in all places and at all times – but the law is, and cannot but be, its vital principle, its organic structure, its essence. Asking whether it is a legal or ethical entity more or less amounts to asking whether the human being is a living or a moral being. Institutions can be defined differently in accordance with their ends, the mission they undertake. In this way, we can have

43 [This observation was neglected by those who objected that my concept of institution presupposes the concept of law, which would then be a *prius* with respect to the former. See e.g. Del Vecchio, 1921b: 11; Ferrara, 1921: 3; Miceli, 1923: 27; Cesarini Sforza, 1929: 12; Volpicelli, 1929: 13ff.; Capograssi, 1936: 6; Capograssi, 1937: 9; Capograssi, 1939: 6 ff.; Crisafulli, 1935: 9; Bobbio 1936: 35–36. On the other hand, some of these authors (Volpicelli, Capograssi and Crisafulli) submit that the law is anterior to the institution only from a philosophical vantage point, while, from an empirical-historical vantage point – which is necessary to an inquiry into the general theory of law such as mine – they acknowledge the correlation or identity between law and institution. If we indeed have to say that a legal order is an institution and an institution *is* a legal order, we can also say that an institution *has* a law, that is, an order, if by this we only mean the principles and norms that belong to it and arise from it, just as we say that a whole has this or that element that comprises it. Similarly, we can also say: 'I have a soul', if we conceive of ourselves as living bodies. On the contrary, we can also say: 'I have a body', if we conceive of ourselves as souls who took up a body. In reality, we are spiritual and corporal entities at one and the same time. A further completely groundless accusation, made by some of the authors mentioned above, is that a contradiction affects my discussion at the end of § 13, where I write that 'the institution exists and can be defined as such only insofar as it is created and preserved by the law'. Saying that the chicken gave a beginning to the egg is not in contradiction with saying that the egg gave a beginning to the chicken: it is all about determining in what sense and why we say the one or the other thing, while both are as true as the fact that chicken and egg are two aspects of the same phenomenon. See also fn. 38].

44 Funnily enough, as far as the state is concerned, the concept that the state and law coincide and constitute the same substance – or, as is sometimes said, two aspects of the same substance – has been often advanced misguidedly and to come to erroneous conclusions, while the right aspect it contains has been neglected. In this way, Kelsen (1911: 245 ff.; 1913: 44 ff., 114) has revived the old theory to maintain that state's wrongs are inconceivable, because the state can only be considered as a legal order. This is evidence that this thesis confuses what the state is with what the state does; for, with regard to its being, the state can never be in conflict with the law [its own law], while with regard to its doing, it can.

45 Lately on this point see Ravà, 1914.

religious, ethical, economic, artistic, educational institutions. However, insofar as they are institutions, all of them are legal entities. The misunderstanding stems from considering the law, too, as one of the ends of the state, one that can be juxtaposed and put in relation with the other ends. This, however, is a mistake: the state exists by virtue of law, that is, the order that constitutes the state, and when the former preserves the latter — what can take the most of the state activity — it does nothing but preserve itself, its structure, its life. Such preservation does not concern its mission and its goal, whatever these may be;[46] for it is just the premise, the necessary condition for state objectives to be pursued further.

§ 16. In a different manner, this attests to what I have already sought to demonstrate by arguments that build on other points of view. The primary and fundamental aspect of law is given by the institution in which it materializes, and not by the norms or generally the precepts through which it operates, as these rather constitute derivative and secondary aspects. This is confirmed not only by the impossibility one incurs of grasping and defining it in its organic unity (§ 3 ff.), by the character of objectivity I delineated above (§ 7), by the feature of sanction that inheres in it and cannot be reduced to the concept of norm (§ 8), but also by the following remark. If we concentrate on the moment at which particular institutions arise and thus their order gets underway, we immediately realize that this order is not determined by a pre-existing norm; therefore, it is impossible to claim that the law is not an institution, but the complex of norms by which it exists and operates. This is evident, for instance, in the case of the state, but not only in this case: it exists because it exists, and it is a legal order because it exists and from the very moment it comes about.[47] Its origin is not a procedure governed by legal norms; as I repeatedly emphasized, it is a fact. Law occurs as soon as this fact occurs, as soon as there is an effective, live and vital state; instead, the norm can be issued afterwards. Hence, law's first occurrence is not determined by the norm,

---

46 Even worse, at times the mistake I discuss above gets mixed up with another one. It is believed that the so-called police state — to which a widespread stylized conception assigns the specific task of safeguarding social peace and the peaceful coexistence of its members — is a state that carries out purely legal tasks. Yet, safeguarding the law is one thing, safeguarding public security or public order is quite another thing. The former is not a state's end, in the proper sense of the word or, rather, an end that exceeds its self-preservation, while the latter is. Against this confusion, prevalent among jurists and philosophers, see Romano, 1912: fn. 201 [; Romano, 1937: 4].

47 In this regard, see Romano, 1901 [; Romano, 1945: ch. 14]. Instead, others contend that 'the state order, when the state first comes about, is but a factual organization [. . .]. Later [. . .] its organization, as well as its overall order, comes to be regulated by legal norms and thus acquires a legal character' (Ranelletti, 1912: fn. 111). Similarly, see Jellinek, 1914: 337 ff. In much the same way, some believe that 'all orders over time go through a phase when, whatever the causes may be, turn them from real into legal' (Marinoni, 1913a: 20). These views clearly depend on the preconception that the law cannot be looked for and found but in a norm. I cannot understand what an a-legal state order waiting to be regulated is and how it should be conceived — as though an order was not, by definition, something already regulated and that, in addition, regulates. [Close to my position, see Biscaretti di Ruffìa, 1938: 11, fn. 11 and *passim*.]

which is a late and subsidiary manifestation. On the other hand, there can be no law before and outside the institution, precisely because there is no organization that makes the norm legal. The law cannot just be the norm established by the social organization, as is often said; for it is the social organization that, among its manifestations, also establishes the norm. If it is true that the legal character of the latter is conferred by the social power that issues it, or at least sanctions it, it follows that this character must be already present in the institution, which could not assign such a legal character to the norm if it did not have it itself.

The truth is that the law is first and foremost an arrangement, an organization of a social entity. If one rejects this postulate, one runs up against the need to explain the foundation and the bindingness of law in extra-jurisprudential ways. From this derive the theories that, despite the elements of truth they contain, cannot be accepted as legal theories, because they portray the law as a purely psychic force;[48] not to mention those that take law to be an individual, merely material force. Now, the organization, as I understand it here, is by no means a norm or a complex of norms: either because, as we have seen, it can be anterior to the norm; or because, when it is posterior to it and is linked with it, it is evidently a phenomenon that occurs as an effect of their enforcement, and thus it is not a norm. The norm might have disposed this phenomenon, but cannot have actualized it itself; nor can it have constituted it automatically, just by way of its own existence.[49]

§ 17. The litmus test for all definitions of law is the so-called problem of international law; consequently, it is worth measuring my definition against it. I take it as a postulate that those definitions that lead us to refute both the existence and – which is not so different after all – the autonomy of international law, are to be rejected because they regard it as an articulation or projection of the domestic law

---

48 See this theory in e.g. Triepel, 1899: 82; Hold von Ferneck, 1903: I, § 20 for a milder version of this theory, also in others, e.g. Miceli, 1906: § 25; Anzilotti, 1902a: 68, as he avers that 'the bindingness of law is more of a moral concept than a legal principle'; etc.

49 [While applying this concept elsewhere (Romano, 1945: ch. 6, § 2, fn. 2) I noted that, as far as the state is concerned, its constitution is often declared and attested by norms; yet, if taken *in se* and *per se*, it is not exhausted by these norms, which are nothing but its exterior signs, its documentation, a form of its affirmation. The constitution will rather concretize in the institutions that it is made up of. In other words, the constitution is an edifice, and this is not the blueprint drawn up by the architect to provide guidance to those who will continue to build it or to those who will dwell in it. With a vivid intuition, the ancient doctrine used to distinguish the constitution from the laws. Aristotle (*Politics*, lib. iv: 1289-a) wrote: 'the laws [. . .] are separate from the declarations that set forth the form of government'; and its commentators and translators confirmed that the laws 'separatae sunt *ab iis* quae declarant rempublicam' (Victorius), 'ab his rerumpublicarum *descriptionibus* diversae sunt' (Ramus), 'abis *rebus quae rempublicam indicant* sunt seiunctae' (Giphanus), in such a way as to 'sane apparet, inter *ea*, quae *constituunt rempublicam*, non numerari leges' (Heinsius). However, such a character of the constitution does not imply, as some believed, that the very constitution is a *prius* of state law, and that it lies outside it. If this were to be true, given that the constitution and constitutional law are one and the same thing, we should then logically deduce the rejection of constitutional law (see Romano, 1945: ch. 1).]

of the various states. The definition of law must be presented in such a way that it might cover what is considered as such not only by scientific tradition, but also by common sense and, above all, by persistent, never invalidated practice. Otherwise, it is arbitrary because, for the jurist, it is not reality that must be subordinated to the concept, but the latter to the former.

For me, this problem raises the question: is the international legal order an institution? There is no doubt on where this figure is to be looked for: we must determine if the community of states shows the constitutional characteristics that, in keeping with the hypothesis I put forward, are the essential characteristics of all systems of law. For now, we can disregard the question of whether such a community should be understood in a broad sense, or rather, if it is cohesive and if the bulk of states partake in it, or whether there are as many communities as the groups of states, which then intersect in many ways and give life to a particular international law.[50] Certainly, the choice between these conceptions is not without consequence, but it is better not to take a position as long as my reasoning applies to both.

While it is known that the doctrine agrees on the quite unquestionable fact that the international society is not a legal person, this is altogether irrelevant for me, as I formulated a concept of institution that does not rely on this feature. Still, another claim that is often raised is that such a society is not legally organized,[51] and this might prevent defining it as an institution, given that the latter is indeed synonymous with organization. Despite this, the meaning of this claim is far from clear. At times it seems meant to reiterate, in a different way, the argument that the international community has no personality. At other times – and this is the meaning that I am concerned with – it is meant to emphasize that there is no common power to which states are subject. But it seems to me that the concept of organization does not necessarily imply a relation, so conceived, of superiority and correlative subordination. In fact, given that all states should be subject to this power, in such a way that none of them, not even a majority of them, might have pre-eminence over the others, this power should belong to the community itself, which should then constitute a person. Based on this, we should conclude that utterly equal communities, like the international community, are organized only as long as they are legal persons. Now, I believe this thesis to be arbitrary and indemonstrable; rather, the condition of equality and mutual independence characterizing the members of these societies is nothing but a feature of their organization, or, if I may say so, an effect of it. The obverse claim is arguably based on the unilateral view that the essential features of a legal concept are deemed to be those accidental features that it deploys in a given field of law: in the present case, domestic state law.

On the other hand, despite scholars' claims to the contrary, it would be easy to identify in the recent literature on the foundations and nature of international law elements that necessarily entail the organization of the society of states. In

50 [Famously, this is Triepel's (1899: 83 ff.) conception.]
51 See Marinoni's (1913a: 31 ff.) objections.

fact, when scholars contend that normative agreement, as the source of international law, produces a will that is no longer the will of the distinct states, but a unified, superior will, where the latter merge together; when scholars contend that, in this way, international law takes on a character of *ius supra partes*;[52] or, more intensely, that international law results in commands and imperatives addressed to the states; this all presupposes an organization, however basic this may be, of the interstate community. The latter might lack internal bodies, those entities that have personality;[53] it might not be founded upon positions of subordination and independence of some states vis-à-vis others; still, it implies a position of subjection of all member states to a non-subjective, impersonal power, one that makes the community possible and brings it about.[54] When I speak of institution I attach no meaning other than this to the expression 'organization'. After all, the quality which is commonly attributed to the states 'members' of this community bears an analogous meaning, if it is true that one can only be a member of a 'body', an 'organism'.[55] Having said that, it is not necessary to recall that often states have common organs or that the organs of various states are assembled in one body or agency; this entails an organization of the international society, always in a figure that is compatible with its impersonality.

Although with different formulations, the early doctrine had captured with clarity the character of institution that I believe is manifest in the community of states, where the international legal order materializes; only recently has this character been neglected or even refuted. This is mainly due to the by now widespread conception that the only source of international law is the collective will of the states, which manifests itself through customs, agreements or normative treaties. In this way, any aspects or elements that antedate those through which, time by time, such a will takes form are excluded from the sphere of law.

First of all, this conception is evidently tied up with the conventional view that reduces law to a complex of simple norms; therefore, it lends itself to the criticisms I have generally made to this view. Yet, in the field of international law it yields more serious consequences than in the field of state domestic law. In effect, there is no denying that the state's distinct laws rest on a unique basis, i.e. the state, which issues them and confers on them bindingness and effectiveness. Instead, the conventional view holds that, as I will explain better in due course, international agreements stand on their own, each of them getting effectiveness out of themselves

---

52 On all these concepts, see Triepel's (1899) work, and among those who generally adopt them, see in particular Anzilotti, 1902a: 71 ff.; 1912: 47 ff.

53 [I now believe that, contrary to the prevailing opinion, in addition to legal persons, also social entities lacking personality can have bodies, whether they are associative or institutional; see Romano, 1937: 95, 100, 102–103; 1945: *passim*; 1949: 213 ff. This position has been adopted by Fedozzi (1940: 472).]

54 'International law expresses a power to which the state is subject' (Anzilotti, 1902a: 74).

55 'Membra unius corporis' (that is, of the *societas gentium*), said Grotius (*De Jure Belli ac Pacis*: II, ch. 8, § 26; ch. 15, §§ 5 and 12.) *apropos* of states.

and constituting the prime principle of the law they produce. In this way, this premise leads to the conclusion – as at least some have indeed concluded – that there is not one international law, but as many international laws as there are agreements.

Furthermore, I would like to point out that the view I am discussing is a reaction against the theories engulfed in the principles of natural law that, in enumerating the sources of international law, exceeded the sphere of positive law. In this regard, it was certainly healthy and made extensive and useful contributions to the revision of a number of concepts and, even more importantly, of the method. Nevertheless, it seems that many of its fundamental parts as well as its structure are beset by a contradiction that gets lessened in some of its developments, thanks to a number of technical expedients, but is not completely expelled. Indeed, while this view was advanced as a positivist move aimed at purging international law of the several natural law influences, it reiterates the same exact postulate of one of the most typical theories by which the natural law tradition had tried to account for state domestic law, to wit, the theory of social contract. The starting point of this theory was individuals thought of as isolated and located in the so-called state of nature, thoroughly free and independent, who at one point, by their own will, subject themselves to the state regime, which they themselves created. Now, by espousing an analogous ideology, it is claimed that states enjoy fundamental independence, establish international law by themselves, and subject themselves to it by agreement, which is a proper social contract, except for the different name and the juridical sophistication in analyzing it. To overcome the corresponding theory of domestic law – and I leave aside its philosophical meaning, which has many more aspects – it sufficed to stress that the legal position of individuals, whatever this may be, is a consequence of the rise of the state, whose order establishes that position. As a consequence, the state order can explain the position of individuals, not the other way around. It is odd that this very objection has not been made to international law scholars. If states are independent from each other, from a legal point of view this position does not pre-exist international law, as it is established by it; and the principle by which states cannot be obliged but by norms that they themselves have contributed to producing through their own will is a principle of positive international law, which then presupposes an already constituted and valid international law. When the opposite is claimed, that is, that the international order is brought into being by an agreement among states, that such an agreement is pre-juridical, and so on, the basis of this order is a natural condition of states. Moreover, the latter is as hard to find in reality as the alleged natural condition of individuals before the state was born: as the view of an isolated human being in the state of nature is purely metaphysical and a-historical, so is the conception of a state isolated from the others, and not living in a community of them, metaphysical, almost mythical. Furthermore, from a historical point of view, it is worth recalling that the international law anterior to the modern one was based on the opposite principle of the subordination of states to the secular power of the Empire and the spiritual power of the Church, not to speak of other particular subordinations to some of them. Today's state independence, then, is not a natural, original, independent condition of international law, but is fully contingent, as it is a consequence of particular characteristics it has assumed in recent times. The further principle of state equality – bound up with that of state independence, but not identical with it – is a rule that even today makes room for exceptions, which are not always appreciated and evaluated.

I believe the conclusion to which all this comes down is fairly simple. As state law comes into being with the state, since the existence of the latter coincides the existence of its legal order, so does international law come into being with the community of states, which necessarily presupposes a legal order that constitutes and regulates it. The principle (and I do not want to investigate if it is so absolute as some contend) that an actual norm of international law cannot subsequently be established without the will of the states that are party to the community and only applies to those that wanted it, is a legal principle. This amounts to saying that it has the same nature of the other – different, even opposite – principle that the legislative power within each state rests not with the citizens, but with some of the state bodies. Therefore, it does not apply to the *original* position of international law, but to a *posterior* phase, when new norms and new institutions are to be produced, existing ones to be amended, and so on. In much the same way, the principle that laws are passed by the Chambers and approved by the Head of State is valid from the moment it is established, but can also be established through a constitution that comes to life at the moment in which the state is founded, that is, on the basis of no previous norms. This brings me back to the view that international law also, like state law, affirms itself as an institution from the very beginning, as a necessary product of the interstate organization, of the structure by which, both *de facto* and *de jure*, it came to take shape.

It is not useless to insist on this point. Undoubtedly, the process whereby a state is formed is pre-legal. But when the state becomes alive, it is already an order comprising the agencies that are granted legislative power. From this moment onward, these agencies possess legal life and all legal directives they issue are legally effective. This also applies to the international community. The formation of its current structure took a long time and was not governed by law; but ever since it took its current form, the principle that states must contribute to the production of new norms with their own will has become legal, as well as the acts issued through such agreements, that will gradually be included in the edifice of international law. The laying of the cornerstone of international law, as the basis on which the other stones accrue, is not marked – as today's prevailing doctrine believes[56] – by these

---

56 It is worth stressing the extreme, perfectly logical conclusions to which some have come by starting from these premises, ones I believe to be a sign of the need to revise the latter. Anzilotti (1912: I, 48, 49, 53 ff.) [differently from the 3rd edition of 1928 and from the German edition] is now of the opinion that the normative agreement, by establishing the law, precedes it and remains outside it; it is not a legal fact, but a pre-legal one. The common sense, on the contrary, and the traditional doctrine consider all treaties as legal acts. Anzilotti (1902a: 48) himself used to think the same. From the same vantage point, it has also been claimed that what is qualified as normative agreement

agreements, but by the emergence itself of the existing international community. Which is to say that these very agreements do not have, as many believe, any inner force, independent of a pre-existing law; nor do they get their effectiveness, as others believe, out of customs. Instead, they rest on the principle that arose as the international community did, and became part of its own constitution, with its current institutional characteristics. In the abstract, it would be possible for this principle to change not only on account of concordant declarations of will on the part of the states, but factually, on account of transformations the international community could undergo: for instance, because of the pre-eminence acquired by one or more states, in much the same way as a change in the constitutional order of a state might be effected not through legal means but also through non-legal happenings. Similarly, while the society of states in the Middle Ages was based on a relationship of subordination of states to the Emperor and the Pope, in the modern era it has taken the shape of a community of peers because of a long chain of historical events. And this consideration also provides evidence that the present condition of state equality and independence is not pre-legal, but is determined by the structure of their community. If then one asks why the latter has been built by establishing that the principle of the agreement among states is necessary for enacting further regulations concerning them, this is an inquiry actually alien to the law; so is the other, analogous inquiry into the reason why a given state confers the legislative power on one body instead of others, or why the unanimity of these bodies is required, rather than the majority, while the majority of their members is enough in case of collegiate bodies.

These claims could be confirmed by foregrounding the existence of other principles of international law that are not established by any agreements and thus cannot be based on them, as they arise from the structure of the international community.[57] For example, the principle that states are allowed to use force to make sure the international order is complied with – as I believe as well as those who claim the international order is based on the common will of the states[58] – is

---

cannot be qualified as such and thus distinguished from contract, in that, as a pre-legal fact, it is not amenable to any legal determinations (Salvioli, 1914: 30). This is also logical, but it recalls the *cave a consequentiariis*. At any rate, it is significant that the theory of agreement, as has been subtly elaborated, which nobody knows whether it has generated the modern views on the foundations of international law or whether it has been generated by them, is now being rejected by them: either Saturn devours his sons, or vice versa.

57 [On these fundamental or constitutional principles, which are established by the existence itself of the international community, which are neither norms of voluntary law nor norms of customary law, see Romano, 1949: 31 ff. For principles with a similar nature, relative to the state legal order, see Romano, 1937: ch. 24, fn. 1; and finally Romano, 1945: ch. 7, § 6, fn. 7. For a substantial espousal of my view on these principles, see Crisafulli, 1941: 186 ff.]

58 See generally Anzilotti (1912: I, 28), who interprets this as the coercion that makes international norms legal. On the other hand, I do not think that the use of force can be considered as legally allowed only because it is a logically necessary consequence of international norms being legal: precisely because they are legal, they are claimed to require coercion, and this is not given by a power superior to the distinct states. Indeed, we cannot say that the use of force is generally

a legal principle. But what agreement does it stem from? Treaties have regulated and delimited it, but they presuppose its existence: none of them has ever established this principle. And I think it pointless to evoke customs. Also in this case we are faced with a principle intrinsic to the institution, as I understand it here.

I could draw this analysis to an end with the following conclusions: international law is the immanent order of the community of states; it comes about with it and is inseparable from it; more than in the distinct norms produced by particular agreements, it is to be found in the institution to which this very community gives form; therefore, it is first and foremost, in its unitary aspects, organization or institution. Further conclusions that should be drawn as to the theory of the sources of international law cannot be developed here, but are to be dealt with elsewhere.

However, it is worth adding a comment. As I said at the beginning of this section, some have denied the existence of an international community encompassing all states, and have rather claimed that there are as many communities as the relationships of each state to the others. Based on what I have pointed out so far, the logical genesis of this theory becomes clear. It is just the corollary of the other theory that conceives of international law as Penelope's web, which gets to be woven *ex novo* at any normative agreement. And, to be coherent, one should conclude that each of these agreements gives form not so much to a community as to a bare relationship, limited not only with regard to the range of states entering into the agreement, but also with regard to the specific subject on which they agree. In this way, one would end up refuting the existence of a general international law, which should then be regarded as a theoretical abstraction, or rather, as the ensemble of principles that are *de facto* shared by the various relationships among states or the majority of them. These principles would not amount to a genuine juridical unity, and they would be exposed together only for the sake and purpose of analysis. Positive international law would be nothing but the specific law of each state with regard to the other states with which it is in relation: of the state A with regard to the state B and then the state C, and so on; even better, it would be the law produced by each concrete agreement. Evidently, this is at odds with reality, and it is easier to advance this view in the abstract than observe the consequences that it brings about in practice. This explains why even those who are on their way to endorsing these conclusions stop midway, proving the unsoundness of this theory's premises that they are forced to neglect. This is at the origin of the common view – which, if those premises were correct, should be jettisoned – that particular international law is considered as a law that is integrated within general law and presupposes it.

From this point of view, too, we are led to reaffirm the existence of a community of states conceived in its integral unity: an institution where new, emerging

---

permitted by international law – except for expressely agreed upon limitations –, since only particular means are permitted that are positively determined, e.g. war. This is evidence that it is a principle or various principles on their own, and that they cannot be evinced from the other principle I mentioned. This is true regardless of other arguments, which I cannot discuss here.

states are included, subject to the so-called recognition;[59] therefore, each of these inclusions widens it in such a way that it does not regenerate but keeps its identity. In this way, international law, in its turn, provides evidence that the general concept of a legal order I advanced is correct.[60]

§ 18. The concept of institution and its equivalence with that of legal order can be confirmed and clarified by distinguishing this very concept from others with which it could be confounded.

To commence, the institution can never be reduced to one or more specific legal relationships (§ 10). The legal relationship has to do with the subjective conception of law, as it presupposes at least two terms as points of reference. I believe one of them is constituted by a person considered either as in its entirety or with reference to one of its specific aspects, or even (if it is a legal person) with reference to one of its bodies; the other term is either this very person – when its aspect or body faces another aspect or body – or finally the object of one of its rights or obligations. Thus the relationship is not an entity in its own right, but a relation among different entities, this word being used in a broad sense. The institution, instead, is objective law, and is objective law because it is an entity, a social body, which, within the legal domain, enjoys an effective, concrete and objective existence. It implies relationships but cannot be reduced to them. Rather, it is foundational to them, in the sense that it represents the organization or structure that is necessary for relationships, if and when they occur within its orbit, to be qualified as legal. The institution is unity; the relationship, whether legal or not, presupposes plurality. This is why, for example, the conception that the state is a simple legal relationship[61] proves not only insufficient but also erroneous – such a conception has to be rejected also in the case of states that lack legal personality.

From this derives the following corollary: in order for an institution to arise, the existence of persons connected to each other through simple relationships is not enough, as there must be a closer and more organic bond. The formation of a social super-structure is required upon which not only their distinct relationships, but also their own generic position depends, or that sway them. Therefore, it is impossible to envisage an institution only composed of two physical persons; for these will remain

---

59 [I subsequently rejected that idea that the admission to the international community hinges on so-called recognition. See Romano, 1949: 60 ff., 106 ff.]

60 [For a conception of international law inspired by the concepts discussed here, see Romano, 1949. Other writers advocate them: Breschi, 1920; Fedozzi, 1940: 15; Monaco, 1932a. Others espouse them with regard to specific topics, among them: 1. As to the relationship between international and domestic laws, see Monaco, 1932b. 2. As to the so-called general principles of international law, see Fedozzi, 1940: 15. 3. As to the unions of states, see Zanobini, 1949: 621; Biscaretti di Ruffìa, 1939: § 78; Schmitt, 1939; 5; 4. As to colonial protectorates, see Zanobini, 1949; Biscaretti di Ruffìa, 1939; Baldoni, 1931; Monaco, 1938: 52 ff.]

61 In any case, it should by no means be confused, as Jellinek (1912: 38; 1914: 167) does, with the other, more correct, which is known as 'Zustandslehre'.

two individualities, unable to morph into one. This, importantly, does not imply that there cannot be institutions where the personal element is represented by two persons only; yet, in this case, this element has to be integrated with some other elements with a cohesive and unifying efficacy, which would otherwise be lacking. Accordingly, the conjugal society, which if considered in itself and for itself is but a relationship, can and usually does adopt the legal figure of family, or rather, an institution. For one thing, state law organizes it on whatever basis, for example, by recognizing the husband as the chief; for another, apart from that, the nature itself of the goals to achieve, to which individuals subject themselves, its possible and normal continuation beyond the spouses, the bond that links its members to past and future ones: this all turns the family into a persistent unity, a social body, whose elements vary in keeping with its constitution, which was and is quite different in different times and places. The Roman family, the royal dynasties, high-nobility families that enjoy wide autonomy, do not fall into one category; but they all are institutions.[62]

On the contrary, two legal persons can, with no external interference and with no other elements being involved, form an institution. This is because their internal structure is a mere creation of the law, which can therefore mould and flex them in such a way for them to constitute a genuine unity, even though, in turn, it is not to be regarded as one person. In this way, the international community and the international law could certainly continue to subsist, even in case the number of states decreased to two. After all, besides the international community made up of many states, there are particular communities, such as federations and real unions of states, that are only made up of two states – what is enabled by the constitution of each of these states. A widespread view interprets these unions between states as a relationship between societies; however, this view is mistaken because, among other things, it neglects the fact of belonging to these unions modifies the states that comprise them, so much so that the one necessarily complements the other, while both of them are constituted in such a way as to become elements of a more complex institution, of a collective entity, without giving rise to a new legal personality. Moreover, those who argue for the personality of these entities intuit the insufficiency of the doctrine that reduces them to mere relationships; and yet this is just as inadmissible, for it attributes to them a character that is not necessary to the existence of an institution, a character that they lack. Finally, the act whereby these unions are created is not a contract [*contratto negoziale*], in a literal sense, but establishes an objective law; therefore, if it is an international treaty, it falls, to use the common terminology, not into the category of treaty-contracts, but into the category of treaty-agreements.[63] Analogously, in the Concordat system, the state and the Church form a union, one that cannot be split in distinct and particular relationships, but gives rise to a genuine institution. Leaving aside other

62 On the modern family as a social organization, see Cicu, 1915: 7 ff., 77 ff.
63 [I have now abandoned the distinction between treaty-contracts and treaty-agreements: see Romano, 1949: ch. 5, fn. 5.]

elements, here emerges the difficulty one always runs into of reducing the figure of the concordat, or at least certain concordats, to that of a common contract.[64]

It is apparent that these examples are the best proof of the criterion that permits distinguishing the institution from a simple relationship: the former is the stable position of an entity; the latter is given by a number of entities that get closer to each other more or less temporarily. A relationship can turn into an institution only when, by internal or external forces, its own terms are altered and stably connected in an organic position, that is, they become members of an entity of its own.

While the institution, as a legal entity, is itself an order, a relationship is not an order, but depends on it, as the order constitutes the environment where the relationship unfolds, or rather, something external to it. This is why a legal transaction [*negozio giuridico*] that only brings relationships into existence cannot alone give rise to law. To produce this effect, an act is required that does not limit itself to constructing a relationship whose various elements dwell in the existing order, but at least in part has to establish the order. What is more, given that a rule, taken per se, in isolation, is not law, as I tried to demonstrate, for a legal act to be considered as a source of law, it has to establish not only rules, but a more or less complex social organization.[65]

§ 19. While a legal order, that is, an institution, cannot be identified with a simple relationship between two or more persons, let alone can it be pieced together and condensed into a physical person. Indeed, it is necessary for this person to tie up firmly with other elements in such a way that the figure of the institution be also reflected in the latter. The elements to which I allude can also be things, namely, objects of a right or of a particular power conferred on someone. But when we look at them as elements of an institution, their legal character cannot be reduced to that of simple *res*. Between a thing as such and a person, between the subject and the object, as I noted above (§ 18), there is a relationship, and this is not enough to generate an institution.

It will be helpful to clarify this concept with a few examples so as to apply it in ways that seem quite interesting, by shedding light on the figure of the institution that sometimes remains in the background precisely because its elements have not been considered in their true position, but in a simple relationship of concrete nature.

To begin with, let us look at that typical, characteristic institution that the state is. By distinguishing states that have personality from states that are not persons, the doctrine has often considered the latter as objects of the law of the prince, the

---

64 [For the same reasons why I no longer believe that, within the category of international treaties, so-called treaty-agreements deserve a figure of their own, I have now come to believe that ecclesiastical concordats also have a contractual character. As to the nature of the concordatarian union between Church and state see Romano, 1945: ch. 10, § 4, fn. 2.]

65 [Also with regard to the nature of legal transactions I have come to a different opinion than that expressed in the text: they bring into being not only relationships, but also norms governing these relationships, and are legal, that is, institutional, in that the autonomy on which they are based derives from the state and is protected by the state. On this topic see many of my writings and, lately, Romano, 1945: ch. 13, § 6, fn. 6.]

monarch, who therefore is outside and above the state.[66] These and similar conceptions appear to me as erroneous, or at least insufficient. Here I cannot account for particular types of states, such as the so-called patrimonial state, which still need to be adequately illuminated. So I will limit myself to observing that the state is always and primarily a regime, a legal order, an institution of which the monarch, the subjects, the territory and the laws are nothing but elements. Thus the monarch is encompassed by the institution, and is never outside and above it, and his position is not independent of it. Indeed, it is one of its particular tendencies, a fundamental feature of the law that crystallizes into the institution itself. From this vantage point, king and kingdom necessarily constitute an indissoluble entity. The kingdom, then, cannot be regarded as a *res* connected to the king through a mere relation of extrinsic belonging: they merge with one another because the state is an institution, of which the monarch is one element among others. The opposite view hinges on an incorrect consideration of the monarch's sovereign position. It is true that sometimes the king qualifies himself as the *dominus* or the lord of the state, but this only means that he is the head, and thus, implicitly, an integral part, not just the owner. Furthermore, the vexed question of whether the king in certain states is above the law does not amount to the question of whether he is above the state. The king can be considered above his subjects, his land, and the laws he enacted and abrogated. If we want to use the modern terminology, we can also say that subjects, land and laws are objects of his power. But in any case these are, not the state as a whole, but distinct elements of the state that encompasses the monarch himself. To put it otherwise, he does not have a purely individual right of dominion, but a right that is endowed on him as the sovereign member of the state and that implies such a position within it. In these orders, this is a dominion that exceeds by far that of a subject with regard to the simple object of his power; this can be inferred by the fact that the effect of its action can eventuate in a transformation of the structure, the organization and the laws of the state, and then in the production of a new law. The alienation or transferral of the state from a monarch to another has exactly this character and implies not only the alienation or transferral of a right, but the loss of a personal status: the exit of the king from the kingdom and the entry of a new king. The truth is that the conception of the state as an object is based on nothing but illusions. Arguably it was suggested by the desire to oppose the figure of the state as a subject, with a figure that might represent, also terminologically, its exact antithesis. Whether or not it has personality, the state is always an institution encompassing its head.

66 On the theory of the state as an object and on the figure of the monarch as placed outside and above the state, see Jellinek, 1914, 164 ff., 669 ff. However, contrary to Jellinek (1914, 165–166), I think it is a mistake to combine the theory of the state as an object with the theory, which scholars allude to but fail to develop, of the state as an institution [istituto] (*Anstalt*), [this is a word that is used in a different sense than my 'institution': they amount to two theories where the one represents a remarkable improvement of the other. See Romano, 1945: ch. 6, § 1, and § 3, fn. 7.]

If this were not the case, it would be impossible to identify the law, of which the leader's rights and powers are but manifestations.

From that legal macrocosm which the state is, we can move on to smaller or even marginal institutions, to repeat the observations I already made with reference to analogous ones. These institutions include some that the jurist's analysis seldom takes into account, but are interesting nonetheless. When a given individual, in the sphere where he can consider himself like a king in his own kingdom, that is, in his home (broadly understood), establishes an order, which is binding upon his relatives, his employees, the things at his diposal, his guests, and so on, in practice he is creating a small institution, of which he is both the head and a member. However, such a figure is not to be found in the laws of the state. These laws consider a person's domicile, distinctly and from other points of views, to safeguard his freedom, his relationship with the other persons who constitute his family, or who work for him, or with the things over which he has a right, and so on. Yet, at least in the first place, this all is not relevant to that "law of the household"[67] that I am speaking of and that state law does not deal with. This is an autonomous, internal order that reduces a set of diverse elements, persons and things to a governmental unit, and considers it from its own point of view. Therefore, for example, state law only considers the subject of a right *in rem* over a house, if this is his property, or of a right deriving from a rental agreement; on the contrary, for this latter order such a relationship is not relevant in itself, and that house will only ever be an element of the institution that lies within it, the scope of a power with which its head is vested as the head, not as a landlord or a tenant.

Analogously, a certain person can give a regime, an arrangement, an organization to a factory, to a school of which he is the head, to a commercial enterprise. Also in these cases, we are faced with small institutions, i.e. legal microcosms, where the personal element – that is in charge as the *dominus* – can well come down to a distinct individual; the latter however integrates with other elements, which, merged together and coordinated, will represent the unity that can be called a company in a broad sense. This is an institution, in light of its inner order, and, as such, it will have a leader, a legislator, subjects, laws of its own, an ensemble of authorities and administrative gears. This is a legal world in its own right, complete in its kind and for its purposes (see also §§ 31, 45, 47). From the viewpoint of state law, it will be something very different. State law will dissect it in the various relationships that exist between its members, or it will take it as a unity and consider it as a *universitas rerum* or a set of assets and liabilities of a company. In this way, while the law of the state will define the position of the proprietor of

---

67 Scholars have dealt with the 'household law' in various respects, although always in a subjective sense and as founded on state law: apropos of the inviolability of domicile (see e.g. Listz, 1905, 401), as well as certain powers that scholars felt the need to distinguish from disciplinary power (see e.g. Hubrich, 1899: 419 ff., 424 ff.; Romano, 1905; Tezner, 1912: 416 ff.; etc.). A "domestic power" has also been attributed to the state within its territory (Donati, 1914). – Fairly different and higher is the relevance of the orders of the Royal House and the Royal Court, the autonomy, which also possesses a particular figure, bestowed on particular noble families by the law of certain states, etc.

the company, which will be the object of a right of his; in the eyes of the inner order, the proprietor can even stay outside this company, when there is a chief in charge other than the proprietor. And, in any case, when the proprietor takes over the government, what matters is not his right of property, but his being the head.

In substance, these and other entities have to be an institution because of their structure, their internal law, and not from the different way the laws of the state depict them. And if we pay heed to this structure, we can see the point of those theories that sometimes have detected legal personality in these entities, and not only in the commercial company in a proper sense, but also, for example, in the ship itself (what came across as very odd[68]). Doubtless these theories are mistaken, because the element of personality is missing both in the eyes of state law and in the eyes of the inner law, but they deserve to be mentioned nonetheless. The same is true for those theories that intuited that, within the inner order, the figure of simple *res* or *universitas rerum* – which certainly does not fit reality and that many deem insufficient – is superseded by the less inert, more lively, more animated figure of the institution. And the laws of the state would do well to take them into consideration.

§ 20. While a legal relationship or one physical person are not enough for an institution to concretize, one legal person is an institution in itself. If we leave aside the thorny issue of legal persons, we can derive a few corollaries from the principles I have developed so far. In substance, legal doctrine has always had the right intuition that it is necessary to formulate a unified concept of such persons and then place them in different categories. However, scarcely can one say that the doctrine achieves this goal the moment it pins down the so-called substratum of corporations in an ensemble of persons, and then looks out for other elements – about which there are uncertainties and disagreements – that constitute the substratum of foundations and institutions in a stricter sense. In doing so, it yields a dualism that cannot be overcome despite the most ingenious efforts. Only the doctrine of organization, which I alluded to (§ 11), solves this problem in a unifying way; however, as I pointed out (§ 13), it draws upon a concept whose legal significance it fails to foreground, and even formulates it in utterly non-legal terms. I think the basis of a legal person is always an order of objective law, which takes shape and is enclosed in itself and for itself, or rather, an institution in the sense I developed above. It is not the persons it comprises, even when it comes to corporations, nor its patrimony, its bodies or offices, its goal, the substratum of its personality, but it is always and only its legal order that binds those persons, allocates that patrimony, specifies its bodies, and coordinates everything with a view to a particular end.

---

68 Ferrara, 1915: 704 [also Ferrara, 1938: 86–87. Some authors have embraced my concept of company, sometimes with a few variations suggested by a misunderstanding of it. See, among others, Ferrara, 1921: 138 ff.; Ferrara Jr., 1939: 137; Ferrara Jr., 1945; Greco, 1942; Messineo, 1943: I, § 77, fn. 17; Valeri, 1945: I, 12. It is apparent that the 1942 Civil code also comes close to it when it defines the enterprise, which was denoted with the term 'company', while the existing code distinguishes between enterprise and company: on this, see Romano, 1944.]

And when I speak of legal order as the substratum of the legal person, I mean the order that can be said to be 'internal', not the one that a superior or broader institution, such as the state, might refer to and that it encompasses. Indeed, personality can then be attributed by the more comprehensive order, but always on the basis of its [the smaller institution's] order, which constitutes a necessary presupposition, an indispensable substratum. In sum – and here I cannot delve further into this topic – an institution takes on the character of person when it is considered as an entity with a will of its own either by its own order or by another order, always on the basis of the institution's order; which is to say, when the will, materially manifested by particular individuals, who are elements of the institution in a broad sense (members, bodies, administrators) with the forms and for the purposes that are imposed by its structure, is considered as the will of the institution itself.[69] This implies that what gets personified is nothing but an objective order, oriented and designed in such a way that it might produce that effect, so as to be considered as an entity that can have a will, either by itself or by others. Such a various source of personality also explains why an entity can at times constitute a person in the eyes of its own order and not in the eyes of another order (as happens with so-called *de facto* entities that are not recognized as legal persons by the state: see § 31) and, vice versa, why an entity does not consider itself as a person (for example, certain states where the will of the sovereign counts as such and not as the will of the state itself), while within another order, such as the international one, they are considered as persons. Nonetheless, the fact remains that the internal order has to be amenable to personification; it has to be an entity that, although it does not attribute to itself any personality, allows others to attribute personality to it.

If all this is true, then we can infer that the act by which a legal person is established is an act that produces objective law, even when, in other respects, it assumes a different figure: for example, that of a private transaction [*negozio privato*]. In effect, this action will remain its 'bylaw' and its 'foundation table'; in sum, whatever we call it, its foundational law. The doctrine was not always capable of distinguishing these two aspects that the same action can assume, depending on whether one looks at it from the viewpoint of the order contained in the legal personality or from the viewpoint of another order that one might consider, and that usually is the state's. From this arises a series of questions that have no reason to exist and that are ill-placed on all counts. This also better explains the reason why the state grants its so-called recognition as the legal person has to exert its

---

69 [Against the opinion I advanced in the text, Ferrara (1938: 25, fn. 2 and 28, fn. 1) observed that there can be a legal person with no will of its own and that, in any case, the will is necessary to the activity and not to the existence of the person. Here I cannot assess the consistency of, so to speak, voluntaristic theories of personality; whether these theories are to be rejected, and I do not think this can be done without preserving the elements of truth they contain, some of my remarks in the text are to be deleted or amended. The fundamental fact remains that the legal person that is a social body (and sometimes legal personality is attributed to abstract or ideal entities, to non-human entities, to gods, saints, etc.) is a legal order, an institution that is considered by itself or by other orders as having powers, rights and duties.]

effects through state law. While I do not mean to say that these concepts give an explanation for the old principle that portrayed the attribution or recognition of personality on the part of the state as a *lex specialis*, yet it seems that this point of view casts more light on the nature of this act.

§ 21. The conception of law that I have developed, in conjunction with some simple corollaries that derive from it, enables us to take a stance against the increasing trend that considers some facts or aspects as meta-legal, ones that the conventional view has rightly included in the domain of law. One only has to recognize that this theory is more exact and alert in the conclusions to which it has come, rather than in the premises it rests upon. Indeed, starting from the latter, that is, from the deficient concept of law which I mentioned, this theory could not justify those conclusions, if it ever felt the need to justify them. On the contrary, while the more recent trend by no means alters the starting point, that is, the notion of law it adopts, it reaches more logical conclusions, which however are less true. These can be considered – certainly against the authors' own intentions – as a demonstration through reduction to absurdity of the inadmissibility of the first postulate.

Among these points, which are wrongly taken out of the scope of law and are put in a sort of limbo, I will now discuss some, while others will be mentioned later on; I already discussed others, such as international agreements, which according to some authors should be left out of international law (§ 17).

1. First of all, I consider the power [*potestà*] of the state, which some writers deem as a *de facto* power, a pre-legal attribute of the state itself.[70] This conception, at least fundamentally, is suggested by the idea that the law is always and invariably constituted by this power, so much so that its position is a term *a quo*, a *prius* of the legal order. These writers concede that, once it has been established, this order is able to limit that power and to turn it into a legal one, a characteristic that state power is believed to lack in its original manifestation. Evidently, this view is premised upon the principle, which I opposed, that the state legal order is nothing other than the complex of rules and precepts established by the state in virtue of its legislative power. Instead, the state and the legal order are not, as I pointed out, two different phenomena; nor are they two different manifestations of the same phenomenon. On the contrary, they are the same thing. This means that an essential attribute of the state, namely, its power, can never be extra- or pre-legal, but emerges with it and its order, which it always disciplines and regulates. Whether this means that this is a

---

70 See Perozzi, 1906: 57 fn.; Petrone, 1897: 140 ff., 149; Marinoni, 1913a: 348, 358; Marinoni, 1913b: 9 ff.; Breschi, 1914: 422. Others (Ottolenghi, 1902: 21) then maintained that the capacity of the state is more akin to the natural capacity than to the legal capacity of the individual. Finally, the theory that contends the state is subject to the law on account of a self-limitation of the former basically amounts to saying that only once it has made its first appearance does the state power acquire a legal character.

power to establish *a* new law, this does not imply that it antedates *the* law. Also this manifestation and expression falls under the scope delineated by a pre-existing law, whose original life is the same as this power's. If this is the case, the consequence is that the theory of the self-limitation of the state, whatever the element of truth it contains, cannot be accepted in the over-extended formulation that has been advanced.[71] While it is true that the state limits itself when it establishes its own legal order, there are no circumstances in which it is not limited, precisely because it is an order from the very beginning: its self-limitation cannot be but a further limitation. Therefore, contrary to what is generally believed, statute law [*legge*] is never the beginning of the law [*diritto*]; rather, it is an addition to the pre-existing law (in the hypothesis that it has gaps) or a modification of it.[72] The legislator, then, is not the creator of the law, in the thorough and absolute sense of the word, that is, its original creator. This implies that the legislator lacks the power to annul the law completely; in order to annul it, the legislator should declare the end of the state itself.

2.   Closely akin to the former, if not permanently tied to it, is the view that has the personality of the state beheaded, in that it denies its utmost manifestations, but acknowledges some subordinate ones. In effect, for some[73] the state could take the guise of a person only insofar as it does not present itself or does not act through its sovereign body, which here [in Italy] is the legislative power, while elsewhere is the constituent power. This is because such a body is claimed to be unburdened from any legal regulation. They fail to notice that, if this were true, the only conclusion one should logically reach is that not only should the state not consider itself as a person in that respect; but it would not be amenable to being taken into consideration by the law: the legislative power (or, in other countries, the constituent power) would not be an object, but a premise of constitutional law. This is contrary to the truth, in that the latter not only regulates the structure of such powers, which it even establishes, but also their function, at least from a procedural and formal vantage point – and in my opinion, as far as the legislative power is concerned, also from a substantial vantage point, although partially (§ 22 *sub* 4).

3.   Based on analogous motives, some authors also denied that, from the point of view of domestic law, the territory of the state has legal value. It is claimed to be a constitutive element of the state, and thus outside and before the law.[74]

71 Jellinek, 1880: 9 ff.; Jellinek, 1887: 199 ff.; Jellinek, 1912: 95 ff., 214 ff.; Jellinek, 1914: 367 ff.; Ranelletti, 1912: fn. 94; etc.

72 From quite a different viewpoint, that is, by building on the opinion that legal orders do not have gaps, Donati (1910: 136 ff.) also states that the new statutory law is always a modification of the preceding law. Yet, this remark, evinced from those premises, could not apply to the first law.

73 Kelsen, 1911: 395 ff., 434 ff.; Kelsen, 1913: 4 ff.; Donati, 1914: 320 (who by mistake also attributes this opinion to me); Falchi, 1914: 28; Anzilotti, 1915a: 2 ff. [yet he appears to have discarded this opinion in successive editions: 1928: 39; and the German edition: 309 ff.]; Anzilotti, 1915b: 10.

74 Marinoni, 1912: 7 ff.

Similarly citizenship, as long as it means state membership, is claimed to be devoid of legal value, a merely political condition of the individuals, a simple presupposition of legal power and duties.[75]

On top of a view that looks unacceptable to me and that I will examine later on, both these opinions are nurtured by the conviction that all the elements that determine the existence of the state are antecedent to the law. This is based on the following line of reasoning: the law is issued by the state; thus the state comes before the law; thus all that constitutes the state comes before the law. This neglects that the various elements that comprise the state is and cannot be but the very legal order. Indeed the legal order determines the state structure and assigns to its distinct parts the condition of its elements; in other words, state and state legal order are the same thing.[76]

§ 22. Yet not only the constitutive elements of the state are claimed to have an extra-legal character because they are believed to pre-exist the position of the law; but also a most important set of aspects of its prior life are claimed either to fall outside the legal domain or to be considered by the law in some secondary respects or by reflex. The theories to which I refer mainly, and implicitly, build upon the usual postulate that the legal order is but a set of norms and, secondly, specify and narrow the end, or, as it were, the object of these norms as they identify it with the relationships that might exist among the various individuals: all that cannot be reduced to these relationships is devoid of any legal significance. It would be pointless to dwell on the confutation of these points of view in any specific way, since in the foregoing pages I sought to demonstrate the flaws of both these presuppositions; which is to say, the identification of law with norms and its reduction to the regulation of the relationships among various individuals. It might be useful, however, to briefly mention some of the most remarkable applications of those theories.

1. I already touched upon the theory (§ 8) that the sanction cannot be considered an essential trait of law. We saw how the demonstration of this theory relies on the idea that the law is nothing but a norm governing relationships among individuals, for whom it establishes duties and rights. Drawing on analogous considerations, others did not deny that the order rests on a system of sanctions and coercions, but contended that this can be relevant to the philosopher, not to the jurist. In other words, the sanction is claimed to be extra-legal, precisely because 'as a guarantee of the legal order, [it] has to be abstractly evinced from the complex of objective norm', and for the jurist there are but such norms, singularly considered with respect to the duties and

---

75 Marinoni, 1914: 147 ff.

76 [On the other hand, that the state is a non-legal entity in itself and for itself, and that a concept of different nature predates its legal concept, is an opinion supported by many authors, as I said before. Among others, Rehm, 1899: 11; Jellinek, 1914: 137, 162 ff.; Seidler, 1905: 17 ff.; Ranelletti, 1912: fn. 87–88; Ravà, 1914: 1 ff.; Marinoni, 1916: 236; Marinoni, 1913a: 20; Donati, 1921; etc.]

the power that derive from them, independently of their end vis-à-vis the legal order.[77] This observation contains some elements of truth that I tried to foreground; yet the conclusion to which it leads is utterly unacceptable, one that disappears once we start from a different concept of law.

2.   The opinion, to which I alluded earlier, that state and citizenship are not to be considered from a legal point of view is premised not only on the contention that they concern constitutive elements of the state and thus, according to those views, anterior to the law, but also on the further contention that the jurist is interested in the distinct relationships that the norms determine with regard to those elements, and not to their general position. It is easy to see that this is conducive to an at least incomplete, and thus mistaken, appraisal of these elements: one only has to think of the views of those who, by discarding the first of these considerations – as they do not believe that the territory is a constitutive element of the state – embrace only the second. Then, the thoroughly nihilist conception that I mentioned is superseded by another one, which certainly corresponds more adequately to reality, as it includes within the law something that pertains to the law, but slips this something into the law through a small fissure and with severe subtractions. In this way, within domestic law, and regardless of international law, the question of the character of the state territory is narrowed down as follows: what is the legal relationship between the state and its subjects with respect to the territory itself?[78] The answer to this question is not relevant here, but it is important to notice that in this way what gets suppressed is the problem, quite fundamental, of the legal position of the territory with respect to the state. Even if it were not one of its constitutive elements (which I believe to be incorrect), the powers of the states over this object have to be assessed in their own right, beyond those secondary and derivative aspects concerning its relationship to its subjects.

3.   In substance, it is always the same mistake, which is reiterated in most areas of public law and, at times, of private law: the failure to grant legal significance to the legal order where an institution materializes except for the relationships among individuals that this order reflects. One of the most absurd consequences of this conception, which nevertheless has quite a few and authoritative supporters,[79] is the one that negates the legal significance of the relationships between the state and its bodies, in the sense of agencies, or among its various bodies. The simple remark that these bodies are not subjects of law, which is entirely correct, when connected to a mistaken conception of law, is sufficient to yield to a series of deductions that deny the reality that I believe is most evident. Under our eyes, among these bodies a host of acts takes place, along with procedures that are crucial to the law, which attends to them minutely and makes them the object of its laws, and measures of all sorts. However, these relationships are claimed

---

77 Marinoni, 1913a: 35 ff.
78 This is how Donati (1914: 535 ff.) couches the issue.
79 Among the most explicit, Jellinek, 1912: 213; and lately Ranelletti, 1912: fn. 116 ff., 174.

to lack legal character – and one is left wondering what character they should have – only because they are exhausted within the state organization. But if they turn into acts that have some bearing on subjects (which is not always the case), then, it is worth emphasizing, not only these acts, but also inter-body relationships that paved the way for them, are claimed to acquire legal relevance. A relevance manifestly indirect and furtive, a shade of life, or better, a momentary galvanization. Once that relationship ceases or dims out of our view, which would be but one of their effects and even not necessary, for those who observe them with fresh eyes, they actually continue to take place, to interweave and not arbitrarily, but in compliance with a more complex order. The jurists see them too, and are compelled to, but they, who have formed an idea of the law that they cannot move away from, believe these are 'empty shades, except in seeming'.[80]

In this context I cannot examine the concept and nature of state bodies, impersonally considered as its agencies, if the relationships among them are to be portrayed as reflexive relationships of the state itself, or otherwise. What matters here is to emphasize that, not only those relations, but even the position of each body vis-à-vis the state cannot be determined if one draws on the common conception of law. For not only does this conception lead to the consequences I spoke of above, but, if rigorously applied, also leads to the contention[81] that the legal significance of the concept of state body is naught. The only thing that might be legally significant is the relation between the state and those who operate its agencies. Still, this view is obviously inadmissible. Insofar as it attributes legal significance only to those aspects of the state organization that involve relationships with officials, this view has the same defect as the one that attributes legal significance to such an organization only insofar as it entails relationships with subjects. These two theories could complete and complement one another, and I fail to understand why some advocates of the latter have rejected the former. Still, even if they merge and complete each other, they do fail to pin down the whole phenomenon of the organization of the state. Instead this phenomenon will appear as fully and intrinsically legal only when we accept the principle, which I have advanced in general, that the law is not only norm governing relationships, but first and foremost organization. Indeed, the primary problem that the state legal order as well as any other entity are faced with is not how to regulate the relationships of the state to its subjects and its officials, but how to distinguish its agencies so as to coordinate, separate and group them, to put them in a hierarchy, to keep them in check, and so on. Only afterwards are officials taken into consideration, and most of the time not as duty- or right-bearers, with whom certain relationships exist, but as a means to make the state will or act. The law (and here comes the weak point of the theory of representation) does not treat them as persons who will and

---

80 [Translator's note: Dante, *Purgatorio*, II, 79.]
81 Ferrara, 1915: 623 ff. [in the most recent work he holds a different opinion; see Ferrara, 1938: 89 ff.].

act on behalf of the state, but as human beings who make the state will or act: they might well be an army of slaves, since what matters – in this respect – is not their legal capacity, but their natural capacity. And this all entails the principle that the law encompasses not only an already formed will or an already performed action on the part of the state vis-à-vis other individuals, but what enables the formation of that will and the performance of that action.

4.   There are many more specific problems[82] reflected in the false conception of which I have spoken. One of the most important and most typical concerns the limits of the legislative function. If and how such a function is legally bounded, in my view, is a question that should be solved not in the abstract, but according to the various positive laws. And, as far as Italian law is concerned, elsewhere I have pointed to the existence of a number of limits.[83] On the contrary, some have generally denied the existence of these limits – in the realm of domestic law – in that they claim the state does not, and could not, have any duty to its subjects to issue or not to issue a law.[84] The norms of constitutional law that mention such constraints are to be interpreted as establishing some duties that physical persons comprising legislative bodies have to the state. Evidently this point of view draws on the conception that the relationships which do not take place between two or more individuals and thus, in the present case, which do not take place between the state and its subjects or its officials, do not fall into the legal sphere. In this way, the correct framing of the question is eluded, one that should investigate if, within a particular order, the legislative bodies – either with respect to the state, or in their reciprocal relations, or even in their position, considered in itself and for itself – are required to respect certain limits.[85]

§ 23. As can be easily evinced from what I said, the definition of law I have delineated and developed is not irrelevant to theories centred on rights. I cannot muse on this topic here, as it involves a variety of thorny issues, but the concepts and institutions [*istituti*] that might be illuminated or even amended are several.

To begin with, the concept of legal relationship, which in today's dogmatics – when it is not overstretched to the extent that it becomes inconsistent[86] – is often

---

82 [Among these problems, it is worth noting that of political representation. See Romano, 1945: ch. 11, § 3, esp. fn. 6.]

83 See Romano, 1902 [see now Romano, 1945: ch. 22, § 1, fn. 2].

84 Triepel, 1899: 268–269. On the same wavelength, Anzilotti (1905: 205, fn. 2) avers that the only legal limits that are imposed on the modern state in its legislative function stem from international law, 'as it is impossible to find, in any other case, a subject matching the legal obligation of the state'.

85 One only has to think of the Church law, where also the supreme legislative authority is legally bounded by the *ius divinum*, with no rights of any subjects matching such a limit.

86 Kelsen (1911: 705 ff.) conceives of the legal relationship as a relationship of a subject to the legal order. This is what Cicala (1909: 10 ff) had already claimed before him. It is not that this view is wrong in itself; yet it appears to have to do with quite a different thing than that which one takes into consideration when one speaks, in a traditional sense, of legal relationship.

reduced to relationships that obtain between two or more persons; at the same time, it is believed that only those relationships are encompassed by the matter that constitutes the object of law, whereas the latter, as we have seen, has a far broader reach. The consequence of such a view is not only that some aspects are taken out of the law as pre-legal or extra-legal, whereas they are essentially comprised in that realm; it also disfigures other concepts as it reduces them to that of relationship, in the abovementioned sense.

Among these disfigurations I can mention those that sometimes are imposed on the concept of *status*,[87] which someone even rejected, as for example is the case with the *status civitatis* and as might be the case with others, precisely because they are not legal relationships, but a mere prerequisite of them.[88]

I believe it is just as incorrect to define rights *in rem* by emphasizing their so-called outer side, namely, the relationship of the right-bearer to other people, his power to exclude others from the thing and to prevent them from using it. On the contrary, in my opinion, the main and fundamental side of rights *in rem* is one's power on things, one that, for the prejudice I just pointed out, is often considered as a legally indifferent *res merae facultatis*. If one wants to conceive of the legal right as a relationship and, at the same time, to latch on its genuine content, then one cannot but recognize that a legal relationship can take place between a person and a thing.

This entails that, on the one hand, as the tradition would have it, the concept of legal relationship can be granted a broader scope than the one some authors attribute to it. On the other hand, it is not necessary to identify this figure when it actually does not obtain, on the erroneous grounds that it would otherwise be impossible to legally appraise particular facts, aspects or positions. From this point of view, I have a few misgivings about such procedural law doctrines that have made use of the concept of relationship in a way that is neither always necessary nor easily justifiable.

Moreover, once we establish that the legal order does not only regulate relationships, let alone in the sense of relationships between matching rights and obligations, this theory founders on the lack of basis – a basis that is commonly acknowledged but is at odds with positive law, according to which one's legal obligation is necessarily coupled with another's right. This theory, which might be true within modern private law, does not make sense as far as public law is concerned, at least in most cases; indeed public law, even today, and more evidently in

---

87 On this issue, see Redenti, 1911: 91 ff.; Cicu, 1914.

88 See Marinoni's view on citizenry I refer to above. And it is understandable that, in that perspective, not only the concept of *status*, but also that of personality gets dismembered, and dissected into distinct relationships that are tied to it. In this way, Marinoni (1913b: 351, fn.) himself affirms: 'The legal personality of a subject – regardless of the legal order that confers it – cannot be constituted but by the attribution, within and for this legal order, of one or more rights, one or more duties; therefore, personality cannot be either attributed or recognized independently of particular rights and particular duties, as only they can constitute and characterize it'. Other authors (Jellinek, 1912: 31) comprehensively conceive of personality as a relationship: it 'is not mainly an entity, but a relationship that exists between a subject and other subjects and the legal order'.

earlier orders, exhibits a series of obligations on the part of public bodies that are matched by no claims to the advantage of the subjects.[89] This is most important to the correct formulation of many problems, both general ones, such as that of the nature of individuals' public rights, and more particular ones, such as the one I mentioned above of the limits of the legislative function. I could go even further, as this conception can help assess more precisely than the way it is currently done the meaning and scope of the reciprocal statement that all public powers are matched to subjects' duties: this correlation is to be understood in a generic sense, and, more than in the specific realm of concrete relationships, in the overall position that public entities enjoy vis-à-vis its subjects and vice versa.

This latter remark, in conjunction with the foregoing ones, could help demonstrate the inadmissibility of the view, recently advanced by many authors,[90] that all subjects are to be considered equal before the law. It is evident that this view rests on the prejudice that the legal order contains nothing but rights and obligations, distinctly determined and attributed by the norm, and that it can disregard the subjects' reciprocal position unless it morphs into one of its many relationships, where rights and obligations match. In this way, individuals' subjection to the state is claimed to be pre-legal, much in the same way as the parallel thesis, examined in § 21, assigns an analogous character to the state *imperium*: where the law rules, there is nothing but the legal relationship, 'relationship of reciprocal and equal imputation'. Such a thesis perhaps is not to be deemed correct, not even from the limited vantage point of the concept of the legal relationship. However, this view turns out to be redundant when it is stated that the state's generic and overall position, namely, its power of supremacy, as well as the position of its subjects, namely, their dependence and subjection, fall under the scope of the legal order or, better, they are and cannot but be determined by the latter.

§ 24. The notion of law that I have deployed, therefore, is justified not only by abstract requirements, but also by the need to avoid offering an incorrect solution to concrete problems – some of which I have discussed. If I laid a claim to the borders that, after all, are those that the tradition has always materially assigned to law – although it never made an attempt to define correctly – nowadays this proves necessary as we are faced with a tendency that severely impoverishes it, and even alters it within the limited field that it grants it. I laid this claim by rigorously positioning myself in the frame of a positivist conception of law and by eschewing any natural law views. The concept of institution, in which I found or, better, with which I identified that of the legal order, is the most positive concept that a legal theory can take as its basis. The institution is not a rational requirement, an abstract principle, an ideal *quid*; it is a real, effective entity. On the other hand, I

---

89 For some observations in this sense, see Cicu, 1915: 143 ff.; Carnelutti, 1915: 59–60 [and nowadays many other authors: see Romano, 1945: ch. 8, § 2, fn. 4 and, lately, Miele, 1945: § 4].
90 Petrone, 1897: 140 ff.; Marinoni, 1910: 260 ff; Kelsen, 1911: x, 225 ff.; Schenk, 1914: 72. Against Kelsen, see Tezner, 1914: 5 ff., and also Nawiasky, 1913: 13 ff.

heeded this entity not from the point of view of the material forces that produce and sustain it, nor in relation to the environment where it develops and lives as a phenomenon intertwined with others, nor with regard to cause–effect relationships that affect it, and therefore, not sociologically, but in itself and for itself, inasmuch as it results from a legal order or, better, it is a system of law. Naturally, I had to go further up to the ultimate reasons, where one can breathe the legal atmosphere, but I never surpassed it. And, while the conventional theory is forced to mark out the field abstractly, and therefore not without uncertainties, I tried to exhaust law in itself, that is, in an objective entity, which is its principle, its domain and its end.

It is not pointless to repeat that the concept of law I formulated does not intend (quite the contrary!) to efface that by which it is represented as norm or set of norms (see above *passim* and in particular § 10). I only wanted to demonstrate the need for the latter to be included in the former, as a less comprehensive and secondary concept, which cannot be rightly defined and assessed if one isolates it from the whole to which it belongs and with which it is organically connected. In my view, all norms that can be found in a particular positive law are nothing but elements of a broader, more complex order and hinge on it, as it is its necessary and unavoidable basis. To limit myself to state law, there are some of its branches where the element 'norm' prevails, so much so that it can be considered – to a certain extent – as the exclusive one. For example, private law and criminal law, although, as we saw, some aspects of the former cannot be pinpointed, or are wrongly pinpointed, if one neglects the broader notion of a legal order. Among these aspects, legal persons and certain other institutions, such as the family, whose unit is affirmed but not exactly defined, or the company, improperly confined to the *universitates* of inert things. As to other branches of state law, my theory acquires more evidence. Constitutional law is not exhausted by the norms that regulate the relationships of the state; on the contrary, it first and foremost encompasses the state in itself and for itself, in its elements, structure, functions, which, like the legislative one, do not generate distinct and concrete relationships. This is the domain where the perspective of law as an institution is so decisive and comprehensive that neglecting or rejecting it almost implies annihilating constitutional law as a whole. But also administrative law, before it governs the relationships generated by the administrative function, is the law that establishes the organization of the entities carrying out this function. Likewise, procedural law, in its further developments, draws upon the organization of the judiciary power, and so on. However, when it comes to scientific treatises about these branches of law, when one moves from the parts dealing with the ways in which an institution presents and affirms itself in its own structure to the parts where the perspective of law as norm prevails, one gets the impression that a change in the atmosphere has occurred and the treatise has adopted a different tone. This is perfectly natural and necessary, as it corresponds to different aspects of law. But those who cannot make sense of this necessity and believe the true, pure law is only where the norm dominates, are placed by that impression in a situation of discomfort or unease, and are often prompted to omit, almost always curtail the analysis of the other parts. In this way, above all in the German doctrine, administrative law scholars often pass over the theory of administrative organization,[91] and, in the field of procedural law, also among us, scholars often neglect the so-called judiciary order and reduce it to a few preliminary notions. These are extrinsic, indirect and often intangible consequences, but they are symptomatic of the one-sided conception of law I strove to complement.[92]

91 See Mayer's (1917: 17–18) remarks on the opportunity of German administrative law to expunge the analysis of administrative organization, as constitutional law and *Staatsrecht* could deal with it. Evidently, this is but a makeshift not to combine two analyses in which one point of view, while prevailing, conflicts with the other. In the first edition of his treatise, Mayer (1895: 14) had gone so far as to say that the administrative organization is not necessarily a legal order [unlike the 3rd edition, Mayer, 1934: 18]. On the other hand, this view has become common currency within German jurisprudence: see esp. Anschütz, 1890 [Translator's note: here Romano makes a mistake, as the correct reference seems to be Bernatzik, 1890].

92 [It is not easy to summarize the various jurisprudential reactions to my view, which identifies the concept of a legal order with that of institution, in the sense that I attributed to this word. Leaving aside a particular literature and particular criticisms, which evidently lack any scientific consistency and show utter incomprehension of the fundamental problems of the general theory of law, I would like to note that my conception has met with resistance especially among legal philosophers and jurists who have dealt with it from a philosophical point of view. See the works I already mentioned in fn. 43 and other junctures, by Del Vecchio, Miceli, Cesarini Sforza, Volpicelli, Crisafulli, Capograssi, Bobbio, and, in addition, Cammarata, 1925: 49 ff., 158 ff.; Cammarata, 1926; Condorelli, 1931: 585; Passerin d'Entrèves, 1934: 44 ff.; Perticone, 1938: 49 ff., and other writings; Battaglia, 1940: 170; Orestano, 1941: 103, 143, 278, etc. Still, it is not always easy to clarify to what extent and in what sense some of these authors contest my conception, let alone if they understood it correctly. In fact, sometimes they reject it in itself and for itself, but then they apply it in a way that logically seems to presuppose its acceptance. Others recognize that, in developing it, I did not pursue any philosophical intent, as I openly declared, and yet they insist in criticizing it with philosophical lens (e.g. Bonucci, Perticone). On the contrary, others, although they denied its philosophical value, adhere to it in the domain of legal dogmatics (Volpicelli, Crisafulli, Capograssi). Moreover, there are authors who accept it for the purposes of legal philosophy: Maggiore, 1925: 127, and other writings, such as Maggiore, 1937: fn. 2 and 3; and, at least in part, Carlini, 1938: 887. Among jurists, if we ignore again quite a few authors who have completely misunderstood my thinking, against my theory: Ferrara, 1921: 13 fn.; Orlando (1926a and 1926b), notwithstanding the fact that he rejected many of the criticisms addressed to me; Maiorca, 1933: 311; Chiarelli, 1936: 135 ff., although he is averse to the normativist theory; aslo Chairelli, 1932: 151; Mortati, 1940: 58 ff., at least substantially; Gueli, 1942: 126 ff., 212; Ziccardi, 1943: 71, although he acknowledges some results that he claims I achieved (see also 108 ff., 120 ff.); etc.

Besides these authors, some scholars adhere to my view, completely or in part, although they reject it from a philosophical point of view and accept it from a legal point of view (Volpicelli, Crisafulli, Capograssi); along with Maggiore, whom I also cited, see Criscuoli, 1922: 32; Mastino, 1923: 187; Ruffini, 1924: 70; Levi, 1924: 70; Breschi, 1920: 87 ff.; Cereti, 1925; Fedozzi, 1940; Baldoni, 1931; Rocco, 1933: 42; Manzini, 1933: fn. 103; Caristia, 1919: 18 ff.; Caristia, 1935: fn. 4; Paresce: 14; Monaco, 1938; Zanobini, 1949: 621; Zanobini, 1936: 10 ff.; Miele, 1936: 418, 419; I, fn. 1; Sinagra, 1935: 18 ff.; Biscaretti di Ruffia, 1939, and now also Biscaretti di Ruffia, 1946: 43 ff.; Schmitt, 1934: 11 ff.; Messineo, 1943: § 1, fn. 10, 15, 16; § 4, fn. 20, 21, 23; etc.

There are authors whose thinking I'm not sure I am interpreting correctly. Piccardi, 1939: 256 ff. and *passim*. Carnelutti, 1939: 40, 65; Carnelutti, 1940: 95, 96, § 54; Ago, 1943: 22 ff. These scholars seem to believe that the concept of a legal order coincides with that of organization, and therefore with that of institution, while the latter concept coincides with that of a complex or system of norms (or commands, according to Carnelutti's terminology, or evaluations, according to Ago's terminology). Nonetheless, I fail to understand how a command, a norm, an evaluation, which in itself and for itself is not legal, can acquire legality because it belongs to a system of norms, of commands or evaluations, that is to say, when it belongs to an ensemble of norms none of which is in itself legal: non-law plus non-law is not tantamount to a law. In addition, if by organization, system, etc., we mean not a simple complex of norms, but something different, do we not fall back into the concept of institution, conceived as a social entity that does not only comprise norms and in which a legal order materialized in its entirety and in its fundamental and primary aspect? In other words, the authors I just mentioned seem to stop halfway to the right pathway. This gets reflected also in the terminology they adopt: the word 'organization', in fact, is used quite improperly if it is meant to design only a complex of norms, which, considered in itself and for itself, it is by no means an organization.

On the relations of this issue with the other one as to whether or not the law has a state character, see the literature mentioned in ch. 2, fn. 31.

In substance, the most important objections to the institutional theory of law, in the way I formulated it, can be succinctly summarised as follows:

1. The concept of institution comes across as not clearly and precisely defined. On this issue, see fn. 37 and also fn. 35.
2. The concept of institution is not a legal concept. This is a blatantly unfounded observation, if one keeps in mind that it has been framed as equivalent to that of legal order, and that therefore it could hardly be more legal. See fn. 38, the pages of the text to which it refers and what I observe in § 24.
3. It is a tautological concept. In the same fn. 38 and in § 24 I observed that, on the contrary, it is a necessary consequence and demonstration of the autonomy of the concept of law, which is not to be defined with reference to non-legal concepts or elements.
4. The concept of institution presupposes that of law, is antecedent to the latter, and therefore cannot coincide with it. As far as this point is concerned, see what I had said in the text especially § 15, fn. 38, fn. 43, § 21 and fn. 75.
5. The law expresses a deontological requirement while the institution is a fact, and what is cannot be identified with what ought to be. It is evident that this does nothing but reaffirm the normative conception of law, without adding any arguments to defend it and to rebut the arguments advanced against it. It is worth noting that I did not expunge the normative and relational character of law, as I only tried to complement it, in the way it looks necessary to me, with the institutional one, by emphasizing the relations of the former to the latter. It is my conviction that such a necessity stems not only from legal considerations, but also from various philosophical considerations, such as those relating to the distinction of law from morality and economy; in a word, from the other manifestations of the so-called practical activity, as well as the explanation of the existence of the *ius involuntarium* and its nature and the problem itself of the function of law. But in this book I do not want to defect from my intention to remain within the purely legal domain. I then limit myself to observing that, when one attributes an exclusively normative character to the legal order, perhaps sometimes this is suggested by the remark that legal science, or better, that legal science that is called jurisprudence, is a normative science: one incurs a misunderstanding akin to that which is incurred when one aims to infer a similar character of language from the normative character of grammar. Indeed, it is well-known that the exclusively normative theory of legal science is on the wane: see, among others, Bobbio, 1934; Piccardi, 1939: 260, 283; Ziccardi, 1943: 113; Ago, 1943: 43; Gueli, 1942: 16 ff.; etc.
6. The concept of legal order cannot refer to all institutions, but has to be limited to the state, or, at most, few other institutions. In the second chapter, I will demonstrate the groundlessness of the narrowest of these opinions and the arbitrariness, even logical, of the others.]

Chapter 2

§ 25. From the concept of a legal order that I offered in the previous chapter we can deduce the corollary that there are as many legal orders as institutions. As I suggested (§ 12), and as I will explain in more detail shortly, they might be connected in such a way that, while their orders keep distinct in some respects, in other respects they constitute elements of a broader order, or rather, of a broader institution of which they are integral parts. However, this is not always the case, nor is there an institution that indistinctly encompasses all the others. Most of the time, each state is without a doubt to be considered an order completely distinct from the other states. And the international community itself, although it is an institution of institutions, consists in an order that presupposes the various state orders; nonetheless, by affirming their independence and autonomy, the international community does not incorporate them in its order. This principle, which might be called 'the plurality of legal orders', is unquestioned when applied to the various states, and also, at least in the most recent doctrine, when applied to the relations between international law and state laws. However, it is often energetically rejected when it comes to other orders. What is more, the state is most often claimed to imprint on them a legal character, either when it directly brings them about or when it simply recognizes them. When this recognition does not occur, as is the case with institutions that are hostile to the state or, in any case, are contrary to the essential principles established by the state as the basis of its law, it is claimed that such institutions are to be considered as anti-legal – not only, as is obvious, with respect to the state, but in themselves and for themselves. The claim is made that there are no legal orders other than the state and the interstate ones: the other orders directly or indirectly fall within the jurisdiction of the state, as complementary elements of its system, or at most its satellites. The law is believed to be but a force or a will radiating from the state (within the international community from more states), and only from it.[1]

---

1   It is almost impossible to mention all the writers who uphold this thesis or adopt it as an indemonstrable postulate. I will limit myself to a few indications. As to the Italian literature: Filomusi Guelfi, 1917: §§ 14, 122; Vanni, 1906: 58, 68, and especially 81 ff.; Miceli, 1906: 127 ff.; Simoncelli, 1917;

To commence, this thesis appears to be in stark contrast not only to the abstract concept of law I delineated, but also to history and to today's legal life, in the way it unfolds within reality.

§ 26. Undoubtedly, this conception is relatively recent, at least as a conception that advances a theoretical principle. This does not exclude the fact that, in certain periods and especially in ancient times, the only legal order that jurists and philosophers took into account was the state legal order. Nor can we regard as an extension of such a limited perspective the fact, however we interpret it, that the Romans had the *ius gentium* or *naturale* alongside the *ius civile*. Indeed, this did not happen on account of a theory, whose traces are nowhere to be found, but on account of a series of factual circumstances that obscured other orders that nobody had the opportunity to foreground and utilize for the purposes of a general concept of law in a positive sense. On the contrary, in the Middle Ages – because of the constitution itself of a society that was divided, riven with many and diverse communities often independent from, or loosely connected to, each other – the phenomenon of the plurality of legal orders manifested itself with such an evidence and force that it would be impossible not to reckon with it. Aside from other orders, which still had a remarkable character of autonomy, suffice it to recall the law of the Church, which could hardly be considered as part of state law. However, the rise of the so-called modern state, and the consequent expansion of its force and its dominance over other communities that had so far been independent and sometimes antagonistic to it, nurtured the illusion that there was a unified legal order. Without blatant and glaring contradiction with reality, this fostered the theory that deems the state to be the lord and the arbiter not only of its law, but of all law.

This theory can be historically explained as an incorrect assessment and an exaggeration of an event that admittedly had a remarkable importance (§ 27), but it has to be doctrinally reconnected to a natural law conception. Even if, at first sight, it seems to be its complete antithesis, it is one of the most conspicuous residues. For such a natural conception typically portrays the law as the concrete actualization – which is supposed to be the only and uniform one – of the transcendent and absolute principle of an abstract and eternal justice. Consequently, this conception rejects the legal character of all social orders that cannot at least be considered as attempts, though imperfect, at such an actualization. Even worse, they are said to be averse to that idea of justice. The doctrine that claims the

---

17; Brugi, 1907: §§ 10, 11; Petrone, 1910: 135 ff.; Dallari, 1911: 422 ff.; Ranelletti, 1912: fn. 39; Chironi, 1912: § 1; Schiappoli, 1913: fn. 15 ff.; Arangio-Ruiz, 1913: fn. 15 ff.; Bartolomei, 1914: 118 ff.; Barassi, 1915: § 1; De Ruggiero, 1915: § 7; [De Ruggiero and Maroi, 1945: § 7;] Del Giudice, 1915: 52 ff.; Maggiore, 1916: 107 ff.; Bonucci, 1915: 44 ff. As to the literature abroad: Jhering, 1897: ch. 8; Lasson, 1882: 412; Berolzheimer, 1906: 322; Jellinek, 1914: 364; Kelsen, 1911: 97 ff., 405 ff.; Kelsen, 1913: 9; [Kelsen, 1920: 13 ff.]. [In the work that appeared after this text was published, the orientation of the literature on the law and the state has remarkably changed; see references fn. 31 below.]

state is the only body, as is usually said, or the only producer of law, is evidently premised upon this type of view, complemented by the other – more recent in some of its developments – that depicts the state as the ethical entity par excellence. It is the coalescence between these two theories that gave rise to the modern one I am speaking of, one that has become predominant at the beginning of the 18th century, and still finds support among those who reject its historical grounds. Yet, it is absolutely inseparable from the theories that laid its foundations. This explains why its latest advocates just enounce it rather than vindicate its truth. And in effect, one would not know how to justify it theoretically if not by making two assumptions: on the one hand, positive law cannot and should not be but the product of natural law; on the other hand, the only entity that, at least today, is well equipped to turn natural law into its positive laws is the state. In this way, one gets to that conception of the state of which Hegel was the most logical and most suggestive advocate. If with this philosopher we admit that the state is an ethical totality, that it represents the entrance of God into the world, that we must honour it as something worldly-divine, and that it is even a real god,[2] then we are faced with a system that cannot be jettisoned without counterposing another. And those who follow it – provided that they, at the same time, totally encompass and enfold the legal phenomenon in its ethical principle – welsh on a more complete demonstration of its tenet. However, not only would the latter become groundless should those premises collapse; but it also proves incompatible with any other premise. Anyway, although still audible, the indistinct and distant echo of Hegel's limpid and precise theory is not enough, if in its latest formulations it only survives as the memory of Hegel's most expressive statements. Parenthetically, there is something I would like to remark apropos one of the latest defences that has been attempted – more than developed – of the doctrine that traces the legal order back to one will, that of the state, by contending that it derives from a mental need akin to the one that leads to the idea of God: the analogy between the legal microcosm and the macrocosm of the order of the universe compels this personification, which enables the conception of one will in a harmonic system.[3]

Based on all this, we can reach the conclusion that those who think of the state as one of the forms, if the most advanced one, of human society and has no reason to attribute a divinity to it (a divinity that they deny to the forms that preceded the state or that are contemporary to it) also have to admit that the orders of these

---

2   Hegel, 2008: § 257 ff.; and additions to §§ 258–272.
3   Kelsen, 1913: 9 [Kelsen (1920: 21, fn.) returns to these concepts in other writings by saying, among other things, that the might of God in the world corresponds to the might of the state, and that the *Summa theologica* and the *Summa juridica* have the same meaning. If I get it right, perhaps this position comes close to Carnelutti's (1939) when, after embracing the principle of the plurality of the legal orders (40 ff.), he comments that the 'law, if we take a closer look at it, shows itself as one immense institution. Nowadays we are more or less aware of this, because we know that the law culminates in the state' (67). See also Carnelutti, 1940, §§ 55, 56, 57.]

societies are to be considered legal – no less legal and not differently than the state order. Indeed, what can be the necessary link between the law and the state, whereby the former cannot be imagined other than as the product of the latter? Not only can we not demonstrate that this link exists, but we can demonstrate that it does not exist.[4] For, while the concept of law can be perfectly defined without the concept of the state, it is impossible to define the state with no reference to the concept of law. The state is not a material union of human beings, a random or casual aggregate: it is an organized community, i.e. a legal entity, one of the various legal orders that reality presents us with.

Thus, the state is nothing other than a species of the genus 'law'. From a philosophical vantage point, the opposite statement proves unacceptable for three reasons. First, because the premises of which it claims to be a corollary are just as unacceptable. Second, because it is incompatible with the concept of law that, as we saw, is logically antecedent to that of the state. Third, because we cannot grant philosophical (i.e. absolute) value to a principle that, especially in particular historical periods, proved to be in the starkest contrast to reality.

§ 27. Very often, however, the notion that, whether directly or indirectly, identifies the law with state orders does not emerge as a philosophical theory. Rather, it is advanced as a principle of positive law evinced from the position that the state is claimed to have acquired in the modern era, remarkably different from its prior position. Even if reduced to such minimal terms, I believe this notion cannot be accepted.

First of all, most probably it originates from nothing else but the desire, albeit unconscious, not to make a shipwreck of those profoundly suggestive philosophical views I mention above. Rescue attempts of this sort are destined not to be successful, and they look suspicious anyway. If a theory that came into life within the realm of philosophical speculation does not prove vital in that realm, it is just as unlikely to survive within the realm of the science of positive law. Indeed, it cannot live unless it gets completely transformed, that is to say, unless it ceases to be that theory.

However, regardless of that, I believe that the way in which the current state is arranged by positive law excludes the fact that it has become the only entity that decides on the legal character of the other social orders. The opposite view benefits and gets arguments in its favour from a historically true fact, which however should be neither exaggerated nor generalized. It is true that many entities that in the past were independent of the state, or at least more independent, today have been embedded within its scope, or, if they were already, in an even narrower scope. It is just as true that, as a consequence, their legal orders in some cases have merged more or less completely with that of the state. Nevertheless, the idea that the state system has become the only system in the legal world is to be most decidedly rejected. What is more, what is to be rejected is the material possibility of such

4   Among others, Stammler (1911: 396 ff., and some preceding works) has tried to argue this point.

a concentration. Should we rely on prophecies, however simplistic, we could stress that in a not too distant future the opposite process is likely to take place. For the so-called crisis of the modern state entails the tendency of an enormous series of social groups to constitute independent legal circles of their own.[5] In any case, if we remain within the terrain of the existing law, my thesis can be readily proven with reference to some orders, although, as we will see, it also applies to others.

§ 28. First of all, with regard to international law. The only truly logical conception that is admissible if one draws on those presuppositions is the one advocated by Hegel. As is well known, based on the principle that the state cannot be subjected to a superior will, he claimed that international law does not consist in a general will constituted above the various states, but comes down to the particular will of each of them.[6] Still, this notion undoubtedly is tantamount to refuting international law, as it is turned into state external public law.[7]

The attempt to find something in between with a view to salvaging, at one and the same time, the dogma that the state cannot be coerced if not by means and with the collaboration of its own will and the autonomy of international law ends up in quite an unconvincing logical trick. Without repeating the observations I made earlier (§ 17), which I am echoing, I would like to add that, in substance, today's most common theory unceasingly teeters between two contradictory statements: that international law depends on the will of the states and that it prevails over that will. To reconcile this antithesis, scholars opt for a makeshift as they distinguish two aspects of the first and the second principles mentioned above. However, it has to be noted that international law appears to be truly law only insofar as it binds and dominates the will of the state, that is to say, insofar as it transcends it and affirms itself as an entity in its own right. In my opinion, this is the order of the international community, to which the distinct states are subordinate, albeit to a limited extent. The broadest constellation of the legal universe, therefore, is not the state, but that community, with which it is intermingled, although to a smaller degree than how other entities, in their turn, are intermingled with the state.

From this point of view, we can better understand the separation, today generally agreed upon, between the state legal order and the international order: hence the possibility for the former to contain elements that are contrary to the latter and vice versa, without this impairing or subtracting anything to their respective legal

---

5   See Romano, 1910: 97 ff.

6   Hegel, 2008: § 333. These theses are now being brought to the fore, from different points of view, by Verdross, 1914: 329 ff. [More in general one has to keep in mind the so-called monist conception propounded by the Viennese school (Kelsen, Verdross, Merkl, Wenzel, etc.), in that some of its members, in various senses and with different overtones, advocate the primacy of state law over international law, whilst others advocate the primacy of the latter over the former].

7   See especially Anzilotti, 1902a: 30 ff.; Anzilotti, 1902b: 26 ff., fn., and the authors cited therein [as well as the more recent ones. Among them, see Romano, 1949 and the authors mentioned in the *retro* of the fn., who have embraced the concepts advanced in the text].

character. Each of them is independent and enjoys its own autonomy, in such a way that, within their own sphere, both freely deploy their lives and their force. If one builds on different premises, the conflict between international law and state law should not be deemed admissible.

§ 29. Secondly, there is another order, that of the Church, which cannot be reduced to the state order without misrecognizing and annihilating it. It even helped those who contemplated it without prejudices to reject the identification between all law and the law of the state. Indeed, many writers have come to a (from this viewpoint) correct conception of the law in general exactly by building upon the analysis of the ecclesiastical order. And it is odd that they have sometimes been charged either with a *petitio principii* or, worse, with malice, or slyness:[8] almost as if law should or could be defined – by the jurist – by ignoring those orders that in reality affirm themselves as legal and have always been considered as such.

The thesis that the order of the Church obtains its legal character from that of the state[9] is blatantly at odds with the most essential elements of both the former and the latter. To begin with, it has to be noted that the law of the state that concerns ecclesiastical matters has – always and in every country – a much narrower reach then that of the order established by the Church. Hence the logical necessity for that doctrine, especially today, to qualify as non-legal a series of institutions [*istituti*] that have traditionally been considered as legal institutions [*istituti*]: matrimonial canon law, criminal canon law, the sacramental law in general, and so on.[10] It is true that they are no longer relevant to state law, at least directly. Nevertheless, it is paradoxical to claim that, because of this, they have lost every legal characteristic, despite the fact that they are still positive institutions regulated and guaranteed by a whole system of norms, bodies, courts, and sanctions internal to the Church. And this should be enough to warn against the premises that are conducive to such a stupefying consequence. Everything makes me think that those who deny these institutions being legal would feel uncomfortable if they were asked not to limit themselves to such a simple denial and to determine that positive character, which I do not know what it would be like.

But there is something more. Obviously, the doctrine that the state grants a legal mark to the order of the Church does not deny that the ecclesiastical law, so conceived – only in part, indeed in the smallest part – arises from the state, and

---

8 See this reproach in Petrone, 1905: 127; Dallari, 1911: 438; Del Giudice, 1915: 45–46 [however, there are later works by this author that go down a different road, which I will have the opportunity to mention shortly].

9 In addition to the authors cited in the previous footnote, see Thudicum, 1887: 6; Jhering, 1897: ch. 8; Jellinek, 1914: 367 (more mitigated in Jellinek, 1912: 302–303); Ranelletti, 1912: 61 ff., 499; Schiappoli, 1913: fn. 15 ff.

10 Lately, in this respect, see Del Giudice, 1915: 48–49.

admits that, on the contrary, it is primarily constituted by the Church. However, the power of the latter to issue that law is claimed to be neither its own nor original, because it is attributed to the Church by the state. When it comes to confessional states, it is believed to be a power of autarchy exercised by the Church as an indirect body of the state through 'delegation', with a view to pursuing interests that are not only the Church's but also the state's. Instead, when it comes to secular states, it makes no sense to speak of autarchy, let alone of a delegation of a power that the state does not possess precisely because it is a secular state. Therefore, we have the figure of autonomy.[11]

The evidence that that this construction is inadmissible can be obtained by the simple observation that it is impossible to conceive a confessional state that disavows a dogma of the Church and that considers as bestowed or delegated something that the Church regards as its own. And as a matter of fact – here I cannot carry out a historical enquiry, however short – no confessional state has ever treated the Church as if it were a municipality or one of those public bodies that the modern doctrine qualifies as autarchic.

In addition, the concept of autonomy, which is believed to define the legislative power of the Church, is not mistaken in itself. However, it does not solve the question. On the contrary, it solves it in the opposite sense to the one with respect to which it is evoked. In fact, among the various meanings that are attributed to the word 'autonomy', for the purposes of the present argument, the one that is implied when we speak of the autonomy of the individuals is to be ruled out. For, even according to the theory I am speaking of, ecclesiastical entities are public entities. I would also exclude – as an assumption – that it is autonomy in the sense of an entity's power to give itself an order, one that belongs to the entities that, owing to their overall position, are said to be autarchic. This means that the autonomy of the Church cannot be but a power that the state does not attribute, but only recognizes, when it does recognize it. This amounts to admitting that this power pre-exists state recognition, that the latter is not its foundation, but the condition for its legitimate exercise under the state order and with the effects that are dubbed 'civil'. Lack of recognition implies lack of these effects, but not its ineffectiveness in the sphere outside the state.

The truth is that the theories that I oppose are suggested and nurtured by a misunderstanding that is worth unearthing. For some scholars maintain that there is *an* ecclesiastical law and very logically point out that its sources cannot be at the same time constituted by the Church and the state, which are in competition, most often even in conflict. If this were the case – they claim – various parts of this law, which might be, and often are, in antithesis to one another, could not be put together if not through a sort of referee called upon to discriminate those norms that, for a variety of reasons, achieve their ends, attain social effectiveness,

11 Jellinek, 1914: 367; Del Giudice, 1915: 56 ff.

manage to impose themselves and therefore are positively legal, from others that, hampered by materially stronger norms, remain dead letter and therefore are to be qualified as a-legal or, at least, imperfect.[12] This discrimination and assessment could not be carried out if not on the grounds of the importance of norms, of their correspondence to the general conscience or to the so-called common senti-ment, that is to say, two criteria that are alien to positive law. For this reason, the concept of ecclesiastical law, which these arguments are meant to combat, could be qualified, and thereby rightly dismissed, as a 'sociological' or a 'relativistic' conception.

It is not for me to investigate whether or not this conception has ever actually been adopted in these specific terms by anybody, or whether, on the contrary, it is rather a windmill, which takes the appearance of an armoured giant because of non-essential elements that are present in the formulation of other theories. It is likely that this guise mainly depends on the fact that often, for the purposes of teaching or with other practical intents, in the ecclesiastical subject-area, the law of the Church and the law of the state are glued together in one enquiry. Occa-sionally some elements of the former that are not relevant to the latter are even omitted, or given less attention. There is no denying that, more often than not, this combination has generated misunderstandings and errors. Anyway, the concep-tion of ecclesiastical law that I believe to be correct is another, quite different one. In brief, it can be summarized as follows.

In ecclesiastical matters the order of the Church and that of each state are too diverse and distinct orders, with spheres, sources, organization, sanctions of their own. They hardly constitute, the one in conjunction with the other, a real unity. Therefore, it is improper to speak of an ecclesiastical law arising from the coex-istence and the combination of the orders mentioned above, no matter how it is obtained. For we are presented with many ecclesiastical laws: that of the Church, on one hand, and that of the distinct states, on the other. Between the former and the latter there can be commonalities as well as antinomies. They can prop against each other, presuppose each other, recognize each other, as well as fight and disavow each other. The relevance and consequences of this are not identi-cal, but similar to those yielded by analogous relations existing between orders of different states or between states and the international order. After all, as we will see, these are relations that do not only take place in the cases I alluded to, but, *mutatis mutandis*, between many other orders of different sort. From a legal point of view, each order, that of the state and that of the Church, should be considered in itself and for itself; and when we consider the one, we have to take the other into account only if, and insofar as, the former implies it for its own purposes and in the sense in which it does so, which might vary significantly. Each order operates on its own, for its own purposes, within its scope and with a force that originates from its

12 Del Giudice, 1915: 43 ff.

organization and from its intrinsic characteristics. The state, then, can claim sovereignty over the Church within the sphere in which this can be deployed, in such a way that the state might freely impose the limits it wishes on the Church's power. And when the state recognizes the Church, the limits and the effect of this recognition are determined exclusively by state law. On the other hand, the Church, by virtue of its autonomy – which does not derive from the state, but rests upon its own order – exercises its power on its members, on the entities that comprise it, and on those with which it is involved in a relation, including the state. Within the limits recognized by the state either as lawful or as otherwise relevant, the Church can also achieve 'civil effects'. Otherwise, it can only count on its spiritual and internal sanctions, which I believe are genuine legal sanctions on account of their nature and their institutional character, whether or not they are backed by civil sanctions (§ 14).[13] In this way, the state can, for example, allow the clergy to marry, while the Church can legally prohibit it; the state can abolish the obligation to tithe, while the Church can continue to impose it, and so on. All these privileges, obligations, exemptions are valid for the order within which they are brought about and subsist independently of any conflicting dispositions of the other order. These are two legal worlds, where the one can materially affect the other, while legally they always remain, or are likely to remain, distinct and autonomous.[14]

§ 30. These concepts apply to the relations of state law to international law also according to today's prevailing opinion, and to the Church's law, although this is often neglected. Yet they will appear even more correct in so far as they, in my opinion, can be applied to the relations between the state and the institutions that the state considers unlawful.[15] Their unlawfulness exists, and can only exist, in the eyes of the state order. The state can persecute them with all its means, and therefore can bring

13 The opposite view, on the contrary, often builds on the principle that genuine sanction is only that which is imposed by the state (Jhering; Jellinek; etc.).

14 [More or less in agreement, see now, among others, Coviello, 1922: 2–3; Jemolo, 1923; Jemolo, 1933: 68 ff., 77 ff.; Del Giudice, 1924; Del Giudice, 1933: 1 ff.; Del Giudice, 1944: 13; Del Giudice, 1939: 2 ff.; Cornaggia Medici, 1933: 71, 107, 238, 244, 282; Zanobini, 1936: 10; Jannaccone, 1936: 19; D'Avack, 1937a: 12, 13, 241; D'Avack, 1939: 313; Checchini, 1937: 10; Piola, 1937; 131; Giacchi, 1937: 327, 328, 330, 333; Falco, 1938: 36 ff., 120 ff.; Capograssi, 1936: fn. 24; Cassola, 1941: 3 ff.; Ciprotti, 1941: 13 ff.; De Luca, 1943: 9 ff.; etc.]

15 For authors who attend to state law and ecclesiastical law, the intrinsic, intimate legality of entities that are considered unlawful, respectively, by the state or by the Church is an insurmountable stumbling block to embracing a broader notion of law, even when they seem willing to admit it as a rule. Strongly averse to this limitation, see Croce, 1915: 331. [Levi, 1914: 285; Levi, 1924: 87–88; Maggiore, 1925: 166; Del Vecchio, 1935: 35; Del Vecchio, 1936: 305; Capograssi, 1936: 11 ff.; Capograssi, 1939: fn. 15; etc.]. Ravà's (1911: § 3) opinion is peculiar, as he distinguishes 'the associations that are contrary to law in force, which do not pursue a particular end, but represent a principle of actualization of a new legal order resting upon different bases then those of the dominating order, that is, upon a different appreciation of the conditions of coexistence. These in some cases could be a secret society or a political sect (for example, a communist one)'. The order

them to an end, as well as produce the consequences, also penal, that fall within its power. But as long as these institutions live, it means that they are constituted, have an internal organization and an order, which, considered in itself and for itself, certainly qualifies as legal (§ 14). The effectiveness of this order is what it is, and will depend on its constitution, its ends, its means, its norms and the sanctions of which it can avail itself. Indeed, the stronger the state, the weaker this order. Sometimes it can be so powerful that it poses a threat to the existence of the state itself. But this has no bearings on the legal analysis of the order. It is well known that, under the threat of state law, many associations live in the shadows, whose organization can be said to be almost analogous to that of the state, though on a smaller scale. They have legislative and executive authorities, courts that settle disputes and punish, statutes as elaborate and precise as state laws. In this way they develop an order of their own, like the state and the institutions recognized as lawful by the state. Denying the legal character of this order cannot but be the outcome of an ethical appraisal, in that entities of this type are often criminal or immoral. This could be admissible if one demonstrated the necessary and abso-lute dependence of positive law on morality – what, in this sense (which I believe to be quite ingenuous), does not hold true. Moreover, for example, a political asso-ciation pursuing the end of disrupting the order of a state that does not meet basic needs and the commands of justice should be judged more favourably than the state that declares them to be unlawful. And certain religious corporations, which sometimes are banned, often reflect, or used to reflect, the general moral sentiment, which is contrary to the ban. After all, everybody knows how arbitrary, contingent and variable the criteria are that the state adopts for considering cer-tain entities as lawful or unlawful.[16] However, this all has to be utterly indifferent to the jurist, who in these cases cannot help but register the existence of institutional, and therefore legal, orders, each one within its own orbit, whether or not they are anti-legal in the eyes of state law, which gets them out of its own sphere, and even combat them.[17]

---

of such associations is claimed to be legal, unlike the order of other particular societies that pursue their own ends and not those of the society at large.

16 See various examples in Ferrara, 1915: 408 ff.

17 [Therefore jurists have no interest in the utterly true remark – which dates back to Plato and has been repeated and developed by many – that even a gang complies with a particular form of jus-tice, so much so that one might refer to them with Bergson's expression, who, while dwelling on dif-ferent topics, spoke of 'a moral organization of immorality'. Jurists can limit themselves to taking note of the observation by which Voltaire contradicted Pascal: the latter defined 'pleasant' the fact that human beings who have forsaken God's laws, such as burglars, produce other rules with which they comply scrupulously. Voltaire replied that this is more useful than pleasant to observe; for this proves that no human society can subsist, not even for one day, without laws, society being like a game that cannot exist without rules. It is worth adding that, if there are societies or institutions that are overtly and entirely contrary to morality, many can conflict with it only in part. This does not mean that the state denies that legal character – one should keep in mind Art. 31, preliminary dispositions to the Civil Code, which limits itself to denying effects on the state territory to the

It goes without saying that what I said about the entities that state law deems to be unlawful applies even better to the entities that the state ignores, or wants to ignore, and that therefore are irrelevant to it.

§ 31. In addition, a phenomenon very similar to that which occurs with unlawful or concealed entities also occurs with institutions – in the way I use this word – that are admitted by the state order. As this happens frequently, it engenders very interesting complications. In general, their regime is directly established by state laws or by private legal transactions that the state permits and regulates. Therefore, regardless of the question of whether these transactions, on the basis of state law, can sometimes be considered as sources of law, we can say that the legal position of the entities of which I am speaking is established and defined by the state order, whether in a mediated or unmediated manner. However, it is often the case that the state order fails to adjust and support the overall position of those entities, because of an inadvertent imperfection or a self-imposed limitation, or the survival of old-fashioned dispositions or the lack of norms more suitable for modern life. In the face of it, these entities create a legal order of their own, an internal one, which is different from the one that the state attributes to them, and that at times does not limit itself to complementing the state order, but clashes with it. And this clash, however concealed, is all the more evident.

As proof of this, I might offer many examples of different significance. It is worth mentioning some of them.

In my opinion, Italian private law does not know any power of supremacy, as this power is nowhere to be found but in the field of public law. Thus, private law governs the relationships falling under its norms as if this power did not exist or were never exercised. Yet, this does not jibe with reality. Every time we encounter a social organism of some complexity, however minimal this organism may be, a discipline is instituted within it, one that contains an overall order of authorities, powers, norms and sanctions. If we leave aside the family, which would require us to resolve a few issues that are preliminary to the question I am tackling here, there is no doubt that every community, whether it is a factory, a firm, a company, whether it is a school or a boarding school, whether it is a club, necessitates 'internal regulations' with a disciplinary character. At times they establish a regime that is utterly indifferent to the state (§§ 46–47), as long as it has never the opportunity to tend to it, whether to recognize or to prohibit it. Yet, at other times the case is more difficult and more delicate. Courts are called upon to evaluate the effects of a disciplinary measure that might have harmed someone's interests. Judges are confronted with the need to recognize these effects as legitimate only insofar as they can also be the effects of the application or the breach of a private legal transaction, most often a

---

orders that it recognizes as such, as well as to the acts of any institutions or entities as long as they are contrary to public decency.]

contract. This means that, for state law, these disciplinary measures – which, for the entity's internal law are measures and imply a power of supremacy and the relative subordination – cannot have any relevance if not from a standpoint that does not pertain to them; which is to say, the fact that, if they cannot be appreciated from this standpoint, then the state is forced to declare them anti-legal (see § 45 below).

There is more to it. Everybody knows that in modern life labour relationships have much more complex characteristics than those inadequately contemplated and regulated by the Civil Code in the few articles devoted to this matter.[18] Without a doubt, these relationships, at least most of them, cannot be addressed by the existing law of the Italian state if not as contracts. It is no less certain that, despite the efforts and resources of the acutest dialectic, both doctrine and jurisprudence fail to put them under this rubric, if not by sacrificing some elements of these relations, or at least by distorting them. In saying this I am not siding with those who, for example, deny the collective bargaining being a proper contract. Still, I believe these views make a point, though inexactly assessed. So, if the theory according to which, in this case, we would have 'an authentic law which will apply not only to those who belong to these groups at the moment of the convention, but also to those who will join later and even to third parties who do not belong to them'[19] has to be rejected and, if it is unclear whether and to what extent one can make use of the figure of the agreement, as has sometimes happened, then the tendency of the order of professional groups to turn from *intra partes* rules to *supra partes* precepts is evident. Hence the inability of the category of the contract to make the organization of unions essentially authoritative.[20] And it does not seem to be a legal order falling into the autonomy that state law grants individuals (art. 1123 cod. civ.).[21] In my opinion, we are confronted with a two-sided legal phenomenon, which cannot be entirely explained unless we admit that it takes place at the same time and with different, perhaps opposite attitudes, within the respective spheres of two distinct legal orders. The one is that of the state, and in its eyes the figure of the contract is by and large the only one that is relevant. All that falls outside that figure cannot be protected by this order and even runs the risk of being declared illegitimate. The other legal order is the particular order that materializes within any institutions or more institutions constituted by the groups of entrepreneurs and workers. For state law, this is a contract; for the particular order, it works as a more or less autonomous system of law, which imposes itself with the means at the disposal of

18 [The observations relating to labour relations and collective bargaining refer to the Italian legislation that existed before the one that now regulates this matter on different grounds, although incompletely. And as far as labour relations are concerned, the foregoing observations on disciplinary powers within private law have to be revised.]

19 Duguit, 1913: 129. After all, it is not an isolated opinion; see references in Geny, 1914: 59.

20 See Messina, 1904: 6 ff. On the uncertainties of jurisprudence on this matter, see Redenti, 1905: 106 ff.

21 On this wavelength Messina, 1904: 5 [Art. 1123 cod. civ. (1865) now corresponds to Art. 1372 cod. civ. (1942)].

the organization and within the organization – means that for the state might be extra-legal or anti-legal, but, on the contrary, are legitimate for the special regime to which they refer. While it is universally acknowledged that the laws of the state on this matter are inadequate, this simply means that, outside and sometimes in opposition to these laws, other orders have been unfolding. These orders claim, to date in vain, to be included within those laws in such a way that the sanctions imposed within industrial enterprises, professional groups, etc., might be backed up by the more effective sanctions of the state. To put it otherwise, there are entities that according to state law are to some extent *de facto* entities; but, if considered in their own right, they possess an institutional character that makes them, based on the concepts I have already developed, legal organisms.

Likewise, according to some points of view, we should analyze another problem, which otherwise remains confused and insoluble. It is the problem of so-called 'non-recognized' associations or institutions, to wit, those that have not been granted legal personality by the state.[22] The difficulty of this problem stems from the fact that, according to civil laws, those entities can by no means be considered as subjects of law. Despite this, for their internal order, for their substantive structure, which they own by virtue of that order, they behave just like subjects of law. For sure, the ideal solution to this antithesis should be found in the distinction between what is relevant to state law and assumes the profile that state law attributes to it and what, on the contrary, is irrelevant to state law and has limited effectiveness within the entities themselves. Naturally, apart from the difficulty of accurately drawing this distinction with a precise cut, in practice it is often the case that the internal order tries to project itself on the outside and to obtain, more or less indirectly, recognition from state powers. Sometimes state law itself, wisely utilized, provides for some expedients – which should not be considered as breaching the law – in order for so-called *de facto* entities to achieve practical results similar, if not identical, to those that are granted to legal persons. A clear example of this, though not the only one, is the expedient of religious corporations that are no longer recognized in Italy.[23] In other cases, on the contrary, this is not viable, and the only solution is to reduce these entities to other figures, more or less analogous, that are admitted and regulated by state law: simple firms, separate patrimonies or patrimonies under special administration, and so on. But it is evident that, given the intrinsic nature of these very entities and their effective constitution, as it is established by their bylaws – that is, by their internal legal order – one cannot go

---

22 On this issue, see a review of the extensive doctrine in Ferrara, 1915: 990 ff. [See the more recent Ferrara, 1938: 299 ff.]. Among the authors who adopted a point of view akin to my own, see Gierke, 1902.

23 [After the concordat with the Holy See of February 11, 1929, in Italy ecclesiastical entities that were denied recognition in the past can now be recognized.]

further than a more or less pale analogy. This brings about a series of difficulties and controversies whose solution reminds me of the squaring of the circle.[24]

Anyway, based on what I said about issues that cannot be tackled in more detail (see § 45 below), it appears also that the entities that are lawful under state law sometimes have their own legal order, one that is alien, at least directly, to state law, and that remains or should remain self-enclosed. The subsequent pages will go into the details of this most interesting phenomenon, which was worth anticipating.

§ 32. Both the theoretical principles I deployed and the practical examples I offered (and many more could have been offered) attest to the thesis that every institution concretizes in a distinct legal order. This might find a basis and might be supported by the state order, but, as I explained above, it might also clash with it.

From this point of view, I come close to the doctrine, strenuously advocated by Gierke and his numerous followers, that 'every organic community is able to produce law'.[25] At the same time, I move away from this theory in many respects. First, I replaced the concept of community with that of institution, as it is broader and, it seems to me, more complete, as well as more intrinsically legal. Second, while Gierke's theory holds onto the common principle that the law is a complex of norms, rules or precepts,[26] I deem law to be not the product of the institution, but the institution itself. Finally, as to the foundation of law, I do not embrace the various opinions that have been formulated by those who espouse this theory.

Later in my studies I will return to this latter point, but for now I am not concerned with it. Meanwhile, I would like to note that, as I extended and completed the theory just mentioned, I am naturally inclined to reject the restrictions imposed

---

24 [It appears that such difficulties have not been completely overcome by the dispositions introduced with the new 1942 Civil Code on non-recognized associations and committees (Arts. 36 ff.), based on the principle that 'the internal order and the administration of associations that are not recognized as legal persons are regulated by the members' agreements'.]

25 Gierke, 1895: 119–120, and many others of his works. See also Thon, 1878: x ff.; Merkel, 1885: §§ 807, 827; Merkel, 1890: 5–6; Preuss, 1899: 201; Bierling, 1894: 19; Meyer, 1899: § 15; Rehm, 1899: 160; Bekker, 1910: 27 ff., 184 ff.; Enneccerus, 1911: § 29; Coviello, 1915: 11; Coviello, 1916: 3; [Levi, 1914: 285 ff.]. Most canon lawyers agree: among many others, Scherer, 1866: §§ 1, 18; Friedberg and Ruffini, 1893: § 2; Stutz, 1895: 37 ff.; Wernz, 1905: 55 [Wernz, 1938: 9–25]; Sägmüller, 1909: § 3; Heiner, 1912: §§ 1, 3; etc. It is also worth recalling that, well before the writers just mentioned, Rosmini (1843: 9–10) contended: 'By social law I do not only mean, as is usually done, the law of civil society, but of any society [. . .]. Any possible society has its own particular law.' For Rosmini, however, social law was not the whole law. There are then many others who reject the identity between law and state law. Yet some scholars do so by opposing natural law to state law and hence leave the field of positive law (see e.g. Cathrein, 1913: 570 ff.). Others adopt particular philosophical stances (Croce, Stammler, etc.). Others restrain their own opinion in various manners (Ravà, 1911: ch. 4, ch. 5, § 4, ch. 7). [See more recent references at fn. 31].

26 Gierke (1895: 113) writes: 'Objective law [. . .] is the epitome of legal propositions' [translator's translation from German], and all the others agree with him.

by the interpretation of some scholars, whether they failed to justify them at all,[27] or whether, as has happened, they have advanced some tentative demonstrations.

In this way, for example, some have recently maintained that only morally necessary communities have a legal order.[28] The principle they build on might even be considered correct, if rightly understood. Where there is a source of law, they claim, there is an authority, and where there is an authority, there is a source of law. This premise does not lead to the conclusion that this is possible only in a mandatory society, let alone that a mandatory society cannot be but a morally necessary one. Leaving aside all other objections, it is easy to observe that, according to this doctrine, the fact of whether or not law exists depends on an extra-legal criterion, which should be drawn from ethics. In my opinion, this is enough to reject this doctrine, at least from the viewpoint jurists are required to take. After all, although this doctrine in general recognizes that the law does not have to be necessarily state law, and that in some historical epochs this phenomenon has occurred – especially with the existence of the spiritual law of the Church[29] alongside the secular law of the state – it comes to the conclusion that nowadays there is, and there can be, but state law. In sum, although framed in a different manner, it is the same thesis I debunked above.

With no reference to any ethical elements, other authors have drawn the same distinction between necessary and voluntary communities.[30] They reasoned that in the former type the individual is subordinated to the social aggregate considered as a superior whole, while in the latter type there is no such subordination. For, there are only limitations on individual liberties, similar to those deriving from a contract, and then maybe a unified will, but not a superior will. Based on these premises, these authors believe that the figure of the organ, in the legal sense of the word, and in general the organization can be found only within necessary communities, while within voluntary communities there is no direct manifestation of the will of the entity, but the sum of distinct wills, or else their representation.

When I identified the concept of organization with that of institution and, therefore, with that of legal order, I myself distinguished the organization from the mere relationship or a sum of relationships (§ 18 ff.). Yet it does not seem to me

---

27 For example, Regelsberger (1893: 85) assertively affirms that the task of establishing a legal order falls to the state, to some small communities belonging to the state, such as municipalities, and to the Catholic Church, 'which has achieved a legal unity that goes beyond the state boundaries'. Based on this, it is doubtful that in this matter Regelsberger embraces a unified principle. A largely analogous position is advocated by Geny (1914: 55 ff.).

28 Sohm, 1915: 10 ff. On the basis of these views, he denies today's Church law being a law on its own, given that at present the Church is a voluntary association. [On the same wavelength, see now Battaglia, 1939: 163 fn.]

29 Famously Sohm (1892: 1) had claimed that ecclesiastical law is in contradiction with the nature of the Church, as the latter has a spiritual character, while the character of the law is temporal. On this doctrine, see also Niedner, 1915: 275 ff.

30 See Cicu, 1915: 16 ff., which deals with it only to draw a distinction between individual law and social law, in that it moves away from the distinction between private and public law. Yet, Cicu's observations have some bearings on the general conception of law.

that such a distinction, or a similar one, has to do with that between necessary and voluntary communities. First, the general structure of voluntary communities – and reality demonstrates this time and again – can be arranged in a way that is analogous to that of necessary communities. It is well known that the state has always served as a model, so to say, for a number of other institutions. Second, I do not believe it correct to say – and I tried to demonstrate this with respect to the international community (§ 17) – that the concept of organization is incompatible with that of a community of equals, one where members are not subordinate to the power of anybody. Finally, we should ask ourselves: in what sense should we understand the necessity and the voluntariness of social entities? Indeed, we should not forget that what appears as necessary from one point of view can be voluntary from another point of view. Can one say, for example, that the community of states is necessary? It seems it is with regard to the current needs of their relations and their life. However, each state, at least formally, joins it and takes part in it on a voluntary basis. And the organization of this community is so evanescent that it is refuted by most writers. Based on the law of the state, which allows for religious freedom, the Catholic Church is a free community, at least in the sense that every member is allowed to leave; but based on ecclesiastical law, baptism has an indelible character and apostates continue to be considered as members of the Church. Is this then a necessary or a voluntary community? And leaving aside the relationship between the individuals and the Church, the latter considers itself as necessary and indefectible as regards its origins and its ends, while of course members of a different religious community will hold a different opinion. The truth is that, since we are within the realm of law, the fact of whether or not a social entity is necessary cannot only be determined with an exclusively legal criterion. And since our problem concerns the entity's intrinsic legality, which has to be determined in itself and for itself, independently of its relations with other entities and with the state, this means that this character can only be evidenced with reference to the internal order of the entity itself. This might be necessary or voluntary, whether one or the other quality is affirmed through its law. From all different points of view, any such classification will be legally indifferent. Once this principle has been established, the conclusion is that it is the law that determines the necessity of the entity, and not the other way around. Moreover, the law can determine its voluntariness. Also voluntary entities, therefore, are systems of law, institutions, organizations, as I understand these synonymous expressions here.[31]

---

31 [The successive literature on the issue of the law always being state law is voluminous and it would be difficult to mention and examine it even cursorily. I will limit myself to a few references.

Among the writers who continue to believe that only states and state-based orders are legal, see Bonucci, 1920; Ferrara, 1921: fn. 1; Mastino, 1923: 187 ff., 210 ff.; Costamagna, 1929, and other writing; Mazzoni, 1934: 29 ff.; Perticone, 1938; 49 ff., and other preceding writings; Ranelletti, 1942: 3; Orestano, 1941: 233 ff.; Scuto, 1941: fn. 3; Rotondi, 1942: fn. 6; Barassi: § 1; etc. I pass over the fact that, while dealing with my ideas on this issue, some of these authors blatantly misunderstood them. The same claim is generally made by many others who advocate such a broad

§ 33. A further development, as well as a proof of these principles, can be obtained by examining the various relations that might exist between the different legal orders. Such an investigation has not been carried out systematically by the doctrine; worse, it has not even been commenced if not with regard to the reciprocal

---

concept of the state that all autonomous and sovereign entities are included, and hence also the Church. In this way, also Volpicelli, 1929: 19 ff., which explores the order of the Church (352) as well as the international order (355 ff.). Analogously, Kelsen (1925: 133) averred that, if 'the Church is a legal order, then it is a state' [translator's translation from German], but then this becomes a terminological issue, as the word state is given a different meaning than the common one, even an arbitrary one (see the correct remarks in Balladore Pallieri, 1935: 47, and Checchini, 1937: 11 fn.). Panunzio (1931a: 183, 184; 1931b: 179 ff.) recognizes the production of extra-state orders, but believes that any order depends on the state at the moment of its creation; in addition, in his view, state is also the family, the *gens*, the city, the corporation, the society of states, that is, the superstate! Moreover, many contend that, whether or not non-state legal orders exist, it behoves the state to glue them together into a legal unity. In this regard, Orlando, 1926a: §§ 1 and 2; Lessona, 1943: 1 (if I got it right); Carnelutti, 1936: 40, 67; Carnelutti, 1949: 97 ff., §§ 56–57; etc. Others, like Rovelli, 1931: 211 ff., point out that all law is state law, even international law, but recognize that the Church is an exception to this rule (226 ff.). Intermediate and less clear-cut positions are advocated, among others, by Grispigni, 1932: 138 ff.; Chiarelli, 1936: 139, 150, 151. Gueli (1942: 212 ff.) only recognizes a merely potential multiplicity of legal orders, but maintains that in the same social environment there can actually be but one order, which turns out to be the state order. Among those who hold onto the distinction, variously interpreted, between necessary and non-necessary societies, see Del Giudice, 1933: 14. While he generally maintains that all time-tested institutional orders are legal, whether they are perceived and retained in the sentiment of the peoples, as a matter of fact he believes that only state orders, the international order and that of the Church are legal on the basis of a criterion that, according to him, could be called the 'necessary sociality of law'.

A special mention goes to those who distinguish the philosophical point of view from the point of view of legal science. According to Cammarata (1925: 49 ff.; 1926) from a jurisprudential point of view this issue can be solved in either way: either in the sense of law being based on the state or either in the sense of law not being based on the state. However, he claims the issue is insoluble from a philosophical point of view. I have already mentioned (fn. 91 above) the opinion of those (Capograssi, Crisafulli) who specifically deal with my concept of institution and do not accept it from a philosophical viewpoint but accept it from a dogmatic one, in a way that impacts on the law being or not being based on the state.

By now there are many more scholars who forcefully and decidedly deny law necessarily being state-based, so much so that it can be said that today this opinion has become prevalent. On top of the writers mentioned at fn. 25 above, and on top of most of those who study international law and ecclesiastical law, whom I had the opportunity to mention, see Levi, 1920: 31; Levi, 1924: 49 ff. (even before in Levi, 1914: esp. § 27); Maggiore, 1922: 111; Maggiore, 1921: 65, 161 ff.; Maggiore: fn. 3 and 4; Ruffini, 1924: 164 ff.; De Francisci, 1924, 80; Cesarini Sforza, 1929: 4 and *passim*; Cesarini Sforza, 1930: 83 ff.; Cesarini Sforza, 1933: 138 ff.; Cesarini Sforza, 1939: IX; Longhi, 1927: 903; Del Vecchio, 1929; Del Vecchio, 1935: 10 ff.; Tedeschi, 1929; Calamandrei, 1929: fn. 2 and 3; Esposito, 1930: fn. 59 ff.; Salemi, 1930: 244 ff.; Salemi, 1935: 153 ff.; D'Eufemia, 1931: 24 ff.; Paresce, 1933: 14 ff., 21 ff.; Ravà, 1933: 8; Maiorca, 1934: 29 ff.; Caristia, 1935: fn. 4; Monaco, 1945: 518; Crisafulli, 1935: 69 ff.; Sinagra, 1935: 18 ff.; Betti, 1943: 5 ff., §§ 3, 4; Betti, 1927: 167 ff.; Invrea, 1935: fn. 159; Capograssi, 1936: 7 ff.; Capograssi, 1939; Capograssi, 1937: 2 ff.; Zanobini, 1936: 39; Zanobini, 1942: 38; Crosa, 1941: 2; Arangio-Ruiz, 1943: 17, fn. 1; Ravà, 1937: fn. 9; Pergolesi, 1938: fn. 52; Levi, 1938: 298; Checchini, 1921: 128 ff.; Checchini, 1937: 10 ff.; Perassi, 1938; Biscaretti di Ruffia, 1938: 11, fn. 11; Biscaretti di Ruffia, 1939; Biscaretti di Ruffia, 1946: § 10; Schmitt, 1934; Piccardi, 1939; Messineo, 1939: § 4; Fragapane, 1944a: 54 ff.; Fragapane, 1944b: 22 ff.; Miele, 1945: § 1 and previous writings; etc.]

relationships between international law and state law.[32] I believe it is necessary to generalize this investigation and to try to draw up a scheme of relations among all possible legal orders, or at least among those that attract the jurist's interest. However, given that this investigation would require highly detailed analyses, it cannot be attempted if not within modest limits; which is to say, as long as it is instrumental in foregrounding the concept of a legal order I have provided. Consequently, it cannot be but the sketch of a few simple lines.

Meanwhile, carrying out this investigation requires keeping in mind the fundamental characteristics of the institutions that can get in touch with each other. And since these characteristics vary indefinitely, so much so that it would be pointless to attempt at a complete classification, my limited goal will be to foreground the figures that appear to be the most important for my purposes. I already mentioned some of them (see especially § 12). I would now like to recall those that I already had the opportunity to speak of and to add a few more. These are the following:

1. First, there can be original institutions, ones within which a legal order concretizes. That order is not established by other institutions and therefore, as far as its source is concerned, is independent. Alternatively, there are derivative institutions, namely those whose order is established by another institution. In this way, the latter affirms its superiority over the former, which in its turn remains subordinate. Between these opposite cases, there is a third, intermediate one, namely, institutions whose order is partly original and partly derivative. In this way, states can take the first and the third figure, in that independence – at least a partial one[33] – is a specific characteristic of theirs, whereas municipalities, for instance, are always derivative institutions in the sense specified above.[34]

2. Second, institutions with particular (and hence distinctly limited) ends are to be distinguished from institutions that pursue general (and hence potentially limitless) ends. In my view, this distinction is interesting in that it postulates a different extension of the sphere in which their respective legal order deploys its effectiveness. As the former institutions only concern an aspect or a few aspects of human life (for example, religion, economy, etc.), they are characterized by a positively circumscribed form of membership. The latter institutions, like the state, can arrange their structure, and therefore

32 [Recently this enquiry has extended to the relations between state law and the law of the Church. See, among others, the already mentioned writings of Jemolo, Del Giudice, Checchini, D'Avack, Ciprotti, Cassola, De Luca, and the references they provide.]
33 [I now believe (see Romano, 1945: ch. 6, § 4, fn. 4) that the order of states, also those that are subjected to other states, such as the member states of a federal state, is always and totally original. The order of the superior state is only a limit – not its source – which is either imposed on it or is recognized by one of its norms.]
34 See Romano, 1908: fn. 25 ff., esp. 44 ff.

their relations, with other entities by counting upon a more extended subjection of its members. However, one should steer clear of the quite common opinion that the legal order of the state encompasses all manifestations of the individual's life that are by nature amenable to being addressed by the law. The state is not, not even in this respect, a universal entity. Saying that the state has general ends means saying that these ends are not positively and distinctly determined, and that, abstractly and potentially, they can always be expanded. Concretely, however, there is (and there has been) no state able to embed among its legal objects all possible deployments of its members' lives. It is imperative to keep this in mind while unpacking some important problems (see below §§ 46–47).

3. In order to fathom the sphere of effectiveness of legal orders in their reciprocal relationships it is helpful to scrutinize, besides the ends of the institutions, also the elements they comprise, which, as I said (§ 12 *sub* 2), can have a different nature. It merits stressing, though, that it is not always and necessarily the case that a legal order is valid only in the domain delimited by the constitutive elements of the institution in question. It can also deploy on the outside, like in the event of an institution whose addressees are outside of it, or a state that extends its power on foreigners or territories that do not belong to it.

4. Moreover, it is important to recall the distinction, which I already mentioned (§ 12 *sub* 3), between simple institutions and complex ones (institutions of institutions). In this latter case, there is generally a broader institution encompassing one or more smaller institutions that are subordinate to it. This subordination might be of varying degrees: it might involve institutions that derive, in the sense I specified above, from the broader one; it might involve partially original institutions; finally, it might involve institutions that are totally original with respect to their internal order, but that nonetheless depend on a broader institution with respect to certain rights or duties that these institutions might have to the broader one or even to other institutions that are outside of them – this is the case with states as long as they depend on the international community. Therefore, the distinction between simple and complex institutions is connected to, but does not coincide with, that between original and derivative institutions. And when it comes to complex institutions, the varying subordination of the smaller ones to the broader one in which they are included is not the only thing that should be considered. For one should also consider the position of the broader one as long as it entails the existence of the smaller ones and, consequently, their order – in this way, for example, the international community entails (we will see in what respect: § 37) the distinct states comprising it.

5. From a similar point of view it is possible to distinguish (§12 *sub* 3) perfect institutions – which are always original and can be either simple or complex – from imperfect ones – which hinge on other institutions with respect to which they are not merely presupposed, but coordinated or subordinated. These are often derivative institutions, but can also be original, if they are simply

coordinated with, or if not entirely subordinated to, the former. Then, as I noted that many a time, there are institutions that prove antithetical to one another, that is to say, in a more or less overt opposition.

6. For the purposes of the present enquiry it might also be of some importance to distinguish between institutions that, vis-à-vis others, have a legal personality and institutions that do not assume this quality. The former ones have a power of their own, to which their members, that might also be other institutions, remain subordinate. This power constitutes the core of their organization. Instead, the latter institutions lack such a power; therefore, either their members are equal, as is usual within the international community, or one or more of its members have supremacy over the others.

7. Finally, as a consequence of what I have said, I would like to remark that there can be mutually independent institutions; institutions where the one claims independence from the other, while the latter, on the contrary, claims the former is dependent on it; institutions that, in their mutual relationships, are variously and to different degrees coordinated on an egalitarian basis, or else are placed in a position of subordination and correlative supremacy.

§ 34. My analysis of the relations between different legal orders necessarily dovetails with the analysis of the ways in which one of them can be relevant to the other. In effect, it is clear that, if an order is irrelevant to another, then there is no relation whatsoever between them. Therefore, for our purposes, it will suffice to bring into consideration the obverse hypothesis, namely, that one or more orders are relevant to others. The first hypothesis will turn out to be negatively determined by the absence of the terms that characterize the second.

What should we mean by 'legal relevance'? It should not be confused with the *de facto* importance that an order could have to another; nor should it be confused with the material uniformity of more orders which is pursued or determined not by a legal need, but by political convenience or opportunity. The rationale of this distinction is not questionable in itself, but it is not always easy to keep it in mind and to understand its true meaning. For now, I will content myself with outlining it generally. To condense my thinking into a quick formula, I can say that in order for legal relevance to obtain, the *existence* or the *content* or the *effectiveness* of an order has to be conditional on another order on the grounds of a legal *title*.[35]

---

35 [As far as original orders are concerned, some have denied that an order can be relevant as such, that is, as a legal order, to one another, on the grounds that original orders are exclusive by nature, and, if considered from within, unique. This opinion, first advanced by Kelsen (1920: 97, 105 ff.; 1925: 102 ff.; 1927: 263 ff.), has also been accepted in different respects and to different degrees by many who disagree with Kelsen's general theories. This has brought about most serious contradictions. Among others, see Ago, 1934: 106; Balladore Pallieri, 1935: 30 ff.; Balladore Pallieri, 1945: 53 ff.; Checchini, 1937: 72; Morelli, 1943: 74, fn. 56; and other references in these texts. On this issue, see also Piccardi, 1939: § 12 ff., 182 ff. It is true that, within a given original order, the norms of a second order only have a value based on the norms of the first. Despite this, I think

§ 35. I would like to begin by examining what this 'title' could be, as its nature varies remarkably case by case.

a. First, I already had the opportunity to note that one order can be in a state of subordination and inferiority to a superior one. This happens when an institution is included into another and contributes to constituting it in such a way that the former's order is, in some respects, surrounded by the latter's more comprehensive order. Or else, this could happen when both belong to a third institution, which puts the one in the position to dominate the other. The ensuing supremacy and the related subordination might not always have the same extent and might not produce the same effects. Sometimes the superior order can determine the conditions of existence and validity of the inferior one, like the state, which comprehensively dominates all the public and private entities that depend on it. In other situations, the sphere of this dominance is more restricted. In this sense, international law hovers over state law, but it can neither suppress nor invalidate it. At any rate, when two orders are in such a position, it is evident that this is a legal title whereby the one is relevant to the other in various degrees and with various effects.

b. Second, an order could be the presupposition of another, which is a complex institution. This could happen also when it remains subordinate to the latter. In this sense, the international community presupposes the states that belong to it. This means that international law presupposes state law, just like the law of the federal state presupposes the member states' law and so on. However, it is vital to distinguish between necessary, essential presuppositions, whose failure draws the other order to an end, and presuppositions that only affect its content or some other aspects.

c. A third figure is given by the hypothesis that two or more orders could be independent from each other as far as their direct relations are concerned,

it is incorrect to maintain that all orders only deem their own norms to be legal and consider all the others as irrelevant. Not only is this view fully arbitrary, but it is also at odds with reality. The principle that every original order is always exclusive is to be understood in the sense that it *can*, not that it *necessarily has to*, reject the legal value of other orders. What would then be the basis of this necessity, and hence this limitation, which turns out to be incompatible with that character itself of original orders, as they are sovereign and know no limitations other than those established or recognized by themselves? See Romano, 1949: 51; Romano, 1945: ch. 6, § 2, fn. 3 and ch. 7, § 6, fn. 11. Put otherwise, an order can ignore or even deny another order; it can address it by granting it a different character than the one that it grants himself, and therefore and, if it wishes, it can also consider it as a bare fact. But I fail to see why it cannot recognize it as a legal order, at least to a given extent and for certain effects, as well as the qualifications that it might want to confer on it. On the contrary, I would like to remark that, for an order to confer on another order qualifications that the latter might not confer on itself, it has sometimes to recognize it as a legal order, not as a bare fact. This happens, for example, when an order that is claimed to be original is considered as derivative by another – I believe this observation is to be kept in mind as far as private international law is concerned.]

whereas together they could depend on a superior order. In this way, they are relevant to each other by virtue of the latter order insofar as it coordinates them. International law, which hovers over those of more states at the same time, offers very interesting examples of this.

d. It might also be the case that an order, without being forced to do so, spontaneously subordinates some features of its content or of its effectiveness to another order from which it is totally independent but that in this way becomes relevant to it. In this hypothesis, then, there is a unilateral relevance, one that does not change its nature, not even when the order, addressed by the other, in its turn treats it with reciprocity – provided that this reciprocity is not the consequence of an obligation imposed by a third order, which would fall outside the hypothesis that I am making. So-called private international law – insofar as it is not supra-state law or is connected to it – occurs exactly when a state, by itself or by its own will, accommodates the order of a foreign state within its own. Below we will see how and in what sense.

e. Fifth and finally, an order can be relevant to another because it is transfused into the latter and hence ceases to exist on its own, but determines the structure of the other order with which it merges. This relationship between two orders, which can be called succession, gives rise to so serious problems that the difficulties in solving them have led the most recent doctrine to deny them by denying the legal relevance of the relation of succession.

§ 36. After examining the titles that make an order relevant to another, it will be easier to analyze how this relevance unfolds and, as I said, how it can concern the existence or the content or the effectiveness of these very orders.

Only in two cases can the existence of an order be dependent on another's: either when the one is subordinate to the other or when the one is a necessary presupposition of the other.

a. The first case does not necessarily occur in all relations of supremacy and corresponding subordination between the two orders, as it is necessary that the one that sways the other dominates it completely. Such a domination bears particular relevance when it has to do not only with the institution regarded as a whole, as a self-sufficient unity, but also with the distinct elements that comprise it. These have to be elements that appertain to both the superior and the inferior institutions. For instance, this happens with the population and the territory of a municipality that are at once the population and the territory of a state. In general, however, even when these circumstances do not arise, the existence of an order could depend on another when it is not original and then rests on the latter, which is its arbiter.

Consequently, we are left with two hypotheses. On the one hand, the superior order itself directly determines the inferior one and therefore constitutes its immediate source. On the other hand, the superior order confers on the dependent institution the power to establish its own order, that is to say, the so-called power of autonomy, in one of the various senses in which this word is used. But also in this latter case, autonomy is always bounded and limited, and, above all, conditioned.

For sometimes the essential principles – those from which the existence of the institution originates – are established by the superior institution in such a way that, not from the beginning and not entirely, the order of the former is established by itself, but only for what concerns some of its more or less secondary parts. In any case, the superior order determines the validity conditions for the inferior one.

We can find remarkable examples of this relation in public or private institutions that are entirely subjected to the state. In this sense, it is the state that brings municipalities into existence. Before that state comes into being, municipalities can be geographical aggregates or different institutions, but they cannot be state institutions as they are at present. It is the state that almost entirely establishes their order and constitutes their immediate source by means of its legislative power. Within modern law, therefore, the autonomy of these entities is not original, but is attributed by the state and can be exercised within particular limits and on specific conditions. Municipal regulations that exceed the sphere that they are granted are certainly null and void of any effectiveness of the state power. In other cases, on the contrary, the state does not create the institution, but allows others to bring it about. For example, this is the case with charities that could also be private organizations. But it is always the state that establishes the terms of validity for these foundational acts. In addition, once they are brought into life, the state regulates their power of autonomy in such a way that the existence of the orders that derive from it depends on the observance of such norms. The same applies to the so-called autonomy of private individuals, in case it entails the production of law.

As can be seen, in all these cases there are legal orders that entirely depend on the state order, in that they substantively belong to it. Either they essentially complement it, like the order of public institutions, or they represent more or less remote ramifications of its trunk, like the order of private institutions. They are institutions that exercise their power on the same persons and the same things on which the state exercises its higher power. This means that the latter can not only get back the power of autonomy that it itself attributed to the institutions, considered in their respective unity; but, in case this power is exercised against the state power, the state can also efface and neutralize the power of the institution by addressing the institution's subjects, who are at the same time the state's subjects. In other words, both the existence of its own legal order in general and that of its distinct developments in particular depend on the state.

In point of fact, it might happen that an order that was initially instituted as subordinate to another – for example, to that of the state – as the latter nullifies it, finds the energies to continue its existence and to withstand the prohibition. At this point, this order will inevitably morph and will assume the character of an order that is not only separate, but is antithetic to the one that it no longer recognizes as superior. Therefore, this case falls under a hypothesis I will examine below.

Furthermore, between two orders there can be a relation of supremacy and subordination that is less extended than the one considered so far. For example, the member state of a federal state – in the hypothesis that they are, as I believe, genuine states – depend on the latter; but their power of autonomy – although within limits that, in the abstract, we can imagine as very narrow – depends on it insofar as it has an original character. It follows that although the federal state is sovereign with respect to them, and although its subjects are also direct subjects of the federal state, notwithstanding this, a complete and absolute subordination is somewhat missing. And the fact that it is missing makes it impossible for these entities to fuse and to give life to a unitary state. Can one, in spite of this, acknowledge that the existence of a member state can be nullified by the federal state? Famously, this issue has been extensively debated with respect to the German Empire.[36] And if the prevailing doctrine tends to provide a negative answer, there are those who provide an affirmative one. For sure, the validity of a member state's order can depend on conditions established by the sovereign state, and it can be denied by the latter's bodies for what concerns those parts that are not original.[37] But the existence of the order, considered as a whole, as an institution that, not only *de facto*, but also *de jure*, is antecedent to the federal state and constitutes a presupposition for it, is generally more unlikely to be deemed as subordinate to it. Nonetheless, there might be exceptions. For example, one might advance the hypothesis that the constitution of a federal state, whether explicitly or implicitly, allows for the possibility of turning the federal state into a unitary state, and only makes this constitutional modification conditional on itself.[38] In this case, one might still regard member states as genuine states, but undoubtedly such a quality is flimsy and conditioned.

Finally, international law offers the example of an order that is superior to the distinct states' orders, while however neither the overall existence of these states nor the validity of their distinct ramifications depend on it. From this principle derives the corollary of the so-called separation of the two legal orders, i.e. international law and state domestic law. And in order for us not to misunderstand it and not to overstate or misapply it, we need to bear in mind the real foundation of the principle from which it derives. This foundation consists in the two following statements:

1. International law does not bestow any power of domestic autonomy on the state. Hence, the power (no matter whether or not we call it autonomy) of the state to establish its own domestic order has an original character vis-à-vis international law, always and completely; whereas, vis-à-vis the federal state, it is only partially original.[39]
2. International law is only addressed to the states, each one considered as a unity, not to their bodies or their subjects (the opposite happens with federal

36 [It goes without saying that what is written in the text refers to the law that was in force when I wrote it and to the state of the art of the doctrine at that time.]
37 [As I noted at fn. 33 above, I now believe that the order of a member state of a federal state is thoroughly original.]
38 This is the case with the German Empire according to Laband (1911: § 13, 128 ff.).
39 [See fn. 33 and 37 above.]

states). Hence, vis-à-vis the latter, international law has no power to nullify the state order that might contest its principles or norms.

The consequence of the first of these two statements is that the emergence and, therefore, the existence or the inexistence of a state, that is, of a state legal order, is totally independent of international law. It is an object alien to its contents, a subject matter that falls outside its scope. The second statement entails that international law does not have the power to deny the validity of the distinct ramifications of the state order, which is located in a different sphere, impermeable to international law.

To sum up and to conclude. In order for the existence of an order to depend on another − except for the case I will examine shortly (*sub b*), whereby the one presupposes the other − the former order has to be in a condition of subordination. This subordination must be affirmed by both orders. Instead, if it is a mere necessity of the superior order, which is not acknowledged by the inferior one, some aspects of the former are likely to depend on other aspects of the latter, especially its effectiveness (see below § 42), but not its existence. Naturally, this does not exclude that the two can engage in a battle that is likely to lead to the collapse of the less powerful. Still, in this case, the existence of the one depends on the latter not in a legal sense, but on account of factual circumstances, extrinsic occurrences, which exceed the present enquiry. In addition, while subordination is a necessary condition for the existence of an order to legally depend on another, it is not a sufficient condition, save for the situation in which subordination is complete and absolute; or better, when the limits imposed on an order are entirely set by the superior order. If this is not the case, then the inferior order can be completely or partly original and, therefore, by definition, it is established at least in part by itself, not by the order that hovers over it − it exists by virtue of itself. However, it might also be the case that an order that is autonomous as to its origin, but is subjected to another order, depends from the latter as to its termination, that is, its further existence. Examples of this hypothesis are member states that may be suppressed by the federal state. Therefore, unlike the derivative character, generally the original character of an order makes it impossible for its existence to be left to another order. Yet, this usually happens only in the initial phase, when it affirms itself, that is, when it first comes into being. Instead, there might be exceptions to it for what concerns the continuation of its existence, that is, its termination. Finally, it is necessary to distinguish between the total and the partial existence of an order, that is, the existence of the distinct elements that comprise it, the existence of this or that group of norms, of this or that particular ramification. If the superior order unfolds within the same sphere as the inferior, if they have the same subjects, the same territory, etc., then − when the circumstances I specified above occur − the superior order is in the position to nullify the overall existence of the subordinate institution as a whole as well as the existence of a part of its order. On the contrary, if the superior order unfolds within a different sphere, then − provided that the circumstances I specified above occur − it can suppress *in toto* the inferior one.

However, as long as the latter continues to exist, the former will not be able to nullify directly the acts, the norms, etc., that are addressed to its subjects or objects, which the superior order does not have the power to oppose, as they are alien to it.

A more detailed development of these principles could be obtained only after outlining a theory of the sources of legal orders, which cannot be done in the present chapter. This could be the subject matter of a dedicated study, included in the series of studies that will follow up the present work.

§ 37. b. The hypothesis about the relations between the orders of the distinct states and international law, and, to some extent, about the relations of member states to the federal state, is opposite to the hypothesis discussed so far. Indeed, the existence of the superior order somewhat depends on the inferior order. Certainly, such a dependence is quite different from that which characterizes the opposite case – though this does not mean that, however indirect, it is less effective and less important. For sure, the inferior order can by no means be considered the source of the superior one, nor does the former have any power over the latter. The relation I am speaking of can be expressed with the formula that the inferior order is the presupposition of the superior order. The law of member states, as far as their original character is concerned,[40] is a presupposition of the law of the federal state. For, if member states vanished, so would the federal state, unless the suppression of the former took place in such a way as to give life to a unitary state with a view to continuing the old federal state – which would actually change anyway. Furthermore, state law is manifestly the necessary presupposition of international law. This is a relation that appears to deserve more attention than ever so far.

Since the state is nothing but a legal order, international law, inasmuch as it concerns the relationships between states, necessarily results in a set of relationships among state legal orders. However, it does not address the distinct elements of such orders, that is, the norms and precepts that comprise them. Indeed, they are addressed as self-enclosed unities – like in some mathematical operations: between brackets. The principle of the so-called separation of domestic state law from international law is correct, because the latter cannot penetrate into these brackets. Nonetheless, the total sum, as it were, of these brackets is a presupposition, and the ensemble of state orders is a condition for the existence of international law. In addition (and more importantly), international law imposes obligations on the states and at the same time confers rights on them. Now, obligations and rights can only be addressed to subjects endowed with a will of their own – not to speak of exceptions that confirm the rule, such as people unfit to plead whose will is replaced, if and when it is believed to be fungible, with the will of their representatives. It follows that, when it comes to nonphysical, legal entities, in order for them to be attributed a will, they have to be legally organized. Still, this organization, based on which the

40 [See fn. 39 above.]

state owns a will of its own, is not provided by international law, but by state law itself. Thus, state law constitutes the presupposition of international law. It should be noted that this presupposition is not merely factual, but is also legal, or rather, one that is addressed by international law, which, on account of it, attributes or recognizes personality to the states in their reciprocal relations. From this point of view, it is commonly said that international law refers to constitutional law for what concerns the competence of the body that is called upon to form, or to express, the will of the state relevant to international relations. Arguably, this expression is not accurate and anyway lends itself to some ambiguities. The figure of *renvoi* of one order to another is more properly at play in two cases: either when the one accommodates the norms of the other by adopting them (material or receptive *renvoi*), or when the one declares that particular measures or relations are taken out of its sphere to be left to the other order (formal *renvoi*).[41] Now, even if we admit that international law takes the will of the state to be that which is constituted by the competent body under domestic law, evidently it does not refer to constitutional law in either of these senses. Neither in a receptive sense, because the norm of constitutional law establishing the competence of a body has to do with a relation between the state and this body, and cannot be accommodated within international law, as it only concerns relationships among states. Nor in a formal sense, because this kind of *renvoi*, in my opinion, implies the legal possibility for the matter apropos of which the law of another order is evoked to be regulated by the order that makes the *renvoi* and that, in doing so, waives its power to regulate it itself. However, in the present case, this is out of the question, as it is a matter that necessarily falls within the scope of constitutional law and that is alien to international law. The truth is that the constitutional norm reads: 'The king, for example, has the power to make treaties.' On the contrary, the international law norm, in keeping with the widespread doctrine, is quite different, as it reads: 'The will of a state is to be considered (by the other states) that which is constituted by its competent body, in accordance with its domestic law.' This last aside is not a proper *renvoi*, not even a formal one. This is even more evident if we accept the opinion,[42] which is not for me to scrutinize here, that, instead, the international law norm is the following: 'It is to be presumed (by the other states) that the will of a state is the one that is expressed as such by its head, by the military command during war, etc.' In this hypothesis, like in the preceding one, international law does nothing but presuppose, to different degrees

41 See, among others, Triepel, 1899: 156 ff., 235 ff.; Anzilotti, 1902b: 179 ff.; etc. Based on the view quickly discussed in the text, which I cannot examine here, I am actually not sure that it is appropriate to identify the recourse to domestic state law on the part of international law – or, vice versa, to international law on the part of state law – with the figure of *renvoi*. I think in these cases it is preferable to say that one order presupposes the other, so as to restrict the concept of *renvoi* to the relations among orders that share the same subjects, objects, and thus norms [see Romano, 1949: 47; Romano, 1945: ch. 7, § 6, fn. 12, 13]

42 Anzilotti, 1910: 124 ff. [differently in the successive editions; German edition: 104, 275].

and with different effects, the organization of the states. It does not deal with such an organization, not even to make it clear that it does not want to deal with it; but it takes it into account. This does not mean that in the eyes of international law the state organization is a pure matter of fact, as some scholars claim.[43] Rather, it is a legal matter, that is, an order that is considered as such. The opposite opinion draws on the usual principle that the law is, entirely and straightforwardly, a norm addressing the relationships by which individuals have rights or duties – and this is a conception that I have tried to debunk in general. By building on the figure that I evoked before, I can say that, insofar as international law confers rights or duties on states, these appear as unities; but one can get to this unity also from international law by using brackets to bracket off some parts of domestic law that are relevant to international law. This does not impact on these parts, and yet it feels the need to address them, precisely because they are presupposed as elements of that unity that the personality of each state is. Nor does it make sense to say that the presupposition of a legal order, insofar as it is a presupposition, is cut out of it and thus has no legal character. For one thing, as long as it is addressed by an order, this presupposition yields an essential character of these orders, one that gives rise to a series of principles. For another, one has to look at how it is addressed, and nothing prevents an order from considering it as an order, and not otherwise.

This is true not only for the organization of the state that is necessary for the constitution or the manifestation of its own will within international law, but also for many other aspects.[44] Those who neglect this principle fail to make out some fundamental characters of international law. If international law does not recognize subjects other than the states,[45] if it considers some states as void of capacity, and so on, these are problems that cannot be conveniently solved unless one pays heed to the states' internal constitution. It is this constitution that, in part, international law relies on in order for its norms to be complied with. Should the state be unable to guarantee this, there would be no suitable subject for international law. This can be, as it is, a law among equals, where no subject exerts power over any others. For the domestic order of each recognized state, whether implicitly or explicitly, contains the fundamental norm that obliges its bodies, at least most of the time, to comply with international law and to introduce the acts that mandate

---

43 Marinoni, 1913a: *passim* and esp. 115 ff. More in general, Marinoni goes so far as to contend that 'the correlation between the internal legal order and the international legal order can only be extra-legal' (162 ff.). This draws on the opinion that the state is a factual entity, which becomes a legal entity in the eyes of each order. Instead, I say: the state can never conceive of itself other than as a legal entity. This does not exclude that, under international law, its legal figure can be different from the one it holds within its domestic law. However, inevitably this latter figure is legally relevant to the former, at least as a presupposition [see also fn. 35].
44 Triepel (1899: 290 ff.) and Anzilotti (1902b: 59 ff.) offer many examples of domestic legal norms that are presupposed by international law.
45 [I now believe that the states are not the only addressees of international law (see Romano, 1949: 58 ff.); anyway, what I observed above also applies to the other addressees.]

its subjects to comply with it. While international law is by no means directly binding on the bodies and the citizens of the state, it presupposes domestic legal norms
designed to make it sure that – at least by and large and in a relative and conditional way – the state does not operate in such a way as to make its commitments
to the other members of the international community unmeetable. In this sense,
when one says that the domestic legal order, as distinct from the international
one, can also be in conflict with the latter, this is all the more true; but it has to be
understood correctly. The divergence can concern this or that relation, this or that
circumstance, but no state can be a member of the society of states, governed by
international law, unless it is organized or constituted in such a way as to ensure –
let me repeat: by and large and as a general principle – the conformity of its
conduct with the rules of that society. As a result, on this account it is by no means
mistaken to say that international law is basically guaranteed by domestic law.
Needless to say, if the guarantee is conceived as a sanction or coercion that results
in a norm ensuring the observance of another one (see § 8), this norm cannot
belong but to the same legal order to which the protected one belongs. But if by
guarantee we also mean indirect and relative ones, which any order can also count
on, these might well be immanent in the internal structure of is subjects, in its own
organization, and therefore in the presupposition of the order itself (§ 18). What
is more, as we have seen and as can be easily imagined, not only the guarantees,
but also the existence of international law is founded on these presuppositions.

§ 38. As to its contents, a legal order can be relevant to another under different
titles and figures.
   a. Again, the first hypothesis I need to address is that of an order that, by virtue of its superiority, directly or indirectly determines the contents of another
order. For example, the state affects the order of municipalities – it could constitute them directly through its laws; or else, it could regulate their autonomy. In this
latter case, when the state establishes the conditions that the validity of particular
deployments of this autonomy depend on, amid such conditions there could be
some that actually concern the contents that need to be included in the order that
municipalities give themselves.
   Also as far as the autonomy of private individuals is concerned – if we hold
onto the hypothesis that it can be a source of law – state law can be relevant to
the contents of this order insofar as it constitutes its prime basis and impacts on
it in all respects.
   Remarkably different is the case of an order that is superior to another, whereas
this superiority is constrained not only by its own characteristics or norms, but also
by the proper and original independence of the inferior order, which tempers this
superiority. This mainly occurs in relations between international law and state
domestic law. As the former cannot affect either the existence of the latter or the
validity of its various manifestations, on account of the same principle, and of a
further application of it, it cannot immediately determine its contents. Nonetheless, international law can affect the contents of state domestic law by obliging the

state to lay down, or by prohibiting from laying down, a particular law, or else, by authorizing the state to lay it down. In any case, the fact remains that if a state contravenes this prescription of international law and gives its order contents that do not conform to the latter, this state violates an internationally relevant duty, although its internal order, in itself and for itself, is fully legitimate. Only from this latter point of view and in this sense can one speak, as many do, of a legislation imposed, prohibited or permitted by international law whether explicitly or implicitly, directly or indirectly.[46] And one should not forget that the right or the duty established by international law to issue or not to issue this legislation is not equal to the state legislative power. This derives from domestic law and cannot be regulated by international law.[47] Rather, it is a right or a duty that the state has towards the other states, one that is exercised, or respectively, observed through the state legislative power. To put it otherwise, the international order can affect the contents of the state, but not through the immediate force of its dispositions, *ipso iure*; rather, it is a consequence of the exercise of a subjective right, or the observance of a subjective duty emerging out of that right, towards the other states. In the end, it is always the state that determines the contents of its own order, but this does not mean that international law cannot affect them, in the sense I discussed above.

As a result, international law, which on account of its nature and its contents never imposes any norms on the bodies of the state and, in general, on the state subjects, is not an integral part of domestic law. The latter, then, is the exclusive source of the norms and the acts that are necessary to the observance of international law. Still, the relationships deriving from international law are to be considered as legally relevant to domestic law: not as its source, but insofar as they can mobilize it and prompt further applications or the compliance with existing norms of domestic law. Among them, the most prominent is the one I recalled above (§ 37), which, in general and save for specific needs, makes international duties mandatory.

Hence the corollary that, when the state, instead of specifically regulating a matter or a case, has recourse to what is established by international law, this does not entail that the latter comes to govern that matter. In fact, as far as its contents and the subjects it addresses are concerned, this matter cannot be but substantively different from that addressed by international law. Instead, recourse to international law − which is often called '*renvoi*', but which I believe not to be so (see § 37) − can be conducive to the indirect production of domestic law in conformity

---

46 Except for particular divergences, see Triepel, 1899: 253; Anzilotti, 1902b: 49 ff.; Anzilotti, 1912: 33 ff.; Donati, 1906: 347; Marinoni, 1913a: 151 ff.; Ghirardini, 1914: 76 ff. [as well as many more recent authors, such as, among others, Perassi, 1937: 26; Romano, 1939: 50 ff.; etc.].

47 In quite a different sense, see Anzilotti, 1902b: 184 ff.; Anzilotti, 1912: 37 [; now in the German edition (43) in a sense that conforms with what I propound in the text]. Cf. instead Donati, 1906: 290; Donati, 1909: 454 ff. [and now also Ago, 1934: 66; Balladore Pallieri, 1945: 55 ff.].

with that which is established by international law or that which it allows to issue.[48] In this way, when a state purely and simply mandates the execution of a treaty, this command implies the production of norms that are necessary for doing so. This does not require any express formulation, as it is the interpreter who evinces them on the grounds of the text that publicizes the treaty.

Analogous figures that the doctrine failed to notice and yet are no less important are those of, respectively, the order of the state and the order of the Church to a law that is superior to both, such as the order established through concordats between these two entities.

§ 39. b. In addition, it might be the case that, through the mediation of an inferior order, the contents of a law are affected by the contents of one or more other orders that could not otherwise claim to be directly addressed by the former. Again, international law offers a few examples of this. International law purports to coordinate state orders in such a way for states to be obliged to give their own orders specific contents meeting various criteria. This might involve the negative duty not to extend the order beyond the state territory and its subjects, or the positive duty to have recourse to the law of other states in some matters. As is well known, the nature of this recourse and the consequences it engenders are highly debated. I will briefly touch upon them in the subsequent section in relation to a further hypothesis in which it appears in a similar manner.

In much the same way, within a system founded on a concordat, the state and, reciprocally, the Church can have the obligation to lay down norms or establish institutions, always on account of, and in compliance with, the concordat, but not necessarily in accordance with dispositions directly specified by the latter, although each of them has to take into account the other entity's norms or institutions to which the very same concordat refers.

§ 40. c. Also the unilateral determination of an order can be a title in order that the contents of another one might exert influence over this order, whether it is independent of, or subjected to, it.

In this way, as state law is relevant to the contents of the municipalities' law on account of its superiority, so also can the municipalities' law be relevant to state law on account of dispositions of the state itself. This is obvious in practice: while municipalities, as well as other autarchic entities, assume the position of state subsidiary entities or indirect bodies, the state, counting on their existence and their activity, does not need to constitute particular direct bodies to carry out tasks that it knows are carried out, on its behalf, by these indirect bodies. Therefore, autarchy offers an interesting example of the mutual influence of two legal

---

48 See for all Anzilotti, 1902b: 74 ff.; Donati, 1906: 285 ff. [and, generally, the latest literature]. It is known that the more ancient doctrine and jurisprudence go in the opposite direction, and, especially as to international treaties, often acknowledge that they become laws of the state.

orders whereby, while the one depends on the other, the former nevertheless acts on the latter in such a way that it has to be taken into account.

Very frequently the state, although it is not specifically obliged by international law, determines its own order in light of the order of other states. So-called domestic law in international affairs, even the one that is not issued in compliance with suprastate international law, postulates that the state is a member of the international society, and hence the recognition of other states as legal orders, along with a series of relations among state orders.[49] Moreover, in particular so-called private international law is, from this point of view, very characteristic. Based on a distinction that has become common, there are genuine international law norms – whether they are many or few in number – relating to the coordination of state legal orders.[50] In the presence of these norms we find ourselves in the preceding case whereby the contents of the state order are relevant to the contents of the order of another state through an order superior to both, to wit, international law. However, there might be a further case. It might happen that, beyond these norms or when no norms are available, the state itself spontaneously coordinates its own law with the law of other states. In truth, it is by no means clear whether between this and the former case there is the substantive and irreducible difference that the modern doctrine identifies too readily. For, this coordination is often conceived, in various senses, not only as a factual or material requirement, but also as a legal one for the legislator of every state. As I said, this requirement introduces an international function, in that it fills the gaps and makes up the deficiencies of suprastate international law.[51] I believe that we have gone too far with the confutation of such views.[52] Much as they need a clearer formulation, they contain an element of truth, which today is straightforwardly neglected. Certainly they cannot be defended, as the traditional doctrine used to do, by drawing on natural law principles: in addition to positive international law, the traditional doctrine claimed that a set of rational norms was binding on the various states, while today most authors concur that these norms are extra-legal. However, this does not solve or, better, overcome the problem as it simply changes its appearance. Indeed, many have noted that, if there is no international law norm that specifies the obligation for the state to have an order that includes specific contents and addresses the order of other states, there would anyway be the generic and vague obligation to exclude the absolute territoriality of a state's law. Consequently, the various states would

---

49 See Ghirardini, 1914: 50 ff., which offers the most recent and widespread analysis of the concept of domestic law in international matters, and the bibliography mentioned there. [See also Romano, 1949: 10 ff., 51, 52.]

50 On this distinction, see in particular Zitelmann, 1897: 73 ff.

51 Anzilotti, 1898: *passim* and 132 ff.; Anzilotti, 1902b: 122 ff., 149 ff.; Fedozzi, 1905: 6 ff.; Diena, 1914: fn. 37; [Diena, 1917: 27, 97]; Diena, 1913: 332 ff.; Ottolenghi, 1913: 10 ff., 70 ff.

52 See, among the latest contributions, Donati, 1906: 440 ff. fn.; Marinoni, 1913b: 457 ff.; Ghirardini, 1914: 13, 36 ff.

only be free with regard to the way such an obligation is interpreted and implemented. While this formula might seem, and actually is, quite vague, I believe it nonetheless offers a glimpse of the right solution. Although I cannot delve further into this particular issue, maybe this solution could be obtained by applying the general concept of law that I have developed. The law does not only comprise norms, and therefore does not only operate through its norms, as is universally believed, but also through its comprehensive existence, that is to say, as an institution that, for the simple fact that it exists, has a legal relevance to those who belong to it. In addition, the international order acts upon states in two ways. 1) With distinct norms that impose on them rights and duties in their reciprocal relationships. In this case international law, as far as the case I am discussing is concerned, can impose on states the clear-cut, strict obligation to coordinate their respective domestic orders by meeting this or that criterion. 2) By simply pointing to the states' general position, their *status*, i.e. their membership to the international society (and this aspect is even logically anterior to the former). And we know (§ 23) that this position, quality or *status*, whatever we call it, is legally relevant on its own, even when it is not unpacked and it is not reduced to specific rights or duties, or better, because it affirms the impossibility of this reduction. A consequence of this (and thus of the international law from which it derives) is that each state remains, as it were, *affected* by this quality. States cannot, or even do not want to, neglect it, and their internal orders take it into account. Therefore, each state gets influenced by international law: in the first case, on account of the *relations* it establishes (ones that gave rise to rights and duties among states); in the second case, on account of a generic *status*, but no less legally relevant, that is bestowed upon the state by the overall institution in which the *societas gentium* materializes.

In this hypothesis, like in the previous one (except for the difference I pointed out), in order for the state to make use of its membership and thus to coordinate its order with the order of other member states, it begins by limiting the sphere not only of the application – as is generally believed – but also of the actual contents of its order. At the same time, it establishes that in the area where its order, so to say, withdraws, the contents of the foreign order come into play – ones that are chosen and determined with varying criteria. Then, we are left with two principles that ideally we should keep separate, although in practice they are interwoven into one disposition:[53] the first signals the boundaries that the state order gives itself; the second refers to the foreign law. Such two principles are intimately linked, as the reason why the legislator declares its incompetence in the regulation of a given matter is that it recognizes the competence of the foreign legislator.[54] In spite of this, it is

---

53 See Ghirardini, 1914: 33 ff., except for the fact that he speaks of a prohibition to *apply* national law and a command to *apply* the foreign law, while, in my opinion, this is a phase prior to the application of the law, that is, a phase in which the law is laid down, with a determinate content, which entails the exclusion of or the *renvoi* to the foreign law.

54 Anzilotti, 1898: 108 ff.; 1902b: 128 fn.

better to distinguish them. For in a different hypothesis than the one I am discussing here, it might be the case that the state withdrawing its own legislative power from a given matter is due to the fact that this matter is deemed legally irrelevant (§ 46), and consequently there is no reference to any other order. In the present case, however, the matter at stake is considered legally relevant to the state order and therefore to the functions that are in potential relation to it: the judicial function, the administrative function and also the legislative one. Yet, as far as the last is concerned, the state does not make use of its power to regulate its contents; the law doubtless deals with it, but negatively, so as to allow another state's order to regulate it. The one and the other principle constitute a domestic law norm that, in this sense, does not tend to settle (as is commonly said, when one looks at the later stage of application) but to prevent the so-called conflicts or concurrence of legislative powers of more orders that apply to the same matter. Of course, this norm, which, by sticking to the prevalent terminology we can call 'collision', is valid only for the state that issues it. The conflict is overcome only with respect to the latter's order, unlike what would happen if an international norm made it binding on all states.

The admissibility of this norm of collision has raised many objections. Some have made the claim that in order for a legal norm to be a legal norm, it cannot address the relation between different laws, the determination of the law that is designed to regulate a given category of facts. For a legal norm can only concern the relationship between law-abiders.[55] This is a consequence of the incomplete conception of law demoting the law to the mere regulation of subjective relationships – a conception that I already debunked (see above *passim* and § 22). Others also contended that no internal norm can, from within the order to which it belongs, impose a limit on a foreign order, because the latter is alien to the former and there is no room for correlation or interdependence. Only international law can, mediatedly, address the correlation of various state orders.[56] It is possible to rebut this line of reasoning by observing that, if one acknowledges that such a correlation can be addressed by international law *mediatedly*, this means that it not only can, but in this case must be addressed *unmediatedly* by domestic law. What would otherwise be the point of that international law norm, so conceived? Moreover, if there were no norm, even if the state order had the legal possibility of completely abstracting from the order of the other states, this does not exclude the point that, for whatever reason, even as a matter of convenience, the state order could decide to take them into account. By dint of this *determination*, the foreign order becomes relevant to the state order. For sure, before this happens, the conflict between state orders cannot be considered but as a practical, factual conflict. However, from the moment this happens onward, it becomes a legal conflict – needless to say, only with respect to the order that considers the conflict as such and issues dispositions

---

55 Donati, 1906: 441 ff. (in footnote, see also Bierling, 1894: 153 fn.).
56 Marinoni, 1913b: 465 fn.

to overcome it. In other words, the state takes into consideration the actual fact that a person, a thing, a relationship can at the same time fall within the scope of several orders. The state takes it upon itself, with the means at its disposal, to regulate this fact, which therefore in its eyes assumes the figure of a legal fact, and chooses one of those orders, which cannot be its own. Such a choice bears no importance for the law of the other states in question, as well as for suprastate international law, but is relevant to the state that makes it. In this sense, the word 'conflict', used by traditional theory, is not to be rejected. However, it is a conflict that does not primarily call into action the judge, as this doctrine claimed by drawing on the natural law notion that the various foreign orders, within the state, have a value of their own, independently of the legislator recognizing them. Rather, it calls into action the legislator, and, only because of this, it assumes a legal value.

The necessary consequence of this is that the foreign law to which the law of a state refers in the hypothesis I am discussing is valid for that state as a foreign law.[57] On the contrary, building on different principles, some scholars believe it is not a formal, but a receptive *renvoi*, and that therefore the foreign law is transformed into a law of the order that invokes it.[58] If this were the case, it would make no sense to speak of conflict, as there would be no opposition between foreign law and domestic law. Indeed, it would be an integral part of domestic law, obviously harmonized with the other parts, that only materially has the same contents of another state's law, to which domestic law refers only for convenience and in order not to repeat *in extenso* its dispositions. However, in my view this conception is absolutely groundless. *Renvoi* to foreign law is in fact connected to the principle that the state order limits itself. This means that the foreign law is called upon to hold sway on a field in which it does not hold sway and that therefore the former cannot be regarded as part of the latter. On top of what I already said, this is proven by the fact that the opposite thesis cannot be upheld when the foreign norm is recognized by the law of the state as a consequence of a suprastate international law precept. In this case, the state is prevented from regulating a matter on its own and is required to accommodate the regulation of another state. In this hypothesis, it has to be at least presumed that the *renvoi* to the law of the latter is performed in compliance with that international precept and therefore has a receptive nature.[59] Now, evidently the same thing can happen when the order of a state deliberately avoids positively regulating a given matter. There is no difference between the two cases. After all, also when the international obligation I mentioned above applies, compliance occurs through a legislative disposition that, like in the second case, recognizes that the legislature has to withdraw from a given field to

57 For all, see Zitelmann, 1897: 257 ff. As a matter of fact, it is the prevailing opinion.
58 Aside from the more or less vague allusions, which I am not sure whether they aim to advance a genuine theory, see Chiovenda, 1912: 303 ff.; Diana, 1905: 73; Bierling, 1894: 153 fn.; Klein, 1903: 353; Marinoni, 1913b: 465 fn.
59 Donati, 1914: 514 fn.

accommodate the foreign law. The only thing that changes is the reason why this happens, whereas the result, from the vantage point of domestic law, is the same.

Nor can one say that, in this hypothesis, it is the state that confers a legislative competence on the foreign state. This is a process that takes place within the domestic law of the state that limits itself, on its own, and attributes some validity to the order of another state without entering in any relationship with the latter. It is a unilateral coordination of the legislative competences of the various states that exerts consequences on the state that sets it in motion, not on the other states, unless they themselves wish it in their turn. Each state solely regulates its own legislative competence, and regulates it even when it restricts it.

It has also been objected that, if the foreign law stayed the same, the consequence would be that foreigners would be subjects of law only according to the order of that state and not according to the orders of the other states, despite the latter's *renvoi* to the former. Therefore, in the eyes of that order, they would be devoid of legal capacity.[60] It could be replied that, at any rate, this would be true if their capacity outside their state had to be only evinced from this *renvoi*. But, on the contrary, it can be declared with another norm that, in my view, does not fall within the scope of so-called private international law and, in some respects, it is a presupposition of it.[61] In effect, within Italian law, such a norm does not feature in the preliminary dispositions of the Civil Code, which are the same as private international law, but in Art. 3 of the Code itself.[62]

In this way, in the hypothesis I am making, I believe that *renvoi* to a foreign law has two implications. (1.) A delimitation of the legal order of a state, as a premise of (2.) the declaration that a particular matter is regulated by the foreign law as such. I will discuss below (§ 42) the further disposition that can be required[63] to attribute to the foreign law an effectiveness within the state that makes the *renvoi*. This effectiveness can be equal, smaller or even greater than the one the foreign law has within its own state. For I think that such a disposition has a relevance of its own and that it not always or not necessarily turns, at least completely, into the so-called norm of collision. While the norm of collision relates to the *content* of the order of a state with respect to that of another state, the disposition relates to the *effects* of the foreign state on the state law that refers to it.

This does not exclude that, in other cases, there might occur a receptive *renvoi* rather than a formal one. In this hypothesis, the content of a legal order becomes relevant to another insofar as the latter wants some of its parts to be uniform to the former. Therefore, the state does not limit itself, as it rather affirms that a

---

60 Marinoni, 1913b: 474.
61 Cf. Zitelmann, 1897: 256; Anzilotti, 1902b: 124 fn.; Ghirardini, 1914: 26 ff., 65 ff.
62 [Instead it has now been included in the preliminary disposition (Art. 16) of the 1942 Civil Code.]
63 Here it is not important to investigate the connection between these aspects – whether both norms are autonomous, or whether they complete each other, if and how they are intertwined with others, that is, those that govern the various concrete relationships.

given matter falls within its scope; it simply does not regulate this matter directly, but through 'blank precepts' that get factually and materially filled by the order to which it refers. Strictly speaking, there is not even a relationship between two orders, but a mere way of expressing and determining itself on the part of one of them.

What characterizes the relations between orders of several states, on the other hand, can also characterize the relations among other orders. This brings about analogous figures that clarify those that I discussed. These relations have not been explored by the doctrine,[64] although they deserve careful consideration.

For example, while the Church claims full autonomy from the state, it none-theless refers to state laws, that is, to civil laws. This *renvoi* can have a different character. Sometimes it can be a receptive *renvoi*, in the sense that these civil laws become an integral part of the Church's internal order. This happened when the old ecclesiastical law referred to Roman law as a subsidiary source for those cases which the former did not directly regulate with formally issued dispositions. And a *renvoi* in this sense occurs in the most evident and most characteristic way with *canonized* civil laws, that is to say, laws solemnly approved, spiritualized and taken over by the ecclesiastical order. Vice versa, often there is a formal (non-receptive) *renvoi*. For there are matters that are of interest to the Church, which are legally relevant to it, but do not fall within the scope of its normative power, in that they concern *res mere civiles*. In this hypothesis, the Church's approving them and refer-ring to them hardly implies that such laws become part of the ecclesiastical law. For this would be in contradiction with the ecclesiastical law principle whereby its legislative competence ends when it comes to matters that it recognizes as the state's concern. This is particularly clear with those civil laws that are contrary to the interests of the Church, although it does not so much openly disapprove them, as it just *tolerates* them. Needless to say, tolerance rules out the possibility of a proper reception.

On its part, the state refers frequently to Canon law. If at times *renvoi* implies the statalization of the latter, at other times this does not occur. For example, when a state recognizes the Church's competence to regulate marriage and attributes civil effects to religious marriage, evidently this does not entail the transformation of religious marriage into a civil one, regulated by the state norms that are only materially identical to the Church's. On the contrary, the state wants marriage to remain a sacrament, that admittedly it is not competent to regulate and to which, however, it grants relevance within its own law.[65]

---

64 See however, among others, Scherer, 1866: § 34; Sägmüller, 1909: 104; Wernz, 1905: 294 [; Wernz, 1938: 369; Jemolo, 1923; Jemolo, 1945: 72 ff.; Del Giudice, 1924; Checchini, 937: 63 ff.; D'Avack, 1939; and other cited at fn. 14 and 32].

65 [It is known that Italy adopted this system in compliance with the concordat of February 11, 1929. The relations between state law and Canon law, compliant with this system, have been abundantly discussed. In agreement with my text, see Del Giudice, 1939: 382 ff. See a review of different

§ 41. d. So far I have examined the relevance of the contents of an order to another one in relation to more orders that are valid at the same time within their own sphere. Yet I also have to address the case of a legal order that, at the moment in which its autonomy or its sources terminate, affects the contents of another order in which it gets incorporated and that, so to say, inherits it.

This hypothesis is usually examined when it comes to subjective relations that take place when an entity, for example a state or a municipality, constitutes or expands itself with all or a part of the elements of another entity. In this way, the former entity either terminates by merging or gets diminished. Here the problem arises of the succession between these two entities, considered as persons. This problem is commonly framed as referring to the fact of whether or not the succeeding entity takes on the rights and the obligations of the other terminated or diminished entity. This issue can assume very particular aspects. For succession can take place among more states, in which case principles of international law have to be taken into account. Or it can take place between entities of a different nature and parts of another organization, as in the case of municipalities with respect to the state or ecclesiastical entities, in which case principles of state law, and, respectively (leaving aside the interference of the state), of ecclesiastical law will be evoked. It is not for me to deal with this problem here, let alone with its various aspects. I am not concerned with succession within subjective relationships, determined by the fact I have mentioned, but with the succession that this fact generates between the legal orders of these very entities. Yet I believe that no satisfactory solution to the first problem can be found unless we correctly solve the second. Such a nexus – sometimes intuited but never unpacked – becomes evident in the light of my concept of law. The union of an entity, that is, of an institution or part of it, with another entity always and necessarily entails the union of two legal orders. The union of their respective territories, populations, patrimonies, etc., is nothing but a consequence of the union of the two orders. A state that annexes another state or a province of the latter does not only annex a number of square metres of land or a few thousands inhabitants, but also a genuine 'social organization', that is, in keeping with my concept, a genuine 'legal order', that comes to be part of its own one. Therefore, it is incorrect to believe that it is an annexation of purely material things and then ask if this implies a transferral of the rights and duties that appertain to the entity that possessed those things. Not at all: a state that, for example, gets broader by incorporating another or at the expense of another, by doing so modifies its own order. This modification mainly occurs by extending its own order on the annexed territory at the very moment of the annexation. As a rule, however, the order in force in that very territory continues to exist, at least in some parts, and to be valid. This means that it is inherited

---

opinions in Ago, 1934: 117 fn.; Checchini, 1937: 124; D'Avack, 1937b: 410 ff.; Vassalli, 1932: 116 ff.; Jemolo, 1935: 72 ff.; Gangi, 1945: 13; etc.]

by the order of the entity that gets broader and comes to constitute a more or less integral part of the latter. In this way, whether this order was autonomous or whether it rested on another order, it now ties to the one of the annexing state, in which it finds its legal basis, as well as the other parts that comprise the latter. In this way there is a novation of its normal source, but it is a subjective one, which does not affect the objective identity of that very order. Certainly the annexing state will be able to modify or abrogate it. However, as long as it does not abolish or, better, substitute it, that order will continue to be valid within the annexed territory, with the effects already produced as well as those that it will continue to produce. Contrary to what is believed, the title of this persistence or continuity is not a special act, whether explicit or implicit, on the part of the annexing state, specifically designed to preserve the validity of such a law, whether temporarily or permanently. There is or there might be no such act, and that title is the annexation itself. The latter yields that effect by nature. On the other hand, the annexing state can remove that effect by means of another act that modifies the contents of the law that it has subsumed. Yet, before this removal positively occurs, the contents of the order of that state get affected by another order.

It is in this sense that we can speak of succession.[66] The successor is the annexing subject with respect to the one that is totally or partially annexed. The object of succession is the latter's order or part of it, more or less organically determined. This implies that, from the point of view of state domestic law, those rights and duties that found, and continue to find, their basis in the annexed order are transferred to the annexing state[67] – except for those that by nature imply a necessary reference to a specific subject (i.e. the annexed or diminished state), which are not transferable to any other subjects. The bearings of this on the relations with other states, that is, from the point of view of international law, depend on the latter's specific principles, which is not necessary to examine here.

§ 42. Finally, the relations among more legal orders can be examined insofar as the effects produced by one of them are relevant to another. As a rule, the effects or

---

66 Against this view, see Marinoni, 1913b: 362 ff. He draws on the concept that a change in the formal source of an order implies its complete termination, and therefore a completely different order supersedes it. This seems unjustified, as demonstrated by what I said as to the character of this, so to say, source novation.

67 In another text (Romano, 1908: fn. 301 ff.) I claimed that the basis of this succession lies in the adherence to the distinct rights and duties of individuals, the goods, the patrimony, the territory, the ends, etc., which are transferred by one entity to another. In practice, this criterion completely and rightly solves the problems engendered by the succession of legal persons. However, from a theoretical point of view, it is worth integrating it by considering it as a consequence of the more general and logically antecedent criterion, to which I allude in the text, of the adherence to a legal order, of which persons, goods, patrimony and territory are but elements, in the sense that I clarified. In this way, this adherence or connection is spelled out, while some authors (Ferrara, 1915: 937 fn.) took it to be too a materialistic concept, unable to justify the title of a legal relationship. [For developments and applications of the concepts mentioned in my text, see Romano, 1925a: 297 ff.; Romano, 1949: 129 ff.; Romano, 1945: ch. 14, fn. 8 and also ch. 7, § 4, fn. 5.]

the effectiveness, no matter how we call them, of an order unfold in the sphere that belongs to it and terminates at the threshold of the sphere of another order. This rule, however, is not absolute. Besides its internal effectiveness, an order could have another type of effectiveness, which can be considered external, i.e., exerted on another order, although it does not affect its contents (which would take us back to the hypothesis examined above). Let us see, as usual, on the basis of what title this can occur, and, consequently, what the ensuing figures are.

a. The first hypothesis we should attend to concerns two orders in a relation of superiority and correlative subordination. When this subordination is complete, in the sense I have frequently referred to, it is evident that the superior order will be able to determine what effectiveness it can or should have also on the inferior order, and, vice versa, what effectiveness the latter has on the former. For example, the value of a state administrative or judicial act on a municipality is as conditional upon the laws of the state as the value of the regulations or an act of a municipality performed on the basis of its own regulations on the state. More complex is the case in which a legal order's subordination to another is only partial. Furthermore, in this hypothesis it is not easy to trace principles with the character of generality. For it all depends on the limit, which may vary, of this subordination as well as on other elements that can be connected to that limit, whether directly or indirectly. For example, the effects produced on the basis of the law of the Church insofar as they are valid for a confessional state; those proper of the order of a federal state with respect to member states, and vice versa. Those of international law on the distinct states and of the distinct states on international law cannot be dealt with like the others, as each category needs to be dealt with specifically, which would be inappropriate in this context.

b. I would like to consider more directly the hypothesis of different legal orders that affirm themselves independently of each other. A typical example is the relation – indeed of independence – that exists among the laws of the various states. Despite this, we have seen that this relation does not prevent states, on their own and through their own dispositions, from assigning relevance to the law of other states by recognizing the way they regulate particular matters and by refraining from positively regulating these matters themselves.[68] Now, such a recognition implies that the foreign law that is referred to is granted a certain effectiveness. However, this effectiveness is yet to be determined, since most of the time it does not coincide with that which the order enjoys within its own sphere. This is particularly evident in the case of an order that does not wish to produce effects outside the territorial area of the state where it

---

68 [On this point, see Romano, 1949: 52. In conformity with my view, Cavaglieri, 1933: 60 ff.; contrary to my view, Ago, 1934: 102; Ago, 1937: 58 ff.; Checchini, 1937: 72. See also the authors cited in the successive footnote.]

arises: in this event, attributing validity outside that sphere obviously means augmenting its effectiveness. But also when the order, for example, wishes to impose itself in some respects on all its subjects, even when they are in a foreign state, and the latter in its turn, based on the relations at stake, decides not to address them with its own laws – also in this case there is no coincidence between the original effectiveness of that order and the effectiveness that it is granted by the recognizing state. Indeed, if the latter does not simply assume a passive countenance and does not simply register its effects, but it itself sees to the application of the foreign law through its force and its authority, and so on, it is evident that it lends an effectiveness that goes beyond the one stemming from its own state, which is the only one that truly belongs to it. On the contrary, the foreign order cannot exert the effects that it believes to be admissible if these prove to be contrary to the public order, public decency and the prohibitions of the other state. In this hypothesis, its effectiveness will get diminished, or even barred, despite the fact that it is generally recognized. From this point of view, at least ideally, a distinction should be drawn between the so-called norm of collision and the norms that ensures the effectiveness of the foreign law, to which the former refers. This does not exclude that, practically and materially, often only the latter norm occurs, although it always presupposes the former. Here I can forgo discussing whether these are truly different norms or two aspects of the same norm. Anyway, it is important to remark that the disposition relating to the effectiveness of the foreign state does not always result in a norm of application, although the doctrine usually tends to place emphasis on it. A norm of application obtains when the foreign order is granted immediate and direct effectiveness, as it is considered as a system of law in its own right. Then it will be necessary to mandate the authorities or even the individuals to apply it, in those cases in which its relevance is admitted. But it might be the case that what has to be recognized is only the validity of the acts (e.g. a judgment) issued by the foreign state itself in accordance with its own law. In this case, the application is already taken care of by that state, while the other state, which attributes effectiveness to these acts, will limit itself to making sure that they have existence and validity based on the law they are premised upon. Naturally, this means that, while the effectiveness of the foreign law is always recognized, it is not applied. It is only its applications that are recognized.

My line of thought implies that not even the disposition regulating the effectiveness of a foreign law 'nationalizes' this law.[69] 'National' is the norm

---

69 [Famously, this point is highly controversial, and so are the principles with which it is entwined. Here I cannot discuss its recent developments, which gesture to the necessity to revise the whole subject matter. I will only make a few quick observations. First, I want to recall what I said earlier (see fn. 35 above) as to the inadmissibility of the opinion that builds on the principle of the exclusivity of original orders and, among other things, denies the order of a state being relevant to the

that establishes its effects, and not the order that this norm takes into account and that claims to be considered as foreign. In the same way, against what some authoritatively argue, I believe that the judgment made in a state that is allowed to be applied in another state does not get 'nationalized'; let alone, for example, the appointment of a consul to whom the state grants the *exequatur*.

In truth, the effects and, in general, the effectiveness of a particular norm or act do not amount to the norm or the act considered in their own right. A legal act (including a norm) can exist and be completely valid and at the same time be ineffective, in whole or in part. On the contrary, an act can continue to be effective even after it has ceased to exist. In addition, one should bear in mind that the effectiveness or the effects of an act (again including the legal norm) do not necessarily derive from other acts or other laws (when it comes to a norm, from other norms). Without insisting on a distinction that in itself is unquestionable, even elementary – although it is difficult to spell out clearly and although it is often forgotten – all that demonstrates the effectiveness of a foreign law is determined by a national law, without the foreign law ceasing to exist as such in the eyes of the latter and without the latter turning this law into a national law. This is a principle that is not only true when the effectiveness that is granted to the foreign law is equal to its original one, but also when it is different, greater or smaller.[70] Partially analogous relations can exist between state law and the law the

---

order of another state. More in particular, I believe it is groundless to object (Ago, 1934: 105) that a foreign norm that only remains a foreign norm cannot have legal effectivity within the order of another state, as this norm is legal only insofar as it is part of an order that grants this character and loses it if the norm breaks away from that order. It is easy to reply that the state that refers to a norm of another state considers this norm in its particular content, and not as divorced from the order to which it belongs. What is more, it considers it as legal precisely because and as long as it is legal within the foreign state, because and as long as it belongs to the latter's order. It should be added that, in my view, there is an irreconcilable contradiction between the opinion of those who deny, in the case at stake, the figure of the receptive *renvoi*, and yet, despite this, keep speaking of a genuine incorporation of the norms that are referred to within the order that makes the *renvoi*. Such a contradiction is not overcome by affirming that the norm that refers to the foreign law is a legally produced norm (Perassi, 1937: 60 ff.; Balladore Pallieri, 1929: 443; Balladore Pallieri, 1940: 25; Morelli, 1933: 12; Ago, 1934: 108; etc.). For, by means of it, one order accommodates norms whose legality within this order is conditional upon these very norms' legality within the foreign order from which they are taken. An infelicitous makeshift is adopted to justify this opinion; which is to say, to claim that in this way an order assumes as its own source of legal norms the source that is entitled to issue legal norms about the same relationships within the foreign order; worse, it is said that in this way legislative competence is attributed within this order to the foreign legislator. Against such specious and illogical conceptions, see Piccardi, 1939: § 13. Among the most recent attempts at revising this subject matter, see lately Balladore Pallieri, 1943: 331 ff., where the author modifies the opinions expressed in earlier writings.]

70 Instead, while he generally believes that reference to foreign law is non-receptive, as to the present case Ottolenghi (1913: 83) holds the opinion that it is a material *renvoi*.

Church.[71] In the previous pages I have already sought to demonstrate that the law of the Church is a legal order in itself, separate and independent from the former. In spiritual and disciplinary matters, the Church enjoys a normative power that certainly does not derive from the state, as it appertains to it and is original. Nonetheless, the state not only recognizes – within certain limits that it is not important to specify – the effects that the ecclesiastical order attributes to its laws and to the acts issued by virtue of such laws. In addition, often these effects are accompanied by others that are actually dubbed 'civil', or rather, 'state-based', ones that the law of the Church could hardly produce on its own. This offers a typical example – which, if I am not mistaken, helps correctly evaluate similar figures – of an order that is relevant to another not as to its existence or its contents, but as to some of its effects. Moreover, for the state, such effects do not coincide with those of that very order, not only because they are greater or smaller, but because they are intrinsically different.

c.   Other cases, in which a legal order might have effects on another, occur when the former constitutes a presupposition of the latter, in the sense examined above. Here I cannot, and do not have to, dwell further on these particular aspects. Suffice it to say, as an example, that sometimes the effectiveness of an international treaty is conditional on the production, on the part of the contracting states, or of third states, of the law that in this way, if produced, has the effect of bringing about the conditions set in the treaty.[72] Similarly certain activities cannot be either performed or omitted by these states, in compliance with international obligations, unless internal legal norms are issued.[73] In this latter case, on the one hand, international law affects, although indirectly, as we saw above, the contents of state law, because it imposes on the state whether implicitly or explicitly, to lay down such norms. On the other hand, state law, whether or not these norms have been issued, exerts effects on international law, as the latter's implementation depends on the former's dispositions.

d.   Furthermore, it can be the case that an already extinguished legal order continues to exert some effects within another that represents its continuation. A few pages above (§ 41) I hinted at the case whereby an order is incorporated

---

71 [See the authors mentioned at fn. 32, 64 and 65.]

72 It is in this sense that Triepel (1899: 290 ff.) speaks of an 'international law that presupposes the law' [translator's translation from German]. See also Donati, 1906: 349 ff.

73 Triepel, 1899: 301; Donati, 1906: 361 ff.; Anzilotti, 1912, 37 ff. [For other applications of these concepts, on top of those concerning the relations between state law and international law, see Romano, 1945: ch. 7, § 6, fn. 14.]

into another and because of this affects its contents. The hypothesis that I am discussing here is tied to the preceding one, but is different. Let us imagine a state that annexes another or part of another state. Not only will the order of the former state end up comprising, in the sense and within the limits already mentioned, the institutions [*istituti*] and the norms of the latter order that are valid at the moment of the union; but, in addition, it might be the case that it sometimes applies and recognizes the general effectiveness of the annexed state's laws that had been aggregated before the union and that therefore it has never take on. This might happen by virtue of the principle of non-retroactivity of laws or, better, of the persistence of laws abrogated with respect to the acts performed under its rule and their effects. In other words, these principles find their application not only within the scope of the same order, when it undergoes modifications, but also in the relations between different orders. When an order inherits another, the latter affects the contents of the former, as at least some norms of the inherited order continue to exist. In addition, the inheriting order in some cases grants the already extinguished parts of the inherited order an effectiveness that is equal to that which, in analogous cases, it grants its own norms that are no longer in force.

§ 43. Based on my analysis of the different senses and the different ways in which a legal order can be relevant to another, we can get to the conclusion that such a relevance can be very extensive. Which is to say, while sometimes it concerns an order as a whole, more often it only concerns part of it. In this way, for example, if the order of a municipality is usually relevant as a whole to that of the state, vice versa only a few elements of the order of the states are relevant to international law; and analogously, the order of the Church to that of the state, the order of a state to that of another state, and so on. It follows that, while at times the relevance I have examined constitutes a rule that is absolute and admits no exception, at other times it itself constitutes an exception, which can be very limited.

It is worth briefly dwelling on one of the many examples that are offered by this latter hypothesis and that looks very interesting to me, if only because nobody thought of framing it in this way, if not in an utterly vague and imprecise manner: so-called natural obligations. Today it is no easy task to condense the concept of these obligations in one exact formula, as some authors have decidedly rejected this concept because they believe it is worthless. I cannot and do not want to embark on such an enterprise which goes far beyond my topic here. Yet, I think it is not pointless to raise the problem of whether or not the natural obligation – within correct limits, which are set by its own original figure – consists in an obligation validly undertaken in accordance with a legal order that is different from the civil one (i.e. the state order) and for this reason is irrelevant (apart from, exceptionally, the effects that everybody is aware of). It might be true that currently the law inclines to a progressive identification of the natural obligation with the moral duty in general,[74] or with patrimonial moral duties.[75] However, we should not neglect that this will bring about, or has already brought about, a new type of natural obligations, substantively different from the old one. Still, it is useful to distinguish the two types.[76] The true, original natural obligation should not be confused with the moral one (while the doctrine that is still dominant has long agreed on this point). I believe it is a perfect and complete legal obligation if one assesses it in the light of its own order, while, when it is subsumed under the civil or state order, the latter recognizes it only in part. The positive non-state order within which the thoroughly legal obligation takes place – which then the state itself considers as 'natural' – can vary. I do not want to investigate in what sense, within Roman law, it was *ius naturale* or *ius gentium*, given that is was indeed counterposed to the *ius civile*; or if we should not take into due consideration, more than is commonly done, the fact that, within classical Roman law, natural obligations only were those undertaken by the slaves and the *filii familias*, which hinged on the order of the family. Within modern law, the sources of obligations that civil law regards as natural can be the following (here I only advance the abstract possibility without predetermining any actual questions, which I do not have the possibility of examining here):

a. the internal order of the family, which can rest on ancient customs. For example, we cannot exclude *a priori* that the parent's obligation to endow the daughter, which Art. 147 of our Civil Code[77] declares to be void of action, is not only a moral obligation, but also a legal one, in accordance with those customs. In the past such customs were included within state law, whereas now they might exist as mere family customs.

b. The order of the Church insofar as it imposes a series of obligations that the state neither recognizes nor prohibits from meeting. For example, while the state has abolished the obligation to give the tithe, the Church continues to impose it on its members. It is my conviction that those who voluntarily give the tithe are not making a donation, precisely because they have no intention of liberally doing something; rather they aim to fulfil a duty arising from

---

74 Not to mention any of the latest writings, see Planiol, 1913: 161 ff., where it is stated that such an assimilation is not complete; Perreau, 1913: 510 ff.

75 Bonfante, 1915: 97 ff.

76 In effect, the doctrine has tried to make this distinction also with respect to those legislations that, like the Swiss Code of Obligations (Art. 63) or the German Civil Code (§ 814), have substituted the expression 'natural obligations' for that of 'moral and social duties'. See the literature cited in Polacco, 1915: 110. [As for Italian law, we now have to keep in mind Art. 2034 of the 1942 Civil Code. On the opinion expressed in the text, see Brunetti, 1920: 201 ff.; Betti, 1920: 128, fn. 21; Cesarini Sforza, 1929: 68–69; S. Romano, 1945: 10 ff. and *passim*.]

77 [The 1942 Civil Code does not contain any definition that corresponds to that of Art. 147 of the 1865 Civil Code.]

positive ecclesiastical law, one that, under state law, might constitute a natural obligation.

c.   The internal order of any private institution [*istituto*], of a class of people that is somewhat organized, and so on. A famous example of this can be the gambling debt, which is not a moral obligation, but is regarded as a clear-cut and strict obligation by the norms recognized by the gamblers, which give rise, as it were, to the regulation of the gaming house.

d.   Other norms arising from private autonomy. Here I cannot examine if and when private autonomy can give rise to a law. But if we grant that the answer to this question is affirmative, this might explain those natural obligations that emerge – unlike those discussed so far – as civil obligations, but are no longer valid as civil obligations and remain sheer natural obligations because they lack some formalities or because of some emerging facts that do not affect their substance (prescription, unjust acquittal of the debtor, etc.). Qualifying them as natural obligations could be based on the following [consideration]: in the end they are obligations whose title persists in itself and for itself either as a 'law' of the contracting parties or as a 'law' of the bequeather, or as any other deployment of autonomy. Therefore, it continues to be capable of bringing about legal relationships. Only the law of the state ceases considering them as thoroughly effective either on account of purely extrinsic and formal flaws, which do not concern their substance or their nature, or on account of those other motives of pure state law that I alluded to.

It goes without saying that this listing of legal orders giving rise to obligations that are natural obligations when they are located within the field of state law does not mean to be strict but only illustrative. The examples I have offered are only meant to suggest a reconstruction of that theory of natural obligations that came to be considered archaic only because it was wrongly framed and misunderstood. It was regarded as the residue of old conceptions. On the contrary, I believe it is not only still alive but is amenable to extensive and productive developments; it could even blossom. If I am right, this might be further evidence that the concept of law I illuminated not only meets the requirements of logic and is necessary to unravel many problems of public law, but is useful in the field of private law too.

I would like to add that state law grants effects to the so-called natural obligation insofar as it considers it as an 'obligation', and therefore also recognizes, although only with respect to these effects, the order on which they rest by giving it relevance. The opinion[78] that portrays the natural obligation as a 'bare fact' producing certain consequences could be true if and only if, within positive law, a new tendency prevails, one that undoubtedly exists but has so far been a mere

---

78 De Crescenzio, 1899: 19 ff.; Simoncelli, 1890: 24 ff.

tendency; which is to say, the idea that natural obligations can only be identified with a purely moral and conscientious duty, and thus with an *in se* non-legal duty.

§ 44. When the circumstances do not arise in which an order is relevant to another, that order is irrelevant to the latter. But while the concept of such an irrelevance is in itself and for itself only negative and cannot be defined otherwise, a more detailed enquiry is not pointless, for it will allow us to distinguish different approaches to it.

First, irrelevance can be total or partial. Partial irrelevance emerges implicitly as a necessary consequence of the partial relevance that I have already examined. Second, it is evident that irrelevance can be reciprocal between the different legal orders involved. However, it can also be unilateral, in the sense that, while an order considers another as irrelevant, the latter instead attributes some sort of relevance to the former.

§ 45. It is more important and more difficult to evaluate the case in which a legal order is, as such, irrelevant to another, while the latter in its turn addresses the former and draws some consequences by attributing it a different figure.

In one of its simplest manifestations, this happens when, for example, the state order considers a given organization as unlawful and imposes penal sanctions on it. In this case, not only are the actions performed in conformity with the order of that organization viewed as crimes; but crime is also the fact itself that this organization has being instituted and therefore ordered. Accordingly, the Penal Code regards certain facts as crimes and in addition punishes the formation of armed gangs to accomplish these facts, as well as the exercise of a superior command or a special function within them (Arts. 131, 253), and, more in general, criminal associations (Art. 248).[79] In these cases, the state order confronts the orders threatening its existence, or at least the most valuable goods it wants to protect, with the maximum force at its disposal. Far from granting these orders the character of 'legal orders', the state treats them as the most serious anti-legal facts, that is, as crimes. In this way, the antithesis between state law and the internal law of these organizations culminates in its most typical manifestation.

Instead, although an order might not be recognized by another – e.g., by the state order – as a system of law on its own, it can nonetheless be considered as a lawful fact and be located, at least to some extent, under some of the figures that the latter order attributes to the facts that are performed under its rule. In this hypothesis, that which, if considered in itself and for itself, is an objective order is converted into something essentially different with respect to another order.

Examples of this conversion can be drawn from those that I had the opportunity to examine from another point of view. The organization of a factory – which

79 [See now Arts. 306 ff., 416 ff., of the Penal Code of October 19, 1930.]

in my view can generate a legal order (§ 31) – where some persons have a power of supremacy over others who are subordinate to them. Under state civil law, this results in a simple contract between persons in a position of equality.[80] Consequently, the rights and duties they claim should be guaranteed and executed with the help of the state are only those that derive from state laws and from the legal transactions allowed by them. And, given that these laws do not allow an employment contract that confers a power of domination on the owners and the entrepreneurs and imposes a duty of personal submission on the employees, no disciplinary power of the former over the latter can be admitted or recognized as such by the state. It can take place, and constantly does take place, in the workplace, with the sanctions that are practically available; but if a dispute arises and is brought before state courts, then the order of the factory is not presented as an employment contract or part of it, the misconduct of the worker is not presented as a breach of that contract, the sanction imposed is not presented as a consequence of penalty clauses or as a termination for default. Obviously, the consequence is that civil law only captures a part of the relationships that really take place and, what is more, captures them inadequately and imperfectly. Everybody is aware of that. This is manifest in the efforts the doctrine makes in trying to calibrate the norms of positive state law to reality, with artifices and sometimes glaring contradictions. Indeed, some authors, with a hazardous conception blatantly at odds with the spirit of current legislation (at least the Italian one), bluntly acknowledge that the employment contract implies a relationship of domination and correlative dependence.[81] On the contrary, other authors make an attempt at a complicated construction. On one hand, they deny there being such a domination;[82] on the other, they do not deny that, in the performance of work, employees are subordinated to the other contracting party. This subordination eventuates in a complex relationship of obligation, which however is claimed to constitute the employee's personal status. For this reason, these authors deliberately formulate a particular concept of status.[83] However, this does not square with reality. Only indirectly and through an extrinsic connection does the so-called discipline of the factory fall into the employment contract. Obviously, without that contract, the employee would not be bound to that discipline, but this is only one of its conditions. This discipline does not arise from the contractual agreement, but from the internal organization of the enterprise to which one comes to belong on the grounds of that agreement. State law does not take into direct

80 [These observations refer to the regulation of labour relations antecedent to that which has been adopted in Italy afterwards and which has sparked a wide literature.]
81 See the authors cited in Barassi, 1915: 473 ff., 622. [See also, as to the new order, Barassi, 1935: 56, and, among others, Riva Sanseverino, 1938: 216, and the various authors mentioned therein]. Also: Cuche, 1913; Nawiasky, 1913.
82 Barassi, 1915: 473 ff. [Barassi, 1935: fn. 80.]
83 Barassi, 1915: 600 ff., 622, 623 fn. [Barassi, 1935: fn. 179 ff., 187 ff., 192 ff.].

consideration such an organization. This is so true that even those who espouse the view that I mentioned admit that the discipline is 'the dominating affirmation of the will of one person: of the head who takes risks and because of that leads and coordinate the activity'.[84] Now, the will of one person is evidently something different from the will that is reflected in the contract. It has to be added that discipline implies a bond of cohesion not only with the chief of the factory, but also among the employees.[85] With the exception of special cases that it is not relevant to take into account here, no contract can be said to exist among the employees. This all confirms my thesis that we are faced with two legal orders: that of the enterprise and that of the state. The former is not recognized as such by the latter.[86] For the state addresses some facts and some relationships that the other order contemplates and regulates in a different way, and attributes to them the only figures that are compatible with some of its basic principles. It is known that the law of the modern state intended to rule out all relationships implying one private individual's dependence on another private individual. Although it was a reaction to the oldest order and the abuses it engendered, in doing so it has gone too far. But in this way the state misrecognizes certain manifestations of social life that still require and will probably require inequality among individuals, the supremacy of some and the subordination of others. And social life, which is more imposing and more powerful than state law, took its revenge by constructing, alongside state law and against it, a series of partial orders within which those necessary relationships can unfold more comfortably and conveniently. For sure, insofar as they are not recognized by the state, these orders are not practically able to attain complete effectiveness. On the other hand, state law continues to ignore them, and by doing so disavows reality; therefore, state law, too, partly loses its effectiveness. The bare concurrence between them brings about many inconveniences, and does not lead to any mutual complement. If one looks at the difficulties encumbering the reform of state law concerning labour contract law, it is evident that some of them are intrinsic and stem from the complexity and the variety of the forms taken by modern labour, while others are due to the persistence of political prejudices – ones that engendered the deficiencies of today's law, which has been forced to apply a relationship of equality even though the terms are unequal.

A further example of relations or facts that state law considers differently than they are considered by the internal order of special institutions (not recognized by

---

84 Barassi, 1915: 632.

85 Barassi, 1915: 755–756. [Barassi, 1935: fn. 80.]

86 There are various figures in the various countries whose legal order regulates the rights of the owners to issue and amend the factory regulation. In this case, some believe this is a right to *imperium* conferred by the state (Jellinek, 1912: 278, and the authors he mentions: Bornhak, Rehm, etc.), while others believe this right arises from the contract (Laband) or locate it within the autonomous corporative law (Oertmann).

the state) is offered by the so-called associations or *de facto* institutions. But what I said about them above is enough (§ 31).[87]

§ 46. In addition, it might be the case that an order, in whole or in part, is irrelevant to another, not only as an order, but under all respects. This means that, unlike the hypotheses examined in the preceding section, the former order is on no account taken into consideration by the latter order. Therefore, the former order does not exist either as an order or as another type of legal fact; nor are the single relations and the single facts occurring within its orbit considered at all.

The possibility of such an extensive irrelevance is not to be doubted, and is clearly manifest in the principles that I have developed so far. There are even orders for which this is a rule, although it does not exclude exceptions. This happens with particular institutions, each of which has a very different end from each other, and therefore does not even have the opportunity to impact on each other. On the contrary, when it comes to institutions with a large scope pursuing ends that cover a broad area of social life – on account of the countless links among its various manifestations, often inseparable from each other – those relations between the institutions' orders might be appropriate or necessary. Yet, one should bear in mind that there is no institution, though broad and comprehensive, that feels the need to consider all social relationships as indistinctly relevant to its order. Consequently, some of these relations are cut out of the sphere of law, although they can fall within the scope of another law that is indifferent to the latter. This also happens when institutions with a universal character, such as the Church, dismiss facts or relations that are not mediatedly or unmediatedly connected to the religious end they pursue, or because of the fact that they are not connected to this end. And this also happens with non-universal institutions pursuing general ends, such as the state (§ 33). For state legal orders also are circumscribed, and thus limited, from many points of view. First, as to the elements comprising them, namely, the territory and the population. While each state has the possibility and the potential to include within its order facts and relationships taking place within foreign territories or between foreigners, as a rule the state does not extend its law so much that it goes beyond its territory and population. It is known that there are many and important exceptions to this rule, especially when it comes to modern states, given that they are not self-enclosed like the older ones. However, this remains a very broad rule, at least as far as certain matters are concerned. The consequence of this rule is that the orders of foreign states as such are indifferent to the distinct states – if not in whole, in no small part – whereas what falls within their scope is

---

87 [A further example: the rules of chivalry, as the norms of so-called 'Gentleman's Community', can be regarded as legal norms in their own right. However, *pace* Calamandrei (1929), this does not mean that the state recognizes them as such. Under Italian law, the breach of them sometimes produces some effects, not however as a breach of law, but as a breach of customary rules. See Romano, 1937: 37–38.]

relevant to them. I believe there is no doubt about that. In this way, for example, in some countries, such as France, it is believed that courts should administer justice only with regard to their citizens and therefore they are not called upon to settle the disputes that only concern foreigners, except for a few cases. And also as regards Italy, some[88] have authoritatively maintained that our judges have no jurisdiction over foreigners except under the circumstances listed in Arts. 105 and 106 of the Code of Civil Procedure. On the other hand, if we do not consider this list as exhaustive, it remains a general principle that the subjection of foreigners to our jurisdiction is subordinate to the occurrence of these specific circumstances, which I do not have to analyze here. When these circumstances do not arise, the issues at stake do not fall into our legal order, be they substantial or procedural.

Moreover, scarcely does the state subsume all the relationships and the facts that take place under its law. Such a subsumption requires these relations and facts to be of interest to the state and the ends it pursues (§§ 33, 40). Now, while we are used to conceiving the state as an institution with unlimited ends, it is evident that this latter expression only has a negative meaning. More precisely, it articulates the concept that there is no social end that cannot become an end of state. Still, this is a potentiality or abstract possibility. In concrete, however expansive and invasive the reach of the state might be, the law of each state is always limited, also for what concerns its matter. This means that there are matters that fall outside its scope, because the state has no interest in them and therefore has no reason to address them either in their own right or insofar as they can be regulated by another order.

§ 47. An opposite opinion has been advocated: 'There is no sphere of individual activity that is not addressed by the law' (viz., by state law). 'A particular action – it has been stated – either is imposed or prohibited by a specific legal norm, or falls within the sphere of liberty, and as such is permitted, provided that it does not entail any limitation on other individuals which is not prevented by any specific legal norms, in which case it is forbidden. The same applies to a particular omission.'[89] Such conclusions descend from the defence of a principle that can be formulated as follows: as the legal order foresees particular cases for which it establishes such obligations and limitations, it implicitly lays down the general norm that, in all other cases, there are no such limitations. This norm is not only negative but also positive, because it would otherwise not be a legal norm. In other words, this norm is believed to positively permit to do or not to do all the activities that are not forbidden or correlatively imposed. Such activities are claimed to provide the contents of the right to freedom and never to be legally indifferent, as they are always relevant.[90]

88 Anzilotti, 1908: 57 ff. fn. [see now Arts. 4 and 5 of the 1940 Code of Civil Procedure, and, as to the doctrine, Morelli, 1941: 104 ff.; Zanzucchi, 1942, 22 ff.; etc.].
89 Donati, 1910: 223.
90 Donati, 1910: 35 ff. and *passim*.

I cannot put this doctrine to the test here. It was constructed to solve the so-called problem of legal gaps. I believe this problem should be framed in a different way, as I aim to demonstrate in my future studies.[91] Yet I think a few quick considerations are not superfluous, as they are also instrumental in corroborating the theory that I have so far exposed.

First, I believe it is incorrect to say that the general and conclusive norm of a legal order has to be a positive norm in the sense specified above, which necessarily attributes a right – a right to freedom – correlated with a duty on others. Rather, it can be a purely negative norm, one that is designed to deny the existence of obligations other than those specified by the other norms. This view is suggested by the prejudice that I rebutted above (§ 22), whereby a right can exclusively be conceived as regulating relationships between persons, constituted by rights and reciprocal duties.[92] On the contrary, I believe it is perfectly conceivable that a legal order declares as one of its fundamental principles the fact that it limits itself to specific matters, in such a way that the others, which it does not address, might be considered legally irrelevant and therefore as a realm in which there are neither rights nor obligations. What is more, this is not a mere possibility, but a strict requirement of all orders, if the axiom I established its true that no order claims to hold sway over all individual activities and manifestations, but only on those that are interesting in the light of its ends.[93]

In addition, I believe it is inadmissible to see a genuine right to freedom in all liberties to do and omit to do deriving from the fact that a legal order does not prohibit or impose certain activities. First, it is easy to observe that if one goes down this road one ends up envisaging a right to freedom everywhere – even though the traditional doctrine, with a correct intuition, or with perfect self-awareness, never dreamt of something like this. And it is understandable why some have gone so far as to envision a state's right to freedom to undertake or not undertake the activities that are not prohibited or imposed by the legal order,[94] while these liberties are nothing other than aspects of its power, which is something more and substantively different than a simple right to freedom. The latter can logically exist with respect to someone that enjoys a higher position, but not with respect to a subject. With respect to one's subordinates, one is not only free, but also (if I may say so) the master.

And, regardless of that, I believe it is incorrect to confound the right to freedom with a series of other rights possessing a figure of their own, whose positive contents are regulated by the legal order. Not only the power of the state, but also, for example, the autarchy of municipalities, the right to public and private property, etc., which also imply the liberty to do and omit to do as well as the claim that the others should abstain from a conduct that might thwart that liberty: these are

---

91 [On this topic, see now Romano, 1925b and Romano, 1945: ch. 7, § 7.]
92 Bierling, 1894: 91 ff.; Donati, 1910: 38 ff.
93 See especially Bergbohm, 1892: 371 ff.; see also Marinoni, 1912: 312 ff. [; and Romano, 1945: ch. 7, § 2 and *passim*].
94 Donati, 1910: 227 ff.

not rights to freedom. The right to freedom can be treated as a right in itself only insofar as it is configured as a right concerning an individual's independence from other individuals, whether superior or equal, who in their turn have an obligation not to interfere in her legal sphere. It is a negative right – a right to a simple omission – while the positive activity correlated to that omission either constitutes the specific object of another public or private law, or is irrelevant. The opinion, today widely agreed upon, that the right to freedom is an essentially unique right, in the sense that it cannot be broken down into as many autonomous rights as the innumerable liberties that are encompassed by it, can be justified only when this right is attributed the negative content I discussed.[95] In fact, such liberties, as long as they turn into positive activities, can give rise to just as many autonomous rights, completely distinct from each other. They can be conceived as manifestations of one comprehensive right only as long as one intends to foreground their common element, whereby in some moments and in some respects they culminate in the affirmation of one's personal independence. Only as long as one wants to bring out this characteristic – such an undifferentiated object – can rights be reduced to the concept of the right to freedom. Otherwise, in themselves and for themselves, either they generate various legal figures that should not be confounded with, and should be distinct from, each other, or are legally irrelevant.

Finally, leaving aside other points that would make me deviate from my path, it has to be noted that the legal order can limit itself in different ways. While these ways can hardly be neglected, the doctrine that I have just referred to does not consider them. Among these different ways, I am particularly interested in the following ones.

a.   First, the legal order can limit the authorities' power without this limitation being matched by others' right to observe such a limitation. In the states prior to the existing ones this was the favoured system. This explains the common, correct opinion that the affirmation of the public right to freedom is very recent and typical of the modern state. Contrary to what has been stated, which is at odds with the historical truth, it is not a necessary affirmation of every legal order. In the end, it would be easy to mention many current cases, drawn from our positive law, in which limitations of public powers are not matched by any citizens' rights. The most salient case is that in which, provided that there are limits on legislative power, nobody is authorized to force the latter to observe them (see § 22 above).

b.   Second, it might be the case that the limits of a legal order generate rights – attributed by the legal order itself – whose content is the observation of these very limits. Or else they might presuppose this observation. The most characteristic of such rights is the right to freedom, conceived in the purely negative sense that I discuss above. It concerns a given independence of each of the subjects

---

95 [Against this opinion, see now Romano, 1925b: 5, fn. 2, and Romano, 1945: ch. 9, § 1.]

who are subordinate to the legal order. This right is matched by the corresponding obligation, binding on the others, not to interfere in the sphere that the state
leaves untouched. This is not the only right that should be taken into consideration. There are others, with an essentially positive content, which therefore cannot be confounded with the right to freedom. These rights ensure that the norms
of a legal order give way to an activity whose performance, within certain limits,
is not addressed by the order itself, in that it is left to one's will: to cite an example
that I have already given, the right to property. Sometimes, instead of rights,
we should speak of the status of some persons based on this presupposition –
for example, the status of autarchy of some public entities. Sometimes, again
from the above mentioned point of view, we have the figure of the discretionary
power attributed to the various bodies of the state or other entities.

Evidently, we are confronted with a whole series of very different cases that,
for my purposes, share the characteristic by which the order considers some of
its activities as legally relevant, but only *to a certain degree*. For, it circumscribes a
sphere that insofar as it is granted and limited by the order, constitutes a right,
a status, a power. One cannot exceed this sphere without carrying out a legally
relevant abuse; yet, the order does not penetrate this sphere, so as for its inside
to be legally indifferent. The incorrect overstatement of this, so to say, legally
indifferent space has led someone to bring into question the fact that, within it,
taken as a whole, we can find the figure of this or that right. Famously some
authors have denied the right to freedom, as they regard it as a simple liberty
or a complex of merely factual liberties. And, from a substantively similar point
of view, other authors have denied property being a right. Now, such opinions,
which overstretch the field of what is legally indifferent, are no less erroneous
than the opposed opinion that all activities are always legally relevant. Both
of them fail to identify the point at which the order stops and beyond which it
never goes. Indeed the order confers the right to freedom, but afterwards the
host of acts that derive from that right, in its eyes, are bare facts; it confers the
right to property, but it does not concern itself with the way in which the owner
enjoys his goods, unless he uses them in ways that are contrary to the laws; it
grants the father of the family parental authority – whose abuse is prohibited
and punished – but it does not consider as genuine rights the various factual
liberties that are encompassed by this authority and are legally indifferent, such
as a father's slapping his son when he gets naughty.

From this sphere, or better, from these diverse spheres, whose inside is
legally indifferent – in the sense I discussed – we can deduce a corollary:
another order might be rooted in their inside, which in its turn is indifferent
to the order that recognizes the existence of those spheres, unless it exceeds
them. As the distinct acts that can be carried out at the will of the *dominus* (so
to say) of those spheres are indifferent, so is the order with which, in some
cases, this very *dominus* will try to regulate those acts. This order might well be
legal in itself if it possesses the necessary characteristics, but it will be of no
relevance to the state order. Just as the state order attaches no importance to

the correction mechanisms adopted by parents toward their children unless they result in abuses of parental authority, so does the state order usually ignore the regulation of a boarding school, an institution [*istituto*], a private hospital. The state order only punishes (Art. 390 of the Penal Code[96]) particular correction or disciplinary mechanisms that it views as abuses. It is worth noting that these abuses do not concern the norms contained in that regulation, which have no importance to it, but with the limits established by the state itself to the rights that allow running that particular establishment.[97]

On the contrary, it might be the case that, for special reasons that vary according to the circumstances, the legal order of a particular entity that takes places within the sphere of autonomy granted to it by the state is not entirely indifferent to the latter. For example, this happens with the regulations of autarchic entities, or with the law of the Church, which the state considers as types of law. It follows that, although generally the state authorities recognize the competence of those entities with respect to their distinct acts, they can decide on the lawfulness of those acts, not only with reference to state law, but also with reference to the internal law of those very entities.[98]

c. Finally, I would like to discuss a further hypothesis. Indeed, it might be the case that, on the one hand, the state legal order does not prohibit each of its subjects from engaging in a particular activity (nor does it impose it) – as a consequence, this activity is free. On the other hand, however, the state legal order might not prohibit other subjects from carrying out an activity contrary to the former. In this case, the state remains indifferent to these conflicting activities being carried out, and hence these activities cannot be considered as the object of genuine rights. Italian law, for example, does not prohibit committing suicide, but in doing so it does not intend to prevent someone from preventing suicide; nor can we speak of a right to free suicide. As I have often said, there are entire matters that fall outside the orbit of the order of the state, and that therefore it ignores, not only in part, as in the cases examined above (*sub b*), but in whole.

Among these matters, some of which I have already explored, it is worth mentioning those with a purely spiritual and religious character. Insofar as it claims to be secular and separatist, the state tends to ignore these matters.

96 [Art. 511 of the Penal Code in force.]

97 I think this gives the lie to those who speak of a legal discipline of private individuals based on positive Italian law. The private discipline is relevant to state law not as a discipline, but under different figures, mostly as sanctions of obligations arising from a contract. In addition, it can be utterly irrelevant but as an abuse of another right (e.g. of parental authority), which is not a right of that discipline. This does not mean that it cannot be sometimes irrelevant to an order other than state law. [I have now come to believe that this problem, which anyway calls for a reassessment, cannot be always solved in such a clear-cut manner.]

98 On this aspect of the relations between the state and the Church, see Scaduto, 1904; Vacchelli, 1904; Schiappoli, 1913: fn. 291–292; Coviello, 1915: §§ 98–99; Jemolo: fn. 85 ff.

The dispositions, which are decreasing in number, that address them are but residues of older orders that have not been abrogated and continue to be valid – and yet they do not disprove the tendency that I pointed out. Religious marriage offers an example of this. Previous state legal norms have been abrogated by new norms instituting and governing civil marriage.[99] Hence, this matter in itself and for itself is alien to state law; likewise, the orders of the various churches or other religious institutions that are meant to regulate marriage are indifferent to the state. This principle might help solve the issue of whether or not, within state law, believers have a right to have religious authorities celebrate their marriage.[100] In my opinion, the answer to this question is negative, based on the simple consideration that this matter is irrelevant to state law. And it is pointless to try to find out, as others have done, if that right, which certainly is not conferred by the state, is attributed by the order of the various religious communities; for, if that attribution could be proved, it is nonetheless to be considered as an order that does not exist in the eyes of the state, which cannot guarantee the rights deriving from that order. The state recognition of ecclesiastical law as a law is conditional upon the *civil effects* that can derive from it; the parts that, on the contrary, do not produce those effects are irrelevant to it unless special dispositions that establish otherwise are issued (ones that can be said exceptional).

It should be noted that this principle applies not only to religious matters, but to any matters. In this regard, I might recall the famous controversy on whether private law – with the exception of family law, that comprises particular norms – contains obligations that do not have a patrimonial character. In this sense, if this question is solved in a negative way, this controversy postulates the principle that a whole series of relationships is irrelevant to state law. Indeed, the matter of these relationships, at least in general, is limited to those relations that have patrimonial value or effects.

An analogous point of view, in my opinion, is applicable to the question of whether or not a member of a private company who is ousted from it has always and in all cases the right to bring a lawsuit in state court against this. At least in general, this right should not be dismissed if it is a trading or civil company, or if it is constituted as a charitable organization, since these are entities recognized by the state and directly or indirectly regulated by state law. But if it is a company that is unable to bring about 'civil' (in the broadest sense) relationships or effects, then I believe state courts are not competent, because that company and its internal order are irrelevant to the law of the state. Therefore, this competence is missing, not only when this latter order contains dispositions that prohibit its members from having recourse to the

99 [Famously, the latest law of the Italian state recognizes civil effect also to marriages celebrated by the ministers of the Catholic Church and of the other recognized religions.]

100 On this topic, see Jemolo, 1915: 133. A quick mention also in Chironi, 1903: 533 and 673.

authorities of the state and task others with settling controversies,[101] but also when its social bylaw does not contain anything of that. In my opinion, it is not possible, in any case, for the judicial authority to decide, for instance, on whether or not a political party did well in ousting one of its members; likewise, it is not conceivable for it to force that party to readmit him.[102] It goes without saying the state is competent to address the questions, connected to the expulsion, which are likely to produce 'civil effects'. Naturally, it is not for me here to investigate the potential consequences of these principles within a theory of associations that is still missing.

§ 48. Finally, it is worth concluding the present chapter by mentioning a topic to which I will return in the future, but that can be anticipated in some points.

I have so far determined the relations among various legal orders by considering the institutions in which they materialize in themselves and for themselves, that is, as legal spheres distinct from each other, regardless of the relationships that exist among them. However, as I have often pointed out, there are institutions that are encompassed by others and are completely dominated by them, in such a way that their legal order has to be considered as part of the order of the former. Therefore, although the distinction between their respective orders is to be drawn and, from some points of view, is always necessary, from other points of view, it turns out to be an *internal partition* of the superior institution's order. The importance and meaning that has to be attached to this partition is a problem that the recent doctrine has examined many times; and yet, no decisive outcome has been achieved. As a matter of fact, such results could hardly be decisive in light of the not entirely correct way in which the problem has been framed.

It is known that within the order of some entities – especially of the state – scholars distinguish two types of norms. First, the norms that are claimed to regulate that position and relationships of the entity to its subjects as well as the relationships among subjects. Second, the norms that, unlike the former type, are called 'internal', which the entity addresses to itself and its bodies. Whereas in these terms this distinction seems *prima facie* very clear, it turns out to be imprecise and obscure if one needs to include among internal norms other norms that evidently concern the relationships between the entity and other persons. For example, the norm comprising the regulation of a state library, or the disciplinary norms that apply to public schools, and so on. Then scholars have introduced a further criterion. They have distinguished norms concerning the entity's general powers of supremacy of and the norms concerning its special powers of supremacy, and

---

101 Lessona (1910: 378) builds on the existence of such dispositions and investigates their effectiveness. Also Bianchi (1901: fn. 17) hints at this question.

102 [This question should be framed differently when it comes to those orders where political parties figure as public entities within the state constitutional order; it is pointless here to determine what solution should be adopted in this case.]

therefore a particular status of subjection in which some people find themselves for a variety of reasons. This latter type of norm is not included in the norms that establish their general subjection. Unlike the former type, the latter type should be included among internal norms. This way of conceiving this distinction, which I myself contributed to clarifying in many works,[103] is not incorrect in itself. However, it seems to me that today it can be superseded and reabsorbed by a more complete, higher point of view, one that better explains the concept of internal norms and at the same time sheds more light on the concept of special powers of supremacy as well as other concepts that have so far remained in the shadow.

The point of view that I am hinting at claims that within some entities with a very complex structure – such as the state, but certainly not only the state – we should distinguish several institutions that, put together, give form to one institution. In this sense, the distinct bodies of the state (the Chambers, the various Ministries, and agencies in general) are institutions: not only those that are *stricto sensu* state bodies, but also so-called state institutions [*istituti*], such as schools, museums, libraries, establishments, and so on (§ 12 *sub* 3). Moreover, any set of these bodies and institutions [*istituti*] can be considered as an institution insofar as they are coordinated with each other, subordinated and unified, and also the so-called three powers of the state – the legislative, the executive and the judiciary powers, that, put together, constitute that broader institution that the whole state organization is. Until we get to the broadest institution, which is the state itself, and encompasses all of the smaller institutions that I mentioned, and therefore, in addition to its specific organization, the other elements that constitute it.

If this holds true, then we come to the following corollary. Any institution is, by definition, based on what I have demonstrated in the first chapter, a legal order. For, in this case, these are institutions that form part of another one, and the legal orders that constitute the former are part of the legal order of the broader institution encompassing them; thus, they are internal legal orders of the latter. With respect to the state (but evidently we can apply the same criteria to any entity with a non-simple structure), I regard as internal norms and (I can now better and more comprehensively say) as its internal orders:

a. The orders of its organization, insofar as they concern the respective position and the relationships of its various bodies and institutions [*istituti*].
b. The orders of its distinct bodies and institutions [*istituti*], both in themselves and for themselves and as regards the relationships with specific officials or with those who, for various reasons, can gain access to those institutions.

103 See Romano, 1905 and Romano, 1912: fn. 7. See also Ranelletti, 1912: 236, 276; Arangio-Ruiz, 1913: fn. 482, 594; Salemi, 1913: 55; Zanobini, 1915: 321 ff.; Presutti, 1917: fn. 40.

These criteria have many advantages. The concept of internal order is clearly delineated and, above all, is unified. The internal order is the institution that is encompassed by a broader one with regard to the order of the latter. Then, the law of a state office with respect to the law of the state considered as a whole, or the law of the state with respect to international law. Second, as far as state law is concerned, the concept of internal order is no longer conditional on the concept of special power of supremacy. On the contrary, the latter is to be evinced from the former, and in such a way that it gets clarified and completed. Indeed, I am now in the position to place due emphasis on special powers of supremacy vis-à-vis general ones, and a whole series of other powers, rights, duties, positions and situations, that can be considered as special vis-à-vis analogous ones endowed with the characteristic of generality. This distinction, which has now become very simple, cannot be but the following: general can be said those statuses, relations, powers, rights, obligations, etc., that are founded upon the order of the state considered as a whole, as the institution that encompasses the others; whereas special can be said the correlative aspects that are founded upon the order of a state institution considered in itself, in isolation. In this way, it is the mentioned distinction of law that justifies and explains the other, which relates to subjective aspects – this is also logically more correct.

Based on this, it is important to distinguish two types of internal orders. First, orders established by the institution that encompasses the others. These are not addressed to the institution itself considered as a whole, but to one of the smaller institutions there are subordinate to it. For example, the norms written down in the Statuto[104] or in other laws concerning the so-called *interna corporis* of the Chambers of Parliament, the disciplinary norms binding on state officials contained in its laws and general regulations, and so on. Second, orders established by each of the smaller institutions themselves. For example, regulations of the Chambers, the instructions addressed by those higher in rank to lower government employees, the regulations of an institution [istituto], a library, etc. Orders of the first type are internal with respect to the sphere in which they are valid, namely, that of the institution encompassed by the broader one, but not with respect to the source from which they arise, namely, the broader institution. Orders of the second type are internal both with respect to the sphere in which they are valid and with respect to their source.

Finally, I should like to note that this nicely solves the question of whether these internal orders are to be considered as legal orders. A negative answer – which I myself in other situations accepted and which is the prevailing one – is correct in the sense that the orders of the second type are irrelevant as such to

---

104 [Translator's note: Romano refers to the Statuto Albertino, which was the constitution that Charles Albert of Sardinia conceded to the Kingdom of Sardinia on March 4, 1848 and that later became the constitution of the unified Kingdom of Italy and remained in force, with a few changes, until 1948.]

the general order, do not form an integral part of it, do not merge with it. This does not mean that they are irrelevant from other points of view. In this way, although the production of the internal regulations of the Chambers of Parliament or of hierarchical instructions is contemplated by the general law of the state – and sometimes is even made obligatory – these regulations do not merge with it, are not connected with the laws and the general regulations to constitute the order of the state considered as one and comprehensive institution. This is a corollary of the principle that they are elements of an order in its own right, of a particular institution, encompassed by the state institution, but distinct from it; these elements concern the institution itself exactly insofar as it remains separate from the superior one and not insofar as it is reabsorbed within it. In this sense, these elements – and this has sometimes been noted with respect to parliamentary regulations – are manifestations of autonomy. After all, when they are considered no longer with respect to the comprehensive order of the state, but in themselves, nobody can deny them being genuine legal orders. This is also a corollary of the definition of law that I have advanced and of the principle that any institution is always a legal order. This is evidence that the two opinions that have so far rivalled each other are both erroneous, whether in a relative or in an absolute sense. For they build on a concept of law that needs amending along the lines of the criteria that I delineated. As to the internal norms of the first type, which are internal not because of their source but because of their sphere of effectiveness, their legal character cannot be brought into question, not even from the point of view I mention above, namely, the full-fledged legality of the organic relationships of the state (§ 22 *sub* 3).

And it seems to me that if we push these principles to their extreme consequences, there would be many advantages for the reconstruction of some general theories. For example, the theory of legal relations regulated by public law and the theory of the division of powers, and so on, might reveal novel, interesting aspects.

Afterword

The juristic point of view: an interpretive account of *The Legal Order*

> Legal truth, or reality, is that which has been accepted or even created by a particular positive law, even if it differs from the reality that, in contrast to purely legal reality, is defined 'effective', 'factual' or 'material'.
>
> Romano, 1983b: 127

Santi Romano was born in Palermo, Sicily on January 21, 1875. His origins had a notable impact on his legal training, as Palermo was the cradle of a host of renewed legal studies that changed once and for all the way of approaching public law in Italy. His master, Vittorio Emanuele Orlando, was both a leading statesman and an innovator of the notion and practice of public and administrative law. The young Romano contributed to a seminal collection of volumes, edited by Orlando, devoted to Italian administrative law, *Primo trattato completo di diritto amministrativo italiano* (*First Complete Treatise on Italian Administrative Law*), published between 1900 and 1915. The importance Orlando and his many collaborators attached to such a monumental scholarly enterprise should not go unnoticed: in his preface to the first volume, Orlando emphasized his and the other contributors' conscious, and eventually successful, attempt at constructing an *Italian* school of public law. This collection of writings, he claimed, was the necessary counterpoint to the growing expansion of the state's competences in the public realm. While in the past Italian scholars had been heavily influenced by the French lawyers who had been working and mulling over the *Code Napoléon* and, subsequently, by the German pandectists, Orlando insisted that the specialization and evolution of the Italian state called for a full-fledged 'home-grown' scholarly apparatus. After obtaining his degree at the University of Palermo, Romano wholeheartedly adhered to this ambitious project.

However, he would soon part ways with his Master (though they remained good friends, with the inevitable ebb and flow of pre- and post-war times) and developed a new, seminal approach to the legal phenomenon. For, unlike his master, Romano had no penchant for the limelight of politics. He entirely devoted himself to legal studies and legal teaching. He taught in Camerino (1897–1902), Modena (1902–1907), Pisa (1908–1923) and Milan (1924–1928). His unconditional scholarly commitment, however, suffered a serious setback from the January 1, 1929, when he had to quit his professorship as he was appointed by Benito Mussolini as the President of the Council of State,[1] the court of last resort in administrative matters. Although his judicial activity took most of his time, Romano did not give up his passion for teaching and gave lectures as an Adjunct Professor at the University of Rome 'La Sapienza'. He first taught Administrative Law, and then moved on to Constitutional Law, as Orlando, who had till then held the chair of Constitutional Law at La Sapienza, nominated him as his successor. Romano resigned from the Presidency of the Council of State in 1944, a few months after the Allied Powers liberated Rome from Nazi occupation. Romano died in Rome on November 3, 1947.[2]

Personally, I am not sure that scrabbling around for biographical details is the best way to make sense of an author's theorizing, but when it comes to Romano, reference to the socio-historical setting is inevitable. The rise of mass-democracy was too great a challenge to Italian oligarchic liberal parliamentary politics that had emerged out of the unification in 1870. Political participation was narrow and the electoral system reflected the liberal nationalist minority comprising the educated and propertied middle class and the liberal aristocracy. Unrepresented constituencies were significantly aggravated by the impact of unification carried out by the Piedmontese political elites. If in the South banditry and crime mushroomed as a response to such disappointing political developments, the Papacy and the Catholic Church were hostile to the new nation-state. In sum, parliamentary politics reflected the interests of a narrow class and was hampered by different forms of aversion and resentment. Meanwhile, two *prima facie* opposite ideologies

---

1   Politically Romano was certainly a conservative, but he did not espouse the Fascist ideology with enthusiasm, although he might have regarded Mussolini's regime as a solution to the limits of 19th-century liberal constitutionalism. Be this as it may, he became member of the Fascist Party in 1928 – 'quite late', Aldo Sandulli (2009: 30) points out, and only to be able to take up the appointment: see A. Sandulli, 'Santi Romano and the Perception of the Public Law Complexity' (2009) 1 *Italian Journal of Public Law* 1–38. In short, the relationship between Romano and Fascism is nuanced, as he never stood up against it in any way, but on the other hand he never allowed the 'Fascistization' of the Council of State: see G. Melis, 'Il Consiglio di Stato ai tempi di Santi Romano', in *La giustizia amministrativa ai tempi di Santi Romano presidente del Consiglio di Stato* (Torino: Giappichelli, 2004), pp. 39–58.

2   Highly detailed bio-bibliographical notes are offered in A. Romano, 'Nota bio-bibliografica', in id. (ed.), *L'ultimo' Santi Romano* (Milano: A. Giuffrè, 2013), pp. 843–885, and Sandulli, 'Santi Romano and the Perception of the Public Law Complexity', cit. For a general outline of Romano's theory see F. Fontanelli, 'Santi Romano and *L'ordinamento giuridico*: The Relevance of a Forgotten Masterpiece for Contemporary International, Transnational and Global Legal Relations', (2011) 2(1) *Transnational Legal Theory* 67–117.

were blending together to give life to the Fascist ideology: nationalism and the kind of socialism that led to revolutionary syndicalism, influenced by French thinker Georges Sorel.[3] But, as David Roberts comments, Italy was particular in its own way, as Italians were developing a radical alternative to the liberal mainstream by combining post-Marxism with radical populism – a combination that would soon culminate in Mussolini's conservative revolution.[4] It is crucial to bear this in mind while making sense of Romano's distinctive contribution to fathoming and taming the heap of ferments that were drawing the 19th-century model of state to a close.[5]

Still, the aim of these pages is not to place Romano in the appropriate histori-cal framework, but to offer a conceptual line that will help unravel some of the interpretative questions raised by *The Legal Order* (hereinafter TLO). This means that I will look at these important historical circumstances through the lens of Romano's texts. I will first consider his writings prior to 1917 and will then discuss *TLO* in some detail.[6]

What to do with the state? Romano's 'The Modern State and its Crisis'

In a seminal essay on the formation of *TLO*, Sabino Cassese contends it is incor-rect to say that Romano deciphered and interpreted the morphing socio-political context.[7] For, 'the new situation is inborn in Santi Romano: he works in sync with the new institutions'. This is no facetious remark, as Romano was at one and the same time an *interpreter* and an *effect* of the new political setting. In a way, he was one of the ways social reality accounts for, and transforms, itself through the refined mediation of an ingenious mind.[8] On the other hand, however, to carry

---

3 Israeli historian Zeev Sternhell traced the roots of Italian fascism to pre-war France, where revo-lutionary syndicalism emerged under the aegis of Sorel's theorizing, as the spearhead of a French-based anti-Enlightenment revolt. See Z. Sternhell, *Neither Right nor Left: Fascist Ideology in France* (Princeton: Princeton University Press, 1996). See also Z. Sternhell, M. Sznajder, and M. Asheri, *The Birth of Fascist Ideology: From Cultural Rebellion to Political Revolution* (Princeton: Princeton Univer-sity Press, 1994).

4 D.D. Roberts, *Historicism and Fascism in Modern Italy* (Toronto: University of Toronto Press, 2007), 19.

5 On the relation between socio-political events and the emergence of new legal paradigms, see the vibrant analysis offered in P. Grossi, *A History of European Law* (Malden, MA: Wiley-Black-well, 2010), 138–152. As a leading legal historian, Grossi is one of the finest interpreters of Santi Romano's work. He puts stress on Romano's capacity to capture the plasticity of law and the plural nature of legal phenomena.

6 On the broader intellectual context and Romano's nuanced relation to contemporary influential theories, see Martin Loughlin's foreword in this book.

7 S. Cassese, 'Ipotesi sulla formazione de 'L'ordinamento giuridico' di Santi Romano' (1972) 1 *Qua-derni fiorentini* 243–283, at 248.

8 Here I am referring to the theorist's 'mediatory function' as it is nicely portrayed in B. Latour, *Reassembling the Social: An Introduction to Actor-Network-Theory* (Oxford: Oxford University Press, 2005), 37–42.

out his mediatory function, Romano availed himself of the tools of legal dogmatics. As I will suggest later, through Romano's theory law could rethink itself in a
way that, unfortunately, would soon be aborted by the Italian leading elites. But
before rushing to conclusions, let me briefly retrace the steps that led to *TLO*.

One of the main issues debated in the rich Italian literature on Romano's
oeuvre is the degree of continuity between *TLO* and his preceding work. As I
will explain shortly, this question begs the further question of Romano's attach-
ment to the *state* legal order and his (allegedly) ambiguous approach to legal
pluralism.

Albeit very young, as I noted, Romano contributed to Orlando's collection on
Italian administrative law, and interpreters disagree on whether or not there is a
link with subsequent theoretical developments. Most of them agree, however, on
the significant connection between *TLO* and a small but germinal text of 1909,
'Lo Stato moderno e la sua crisi' ('The Modern State and its Crisis' – hereinafter TMS), which was Romano's inaugural lecture at the University of Pisa.[9]
The title signals his deep awareness of a set of epochal transitions that would
rapidly change the nature and practice of the liberal-constitutional state. While
some writers regard this text as a proof of Romano's unquenched passion for the
marvellous machinery of the state,[10] others stress that his fine-grained analysis of
the gaps of the state order gestures towards a new way of conceiving the state and
its tasks.[11] While both readings capture important points, it is my claim that a different interpretation of this text might offer a first glimpse into the particular way
law was changing *through* Romano's theorizing.

To commence, I would first like to examine the reasons why Romano is believed
to reassert a conventional idea of the state endowed with a legal personality that
makes it a truly self-sufficient entity, one that is not reducible either to its sovereign or to its subjects.[12] TMS begins by claiming that the state – a 'magnificent
creation of the law'[13] – is able to assemble 'the various elements that comprise it'
on account of its personality as well as a power that is rooted in its own nature
and force, which is to say, the force of law. In doing so, the state 'goes beyond the
individuals' transient existence [. . .] and rises above, and balances, particular
interests'.[14] Although he did not disavow the origin of the state, which he traced
back to the French revolution, he averred that that particular form of state had a

---

9 See e.g. Cassese, 'Ipotesi sulla formazione de 'L'ordinamento giuridico' di Santi Romano', cit.,
   246.
10 See e.g. A. Morrone, 'Per il metodo del costituzionalista: riflettendo su 'Lo Stato moderno e la sua
   crisi' di Santi Romano' (2012) 2 *Quaderni costituzionali* 369–387, at pp. 377–378.
11 Cassese, 'Ipotesi sulla formazione de 'L'ordinamento giuridico' di Santi Romano', cit., 276.
12 See D. Runciman, *Pluralism and the Personality of the State* (Cambridge: Cambridge University Press,
   1997).
13 S. Romano, 'Lo Stato moderno e la sua crisi', in id., *Lo Stato moderno e la sua crisi. Saggi di diritto costituzionale* (Milano: A. Giuffrè, 1969), pp. 5–26, at p. 8.
14 Ibid., 7.

major flaw. Romano did not censure the establishment of the new political structure at the expense of the Old Regime. For, if it is true that the Revolution drew to an end the traditional pluralistic order unfolded throughout the Middle Ages, this happened because in the interstices and fissures of society other institutions and forms of government had been emerging. In short, the Revolution brought to the light, and sanctioned, a much slower process of socio-political, cultural and economic change. Instead, the main mistake of the French revolutionaries was to ignore those institutions and forms of government. The new order's 'original sin' was to believe 'it could neglect a host of social forces' that it ingenuously thought 'would collapse [. . .] in that they were considered as mere historical remnants destined to wither away shortly'.[15]

In other words, the newly minted state was unable to appreciate the developments occurred within other, non-state institutional contexts and decided to do away with them once and for all. It staunchly foisted upon the manifold political setting the all-encompassing, ideological dyad state-individual. The state and the individual were the only actors at play, as though the individual were truly vested with 'an infinity of rights emphatically proclaimed and conferred with such a costless generosity'.[16] In this way, the individualistic ideology that breastfed the revolutionary state made it blind to the existence of non-state aggregates, that could hardly be effaced with recourse to bare force. For Romano went on to say that those institutions and forms of government did continue to exist and to nurture the aversion and resentment against the new state order. Based on these considerations, he offered an analysis of the rise of turbulent non-state formations that were threatening the state.

Needless to say, one's interpretation of Romano's diagnosis of the new ferments depends on whether or not one views him as an advocate of the traditional state-person. But let us have a dispassionate look at what he wrote. Like such contemporary authors as Maurice Hauriou, Léon Duguit, Eugen Ehrlich, Harold Laski and others,[17] Romano's attention was drawn to the heap of sub-state and suprastate associations and organizations that, whether peacefully or not, were making the claim that the state was unable to organize and regulate social life and were developing alternative forms of self-government. They 'tend[ed] to join together' and, although they 'pursue[d] diverse ends, they share[d] a common trait',[18] as they fostered a regulatory framework that according to many scholars was irreconcilable with the state legal order. These were labour-based organizations, such as workers' federations and various kinds of trade unions, whose imaginings about

15 Ibid., 13.
16 Ibid., 14; see also Grossi, *A History of European Law*, 138–139.
17 See Runciman, *Pluralism and the Personality of the State*. See also S. Cassese, 'Ipotesi sulla fortuna all'estero de 'L'ordinamento giuridico' di Santi Romano' (2015) 1 *Rivista trimestrale di diritto pubblico* 177–182.
18 Romano, 'Lo Stato moderno e la sua crisi', 12.

social organization hinged on a patrimonial, status-based and corporatist political structure. While Duguit was elaborating the notion of functional representation as a way to reform the Senate, which would be elected through indirect suffrage to represent these associations and organizations,[19] Romano believed the emphasis on labour-based and profession-based criteria should not wipe out traditional features of the state, such as territory and population. In his view, a tension was mounting between the nation state and the corporatist state.

Apparently Romano's conclusion was that the state should not be jettisoned, as it is the only organizational form that secures individual and political equality. He recognized that it should cease to be blind to aggregates that are neither official bodies nor individuals. The state should be able to accommodate the various sub-state and supra-state self-organized entities that the Revolutionary state ignored. Yet, he concluded by saying that less extremist associations and organizations should break their ties with revolutionary ones to contribute to a far-reaching state reform. If this were the correct exegesis of Romano's view of the matter, it would doubtless be difficult to reconcile this position with the clear-cut passages of *TLO* where it is stated that 'the idea that the state system has become the only system in the legal world is to be most decidedly rejected' and that 'the state is nothing other than a species of the genus "law"'.[20] But the reason why I used a distancing expression like 'apparently' at the beginning of this paragraph is that I believe these junctures of *TLO* gesture to an alternative route to Romano's genuine view of the matter in TMS, one that centres not so much on the factual circumstances he discussed but on the distinctive nature of law and legal theory.

Indeed, it is very significant that TMS opens with the sentence: 'Every science finds in its own nature and the procedures that characterize it particular and specific causes for error', while a few pages below he writes 'there is no law that does not reflect an actual social condition'.[21] Can these statements suggest that Romano was more preoccupied with the (legal) framing of the issue of social change more than with social change itself? In effect, his focus was the way legal theorists make use of the conceptual tools of their discipline to account for a society in transition. Can Romano's words imply that the way social change is accounted for impacts on society? That this reading is not entirely misplaced is confirmed by Sandulli's survey of Romano's overall theoretical trajectory.[22] He writes that Romano's main concern was with the particular approach to reality that jurists should take *qua* jurists and, consequently, with the distinction between the legal and the non-legal: 'What are, according to Romano, the qualities of the real jurist? The capacity to

---

19 See e.g. C. Laborde, 'Pluralism, syndicalism and corporatism: Léon Duguit and the crisis of the state (1900–1925)' (1996) 22(3) *History of European Ideas* 227–244.
20 S. Romano, *The Legal Order* (Abingdon: Routledge, 2017), XXX.
21 Romano, 'Lo Stato moderno e la sua crisi', 5.
22 Sandulli, 'Santi Romano and the Perception of the Public Law Complexity', cit.

dominate and carefully scan the horizon of the whole social phenomena, managing to identify what is legally significant.'[23]

It is my contention that this interpretation could be strengthened in two steps. First, not only did Romano believe the real jurist should identify what is legally significant, but he thought the jurist should avoid any contamination of the *juristic point of view* with non-legal concepts and methods. Second, this purity is not so much meant to preserve a special path to social reality, as it is meant to *affect* reality in a very particular way. In sum, although, unlike Hans Kelsen, Romano never explicitly theorized the separation between legal theory and other disciplines, the specificity of jurisprudential devices seems to be a main presupposition of his conceptualization. At the same time, he thought the juristic point of view is the only one that, by *describing reality through the prism of law*, is likely to exert particular effects on reality.[24] For the juristic point of view makes the coexistence of different institutions and organizations possible as it captures their common element, that is, the capacity to self-organize.

As a result, legal theory in Romano's work plays out as a *technique of description* that is capable of engendering specific social outcomes. On this reading, it makes sense to conclude that TMS does not defend the state as a special political form but the juristic way to account for the particular organization the state ensures. Thus, it is not the state itself that is likely (or unlikely) to enable the peaceful coexistence of non-state associations and organizations. Instead, it is the juristic (i.e. non-philosophical, non-sociological, and so on) description of the state and its relation to non-state associations and organizations. This explains why Romano said it is a good thing that, whereas modern constitutions are supposed to encompass all the fundamental principles and institutions of law, in reality they turn out to be replete with gaps. Indeed, this makes sure that 'the battle that now seems to be fought against them may take a different configuration, as it will be evident that it is taking place in a field where there are no trenches to destroy but shelters to erect'.[25]

Law as an intelligibility condition: the ordering function in The Legal Order

In *TLO* Romano was at pains to clarify that he had no intention of crossing the border between legal theory and other disciplines. Certainly he explored phenomena that were the obvious focus of philosophy and sociology, but he aimed to provide a legal analysis of them, for legal purposes and with legal outcomes. In the

23 Ibid., 35–37.
24 For the idea of Romano's theory as a 'complex self-description of society', see G. Teubner, *Constitutional Fragments: Societal Constitutionalism and Globalization* (Oxford: Oxford University Press, 2012), 21.
25 Romano, 'Lo Stato moderno e la sua crisi', 20.

vein of what I argued above, Maurizio Fioravanti's instructive account suggests that Romano's objection to his contemporaries' accounts of the surge of belligerent non-state entities was genuinely methodological.[26] Indeed, Fioravanti comments, Romano's claim was that only the juristic point of view allows realizing that 'there is no contradiction between the new socio-political pluralism and the basic characteristics of the modern state'.[27] For legal analysis illustrates that 'no system of public law is conceivable as a complete and coherent whole that makes no room for "society" as an indirectly productive source of continuous integrations to the legal order'.[28] This means that, although the law provides a point of view that disavows all contaminations, it however serves as a point of view on society as its chief focus. Law is a self-enclosed field whence the jurist observes social reality and reframes it in a legal manner, and this is exactly what tempers social conflicts and enables peaceable coexistence among societal parties. The pureness of legal theory, then, is not self-oriented, as it is instrumental in a specific, proactive account of social reality.[29]

If we approach Romano's institutionalism through this lens, arguably many of the objections against it lose their critical momentum. For critics argue that his timid defence of legal pluralism was completely hollowed out by his state-based legal institutionalism.[30] From a reverse angle, other critics maintain that his legal pluralism pursued conservative goals, as Romano's image of law was modelled on state law.[31] In effect, the reader who first ventures into *TLO* is left with a sort of interpretative conundrum. No doubt, Romano's institutional theory of law opens up to a pluralist understanding of the legal realm. Yet, when it comes to providing examples of law's plural nature, he constantly referred to state law and other (more or less recognized) legal regimes such as international law and the law of the Church. As a consequence, his pluralism turns out to be impaired by the conventional character of the legal frameworks he spoke of. Critics take this as a pointer to a contradiction or, better, a serious clash between Romano's deft reading of the jurisgenerative force of social groups and his loyalty to the state as the utmost

26 See M. Fioravanti, 'Per l'interpretazione dell'opera giuridica di Santi Romano', 10 *Quaderni fiorentini per la storia del pensiero giuridico moderno* (1981) 169–219.
27 Ibid., 217.
28 Ibid., 218.
29 Fioravanti suggests this depends on how Romano's theoretical background gets reflected and incorporated into his texts. First, his preference for the English, unwritten constitution emerging out of a time-tested development of its institutions in comparison with the abrupt establishment of revolutionary written constitutions. Second, the idea, drawn from Friedrich Carl von Savigny, that the legislator is somewhat powerless vis-à-vis the steady development of the social body through time. Third, the idea that the state-person would soon evolve into a law-based state, one that is able to grant legal recognition to a variety of orderings and entities *through* state law. See ibid., 189.
30 See e.g. N. Matteucci, *Positivismo giuridico e costituzionalismo* (Bologna: il Mulino, 1996).
31 See e.g. G. Tarello, 'La dottrina dell'ordinamento e la figura pubblica di Santi Romano', in P. Biscaretti di Ruffia (ed.), *Le dottrine giuridiche di oggi e l'insegnamento di Santi Romano* (Milano: A. Giuffrè, 1977) pp. 245–256, at pp. 249–254.

legal system. Thus, most critics concur with Norberto Bobbio's incisive formula that 'Romano was a pluralist from a theoretical standpoint, but a monist from an ideological one.'[32]

Against these sceptical accounts, my contention is that there is no clash between Romano's institutionalism and his pluralism, although his theorizing eventually did get caught in a dilemma. To be clear, it is not his conceptualization that ended in deadlock. Rather, his penetrating, strictly legal and highly consistent analysis brought to light an inborn characteristic of law, which Romano did not intend to solve (I will elaborate on this point in the concluding section). To make my case, I would like to begin by pinpointing the main elements of Romano's conceptualization of law with a view to determining what idea of law he left us with. Based on this analysis, I will explain why his aporetic conclusion is so relevant to the understanding of present-day socio-political phenomena.

Romano anticipated a few tropes of 20th-century jurisprudence, particularly the notion of legal rules, the role of coercion, the relation between law and morality and the practice-based concept of law. The first sections of *TLO* take issue with the widespread view that law is a set of rules. He mainly thought of two strands of legal theory: on the one hand, the view that law is an ensemble of primary rules mandating conducts and backed by threat of sanction; on the other hand, the view that law is the regulation of normative (for some authors, pre-legal) relationships between individuals. It is pointless to recapitulate his argument here. What matters is that Romano's debunking these two alternative lines of reasoning raised a compelling point as to the source of legality. For he argued that for one to determine that certain rules belong to the legal system, one has to postulate a point of view or at least a unifying element that brings them together under the same category. It should come as no surprise that this was Hans Kelsen's, Carl Schmitt's and Herbert Hart's resolution as they advanced the notions of *Grundnorm*, concrete order and the rule of recognition. Kelsen's neo-Kantian approach depicted the *Grundnorm* as a point of view for the legal scientist to make sense of the unity of the legal system.[33] Schmitt demoted rules to legal 'normality' and claimed that the legal order can hardly be understood unless one looks at the institutional practices that the law incorporates and qualifies as legal.[34] Hart's praxiological account locates the rule of recognition in the judicial practice where officials can employ primary rules of conduct by way of power-conferring secondary rules.[35] Each of them, in their distinctive way, strove to identify the feature that allows defining a set of rules as legal.

---

32 N. Bobbio, *Dalla struttura alla funzione. Dalla struttura alla funzione* (Broma-Bari: Laterza, 2007), 154.
33 See H. Kelsen, *Introduction to the Problems of Legal Theory: A Translation of the First Edition of the Reine Rechtslehre* (Oxford: Oxford University Press, 1992).
34 See C. Schmitt, *On the Three Types of Juristic Thought* (Westport, CT: Praeger, 2004).
35 See Hart, *The Concept of Law*, cit.

Romano rejected Kelsen's theoreticism and offered a solution that falls midway between Schmitt (who actually drew from Romano) and Hart.[36] In *On the Three Types of Juristic Thought*, Schmitt quoted a passage of *TLO* that reads: '[T]he legal order, taken as a whole, is an entity that partly moves according to the norms, but most of all moves the norms like pawns on a chessboard – norms that therefore represent the object as well as the means of its activity, more than an element of its structure.'[37] Schmitt was attracted to the emphasis on the 'concrete' character of the legal order and the ensuing devaluation of rules as second-order effects of law. Yet, his interpretation misread Romano's juncture as saying that the law always rests on factual (institutional) contents that it is up to a political authority to select. Romano's institutionalism is not concrete in this sense, as this would compromize the separation between the legal and the social that he clung to. According to Schmitt, institutional (i.e. social) patterns of conduct become legal as they are selected as relevant to the identity of a political community and are endowed with the binding force of positive legality. As Romano repeatedly pointed out, the institution is not a social entity that acquires legality through official recognition. Rather, it is a legal entity as such. Unlike Hart, Romano did not pay special attention to the activity of state officials. Yet, Hart's seminal account of rule-governed practices resonates with Romano's notion of what qualifies an institution.[38] In *The Concept of Law* the legal system is portrayed as a combination of primary and

36 In this context I can hardly do justice to the enormous amount of works produced on these leading authors. On the neo-Kantian sense of the *Grundnorm* as an epistemic presupposition, see S.L. Paulson, 'Four Phases in Kelsen's Legal Theory? Reflections on a Periodization: A Review of Carsten Heidemann, Die Norm als Tatsache. Zur Normentheorie Hans Kelsens ('The Norm as Fact. On Hans Kelsen's Theory of Norms') (Baden-Baden: Nomos, 1997)', (1998) 18(1) *Oxford Journal of Legal Studies* 153–166; S.L. Paulson, 'Introduction' to H. Kelsen, *Introduction to the Problems of Legal Theory: A Translation of the First Edition of the Reine Rechtslehre* (Oxford: Oxford University Press, 1999). On Schmitt's concrete order see M. Croce and A. Salvatore, 'After Exception: Carl Schmitt's Legal Institutionalism and the Repudiation of Exceptionalism' (2016) 29(3) *Ratio Juris* 410–426; M. Loughlin, *Politonomy*, in J. Meierherich and O. Simons (eds), *The Oxford Handbook of Carl Schmitt* (Oxford: Oxford University Press, 2014). On Hart's combination of primary and secondary rules, see N. MacCormick, *H.L.A. Hart* (Stanford: Stanford University Press, 2nd edn 2008); R. Sartorius, 'Hart's concept of law', in R.S. Summers (ed.), *More essays in legal philosophy: General assessments of legal philosophies* (Berkeley-Los Angeles: University of California Press, 1971), pp. 131–161. On the convergences and divergences between old and new institutionalism see Martin Loughlin's foreword in this book and M. La Torre, *Law as institution* (Dordrecht: Springer, 2010).

37 Romano, *The Legal Order*, cit., XXX. Here I quoted this passage as it appears in the present translation of *TLO*. Yet it is worth noting that Schmitt's translation of Romano's wording is different from the original version in some telling respects – see Schmitt, *On the Three Types of Juristic Thought*, 87, and see comments on this in M. Croce and A. Salvatore, *The Legal Theory of Carl Schmitt* (Abingdon: Routledge, 2013), 116–121.

38 In his perceptive interpretation of Romano's pluralistic theory and his relevance overall, Jan Paulsson comments on the affinities between Hart and Romano: '[A] close reading of Herbert Hart shows that he moved, doubtless unconsciously, some distance away from Kelsen and toward Romano' (J. Paulsson, *The Idea of Arbitration* (Oxford: Oxford University Press, 2013), 47).

secondary rules, the latter type of rules being meant to establish how primary rules can be recognized, issued and amended. Romano's institutions are precisely characterized by this second layer of control whereby a set of specialized roles is established that permit role-players to administer rules of conduct.[39] In a way, his conception of law posits that all normative entities that possess such a second layer of administrative control can be regarded as legal – although they do not have to be as specialized as state administrative bodies. And this latter consequence, of course, is something that Hart's state-based positivism never conceded.[40]

This explains why Romano's institutionalism cannot be severed from legal pluralism. For he rejected two typical ways to unravel the 'panlegalist' conundrum whereby all rule-governed contexts are legal orders: the special relevance attached to the state monopoly on force and the relation between morality and the law. Romano regarded coercion as a basic function of all normative contexts. When he claimed that 'when one says that the law is a norm backed by sanction [. . .] in no way [. . .] can this mean that the law is a norm accompanied by another norm threatening sanction',[41] he aimed to reject conceptions, such as Kelsen's, that envisaged a special tie between law and state force – in the sense that law *is* force *conferred* on a particular norm, which in its turn becomes legal on account of this conferral. Like other forerunners of legal pluralism, such as Eugen Ehrlich and Bronisław Malinowski, Romano thought of coercion as an inner mechanism of all normative practices, regardless of the context in which rules are at work. Therefore, the force the state associates to legal rules is a factual element that (conceptually) has nothing to do with the natural coercive force of rules. The sanction is 'a constraint which is inborn in, and necessary to, social power',[42] or rather, any power operating in the social world. If this were not enough, in Romano's

---

39 Romano offered a compelling, critical analysis of the so-called 'bandit model' and other command-based theories of law in *Frammenti di un dizionario giuridico* (*Fragments of a Legal Dictionary* – hereinafter *Frammenti*), first published in 1947, where he analyzed the peculiar nature of secondary rules as rules that do not prescribe conducts but define specific procedures and are addressed to state bodies – see S. Romano, *Frammenti di un dizionario giuridico* (Milano: A. Giuffrè, 1983), 135–144.

40 It should be noted, though, that Hart oscillated between a 'pluralist' conception and one indebted to traditional monism. He even seemed to be aware of this theoretical outcome. In the 'Postscript' to *The Concept of Law* he wrote that it is 'quite vain to seek any more specific purpose which law as such serves beyond providing guides to human conduct and standards of criticism of such conduct' (H.L.A. Hart, *The Concept of Law* (Oxford: Oxford University Press, 1994), 249). Importantly he adds: 'This will not of course serve to distinguish laws from other rules or principles with the same general aims' (ibid.). Still, Hart continued to support the idea that it is possible to identify a distinguishing line between law and other rule-governed practices, as 'distinctive features of law are the provisions it makes by the secondary rules for the identification, change, and enforcement of its standards' (ibid.). Romano never fell prey of this ambiguity as he straightforwardly recognized that, as many practices do have secondary rules, the presence of this type of rules can hardly denote the *differentia specifica* of law.

41 Romano, *The Legal Order*, cit., XXX.

42 Ibid., XXX.

eyes saying that legal *norms* are *legal* norms because the state backs them up with its coercive force would unwarrantedly imply that the state is the source of legality – what he believed to be utterly mistaken based on the institutional conception I summarized above.

Romano was just as blunt when it came to the connection between law and morality. He did not reject the potential tie between them, but claimed it is by no means a conceptual requirement of law. He treated law and morality as two distinct normative practices that most often overlap because of the sphere of action they cover and the agents they address. He argued that, while morality claims a special pre-eminence by which law is supposed to conform to moral norms, this conformity is conceptually indifferent to the notion of law. Romano wrote that it is correct to say that law should never be at odds with morality, but this does not imply that

> The law that does not fit morality is not law. [. . .] That law has to be moral is a requirement (I do not mean a practical, but a conceptual requirement) of morality, not of law; and, so to say, immoral law is just as legal as moral law. While it is often the case that the law prohibits actions, manners, norms, and so on, that conflict with morality, evidently the anti-legal character of these manifestations does not derive from morality, but from law's own force that establishes this (although it may establish otherwise). And when, as is just as often the case, legal norms specify their contents and dispositions by referring to the norms of morality, this does not entail that the latter become legal norms [. . .].[43]

In short, Romano is as far away from sanction-based conceptions of law as he is from natural law theories. But what is it, then, that characterizes law? Romano's consistent answer is that law is an organizational activity, a complex practice (although this is not a term of his). Arguably his clearest account of what law is – one that can be found in many passages of *TLO* – is offered in *Frammenti*, in an entry where he tackled the question of the 'function of law'.[44] In this framework, the word 'function' implicates no functionalist biases, as it echoes a type of functionalism that William Twining calls 'thin functionalism'.[45] If law 'is a species of social practice concerned with the ordering of relations between subjects at various levels of relations and of ordering',[46] then what distinguishes law from other practices pursuing the same objective is its 'orientation'. As Twining avers

---

43 Romano, *Frammenti di un dizionario giuridico*, cit. 72.
44 Ibid., 76–86.
45 See W. Twining, 'A Post-Westphalian Conception of Law' (2003) 37(1) *Law and Society Review* 199–258; W. Twining, *General Jurisprudence. Understanding Law from a Global Perspective* (Cambridge: Cambridge University Press, 2009).
46 Twining, 'A Post-Westphalian Conception of Law', cit., 240.

by drawing on Karl Llewellyn's notion of law's jobs, what is special about law is 'its orientation towards the doing of a cluster of jobs – dispute prevention, dispute settlement, allocation of power and authority and so on'.[47] In *Frammenti* Romano moved away from all thick functionalist notions of law, as he wrote that law is not designed to achieve justice or implement natural law, nor is it designed to enforce contracts and punish their infringement. According to Romano, the law stabilizes social practices by establishing a set of powers and authorities – and, conversely, all the practices that carry out such a stabilizing function are legal practices. However, it is imperative not to separate either conceptually or pragmatically this ordering activity from the entity that is ordered. He dismissed as naïve and untenable the idea that an entity emerges as a factual entity and then gives itself an order by developing a set of legal rules. He insisted that the moment when the entity is created and the moment of its ordering via law are indistinguishable. How does, then, the law carry out its ordering function?

I would like to insist on the notion of law as a juristic account with performative effects. In *TLO* Romano never gets tired of saying that there is no distinction between the existence of an institution and the establishment of a legal order. In other words, the law is knotted into the entity it regulates. Codified rules are nothing but the verbalization of something that can never get entirely verbalized. They are fallible approximations. If this is so, then there is no ostensible separation between the law and the structure it governs. If I may use a non-Romanian lexicon, the law provides the *intelligibility condition* for one to conceive an entity as that particular entity – one that can be partly and tentatively encapsulated into a particular practice, such as an unwritten constitution, or a text, such as a written constitution. In its turn, the ostensible phenomena one accounts for (that is, the entity that is being described from a juristic point of view) provide the *existence condition* for the law. This is the nuance that is enshrouded in the term 'order', which is scarcely equivalent to system: it is an ordering force that is (at least in part) ineffable in that it is a dynamic, unceasing process that cannot be congealed into a fixed, rigid form. The law is nothing but a complicated interaction between the factual existence of a normative entity (existence condition) and that normative entity's accounting for its own existence with reference to its internal law (intelligibility condition) – this activity of accounting of course requires mediators, that in Romano's mind are the jurists. This explains, for example, why denying that organized criminal gangs have a law of their own looked meaningless to him – it would be contradictory to deny that organized gangs are organized. Law is something that either exists (in the practice and verbalizations of a normative entity's members) or does not. This also explains why the law, as he pointed out, is inherently

---

47 Twining, *General Jurisprudence*, cit., 111.

'conservative',[48] although in a way that structurally opens it up to change, even radical change. It is worth quoting Romano:

> Like all buildings, [the law] has foundations, walls, roofs that ensure its stability, and in a way close it off. But it has doors, windows, pipes, fans that keep it open to the external world. And as a building is always amenable to enlargements, reductions and transformations, so is the legal order – the institution – an entity that, although it remains identical to itself, as long as it is alive all its elements get continually renewed whether abruptly or gradually.[49]

The ordering function of law and its conservative nature are framed by Romano as a filtering activity that oversees social change. It is the specific nature of the juristic point of view that allows seeing change as something that is potentially instrumental in the ordering of society. As an intelligibility condition, the law can never be set against change. The law makes potentially threatening phenomena cognizable, and when the jurist reads them from the juristic point of view, she deciphers (or even constructs) their compatibility with the elements of the order they threaten. The juristic point of view lies in the ability to play with the fine line between crisis and change. Indeed, Romano went on to say that social change 'is regulated and tamed by the proper function of the law, but this function should never exceed certain limits, in order not to jeopardize the life itself of the entity' that law governs.[50] As is the case with TMS, both *TLO* and *Frammenti* put forward a notion of law as a special place from which society can be described in a way that affects it. This is why law is neither norm, nor coercion, nor morality. Law is a practice carried out by adopting a particular point of view, which involves a technical language and categories of its own.

A knotty legacy: the Romano dilemma

In the second half of the 20th century – quite a different socio-political scenario than Romano's – legal anthropology and socio-legal studies began to pave the way for an alternative understanding of law as conceptually and (at least in some geo-historical contexts) practically independent of the state. As early as the late 1920s Malinowski advanced the theory that the legal body of the 'savages' was not comprised of rules prohibiting specific conducts, as other colleagues of his had suggested.[51] He argued that primitive law (or, more precisely, the law of the Trobriand Islanders he was studying) should be described as of a 'civil law' type,

---

48 See Romano, *Frammenti di un dizionario giuridico*, cit., 86.
49 Ibid., 86.
50 Ibid., 86.
51 See B. Malinowski, *Crime and Custom in Savage Society. An Anthropological Study of Savagery* (London, Routledge & Kegan Paul, 1926).

understood as a 'body of binding obligations, regarded as a right by one party and acknowledged as a duty by the other, kept in force by a specific mechanism of reciprocity and publicity inherent to the structure of their society'.[52] His all-embracing definition of law minimized the relevance of 'Western' notions such as coercion and authority for the analysis of non-Western normative contexts. Malinowski believed that the mechanism meant to ensure compliance was the publicness of rules and the reciprocity among community members. The image of law that emerged was that of an internal mechanism of social life, inscribed in the web of interactions developed by social agents.

In her seminal article on semi-autonomous social fields, Sally Falk Moore seized on Malinowski's openness to non-state law to extend its heuristic scope, and proposed a methodological amendment to it.[53] Whereas Malinowski explored a community's organizational system as a unified whole, Moore, by drawing on Max Weber and Leopold Pospisil, questioned the unity of the anthropological 'subject of study'. In a way that echoed Romano's TMS and *TLO*, she commented that '[i]t is well established that between the body politic and the individual, there are interposed various smaller organized social fields to which the individual "belongs"'.[54] Social fields are contexts having rule-making capacities and the means to induce or coerce compliance – in short, said Moore, they have a legal order of their own. On this account, state rules can still be distinguished from non-state rules in terms of reflective, emancipative, transformative, but also artificial and technological character; yet these characteristics are a matter of degree, unable to determine either a conceptual or an ontological difference.[55]

Former legal pluralists were fully alert to the problem of an overextension of the concept of law, as Sally Engle Merry remarked in her influential article on legal pluralism: 'Why is it so difficult to find a word for nonstate law? [. . .] Where do we stop speaking of law and find ourselves simply describing social life? Is it useful to call all these forms of ordering law?'[56] If some critics regard this issue – which Twining eloquently labelled 'definitional stop'[57] – as a symptom of a conceptual

52 Ibid., 58.
53 See S.F. Moore, 'Law and social change: The semi-autonomous social field as an appropriate subject of study' (1973) 7(4) *Law & Society Review* 719–746.
54 Ibid., 721.
55 More recently this view has been compellingly advanced by Gordon Woodman – see e.g. G.R. Woodman, 'Ideological combat and social observation. Recent debate about legal pluralism' (1998) 42 *Journal of Legal Pluralism* 21–59; G.R. Woodman, 'The idea of legal pluralism', in B. Dupret (ed.), *Legal Pluralism in the Arab World* (The Hague: Kluwer Law International, 1999), pp. 3–19.
56 S.E. Merry, 'Legal pluralism' (1988) 22(5) *Law & Society Review* 869–896, at p. 877.
57 'If one opens the door to some examples of non-state law, then we are left with no clear basis for differentiating legal norms from other social norms, legal institutions and practices from other social institutions and practices, legal traditions from religious or other general intellectual traditions and so on' (W. Twining, *General Jurisprudence. Understanding Law from a Global Perspective* (Cambridge: Cambridge University Press, 2009), 369).

failure,[58] others, like Simon Roberts, raised a question that is more important for my purposes. While in 1978 he had voiced a conceptual and heuristic concern relating to anthropological inquiry, lately he was more preoccupied with the practical consequences of the definitional stop. Indeed, Roberts' initial treatment of legal pluralism had mainly to do with the 'exportation' of folk concepts while studying how non-Western populations use rules and settle disputes.[59] He contended that one's applying the conceptual devices of Western jurisprudence to non-Western settings leads to a fundamental distortion of one's research, as it drives attention away from people's actual performances in dispute-settling contexts and the way values and rules are framed and reframed in those contexts. He concluded that legal pluralism was an invention of legal scholars who believe they see law everywhere only because they are unable to distinguish between their folk categories and the categories developed and applied by non-Western populations.

Recently Roberts returned to the issue to advance a different critique concerning the pragmatic effects of legal pluralism.[60] He contended that legal pluralism has now become a new orthodoxy that represents law as existing beyond and above the state. The main mistake, according to him, is that this conceptualization fosters a notion of law as separated from the activity of governing. One of the consequences identified by Roberts helps me introduce an important issue that can be dubbed 'the Romano dilemma'. Roberts remarked that at present what he called 'essentially negotiated orders', whether at local or global level, fall into the overextended category of *legal* orders. In his view, stretching the label 'law' runs the risk of eroding the relation between law and justice. Indeed, negotiated orders, and above all transactional social orderings that dwell in the global scenario, have rationalities of their own, which presuppose a different orientation to rules from those of state law.[61]

I think the interpretation of *TLO* I have elaborated so far helps dissolve the dilemma – since I doubt it can be solved once and for all. Legal pluralists have set the record straight by unveiling the historical and context-specific connection between the law and the state, as Marc Galanter nicely summarized when he wrote that Western state legal systems are nothing other than 'institutional-intellectual complexes' claiming 'to encompass and control all the other institutions in the society and to subject them to a regime of general rules [. . .]. These complexes

---

58 See above all B.Z. Tamanaha, 'The Folly of the "Social Scientific" Concept of Legal Pluralism', (1993) 20(2) *Journal of Law and Society* 192–217.

59 See S. Roberts, 'Do We Need an Anthropology of Law?' (1978) 25 *RAIN* 4–7.

60 See S. Roberts, 'After Government? On Representing Law without the State' (2005) 68(1) *The Modern Law Review* 1–24.

61 It is worth stressing that this is a risk that Kelsen had ridden roughshod over: 'If we ignore this specific element of the law [i.e. coercion], if we do not conceive of the law as a special social technique, if we define law simply as order or organization, and not as a coercive order (or organization), then we lose the possibility of differentiating law form other social phenomena' (H. Kelsen, *General Theory of Law and State* (Cambridge, MA: Harvard University Press, 1945), 26).

consolidated and displaced the earlier diverse array of normative orderings in society, reducing them to a subordinate and interstitial status.'[62] Nonetheless, Romano's reading of this historical fact turned the table of legal analysis. For he never claimed that the state should prevail over other institutions; nor did he ever claim that other institutions should prevail over the state. As I strove to demonstrate, he was concerned with a *perspectival* matter: what is the point of view from where the 'matter-of-factness' of the conflict between institutions can be reframed in legal terms? Can *practical* conflicts be transformed and tamed as they are turned into *legal* ones? If this is the question Romano was trying to answer, then he never pitted the law of the state against the law of other institutions. Instead, he intended to task jurists with providing an account of social reality that might find a route to make the various legal orders compatible with each other. Therefore, in the end the Romano dilemma is destined not to be solved, as it is not a genuine dilemma. Instead, it is a space, or a lexical circuit, that jurists have to inhabit as they perform their jurisprudential practice. Doing away with fictitious portrayals positing an alleged natural superiority of the state legal order is only one of the premises to fulfil this task – it is but a step to a better understanding of the state as a legal order that is able to accommodate (and be accommodated by) other, non-state orders.

Therefore, the gist of Romano's analysis is the jurists' awareness and the precise conceptualization of the juristic point of view. Certainly he was conscious of the political outcomes of this activity, which is supposed to produce effects on reality. And yet jurists should not so much be concerned with these political outcomes as such, as they should pay heed to the purity of legal analysis. The question posed by Roberts, then, of a connection between justice and state law does not fall within the scope of legal analysis (as far as Romano conceived of it), because it is a pragmatic effect that the separation between law and justice prevents approaching as a conceptual issue. And I think Romano is correct, if, *pace* Roberts, many scholars have shown how the state and the rule of law have played as instruments to foster the neoliberal agenda and to promote greater inequality.[63] At the same time, *TLO*'s methodological pureness was not instrumental in furthering the project of a specific conformation of law, as some positivist theories might have been.[64] Romano's theorizing of the juristic point of view delineated an image of the law as a virtual

62 M. Galanter, 'Justice in Many Rooms: Courts, Private Ordering, and Indigenous law' (1981) 19 *Journal of Legal Pluralism and Unofficial Law* 1–47, at p. 19.

63 See e.g. W. Brown, *Undoing the Demos: Neoliberalism's Stealth Revolution* (New York: Zone Books, 2015); U. Mattei and L. Nader, *Plunder. When the Rule of Law is Illegal* (Malden, MA: Blackwell Publishing, 2008); A. Ong and S.J. Collier (eds), *Global Assemblages. Technology, Politics, and Ethics as Anthropological Problems* (Malden, MA: Blackwell, 2005); S. Sassen, *Territory, Authority, Rights: From Medieval to Global Assemblages* (Princeton: Princeton University Press, 2006).

64 I elaborate on this point in M. Croce, 'Is there any place for legal theory today? The distinctiveness of law in the age of pluralism', in U. de Vries and L. Francot (eds), *Law's Environment: Critical Legal Perspectives* (The Hague: Eleven Publishers, 2011), pp. 19–44.

place from where the state can be reimagined: a space where the state appears as a concept rather than a thing[65] and thus can be reframed in many different ways.

In the end, dissolving the Romano dilemma is something that cannot be done theoretically. For it is a conceptual line itself, more than a riddle to solve. Instead, approaching social phenomena *through* the Romano dilemma as a conceptual line is the jurist's main objective, as the language and categories she applies are intended to produce a revision of the state in the sense of its compatibility with other orders and the conceptual frameworks these orders are rooted into. This does not imply that peaceful coexistence will always be the natural upshot or that justice will never be harmed. Nobody can predict where the juristic activity will lead to, and, as Romano's historical circumstances convincingly illustrate, actual politics can always spoil the result of juristic inquiry. Yet, as long as law offers a categorial space for rethinking the state, it does not produce or construct it, but opens up further spaces for lay people to produce or construct it under the aegis of new legal imaginings.

Mariano Croce

---

65 See e.g. D. Cooper, *Everyday Utopias: The Conceptual Life of Promising Spaces* (Durham and London: Duke University Press, 2014); C. Hay, 'Neither Real nor Fictitious but 'as if Real'? A Political Ontology of the State' (2014) 65(3) *The British Journal of Sociology* 459–480.

Bibliography

Ago, R. (1934) *Teoria del diritto internazionale privato*, Padova: CEDAM.

Ago, R. (1937) *Règles générales des conflits de lois*, Paris: Librairie di Recueil Sirey.

Ago, R. (1943) *Lezioni di diritto internazionale*, Milano: A. Giuffrè.

Anzilotti, D. (1898) *Studi critici di diritto internazionale privato*, Rocca San Casciano: L. Cappelli.

Anzilotti, D. (1902a) *Teoria generale della responsabilità dello stato nel diritto internazionale*, Firenze: F. Lumachi Succ. dei Fratelli Bocca.

Anzilotti, D. (1902b) *Il diritto internazionale nei giudizi interni*, Bologna: N. Zanichelli.

Anzilotti, D. (1908) *Il riconoscimento delle sentenze straniere di divorzio in ordine alla seconda Convenzione dell'Aja 12 giugno 1902*, Bologna: Tipografia Gamberini e Parmeggiani.

Anzilotti, D. (1910) *Volontà e responsabilità nella stipulazione dei trattati internazionali*, Roma: Tipografia dell'Unione Editrice.

Anzilotti, D. (1912) *Corso di diritto internazionale*, Roma: Athenaeum.

Anzilotti, D. (1913) 'La questioni di diritto sollevate dagli incidenti del Carthage e del Manouba', *Rivista di diritto internazionale* 2(3–4).

Anzilotti, D. (1915a) *Corso di diritto internazionale*, Vol. 3, Roma: Aethenaeum.

Anzilotti, D. (1915b) *Il concetto moderno dello Stato e il diritto internazionale*, Roma: Tipografia Fratelli Pallotta.

Anzilotti, D. (1928) *Corso di diritto internazionale*, 3rd ed., Roma: Athenaeum.

Arangio-Ruiz, G. (1913) *Istituzioni di diritto costituzionale italiano*, Torino: Fratelli Bocca.

Arangio-Ruiz, V. (1943) *Istituzioni di diritto romano*, Napoli: E. Jovene.

Baldoni, C. (1931) *Le unioni internazionali di Stati*, Roma: A. Sampaolesi.

Balladore Pallieri, G. (1929) 'Il concetto di rinvio formale e il problema del diritto internazionale privato', *Rivista di diritto civile* 4.

Balladore Pallieri, G. (1935) 'Le dottrine di Hans Kelsen e il problema dei rapporti fra diritto interno e diritto internazionale', *Rivista di diritto internazionale* 27(1–2).

Balladore Pallieri G. (1940) 'I limiti dell'efficacia dell'ordinamento italiano', *Jus* 1: 25–92.

Balladore Pallieri G. (1943) 'Le varie forme di rinvio e la loro applicabilità al diritto internazionale privato', *Annuario di diritto comparato e studi legislativi* 16.

Balladore Pallieri, G. (1945) *Diritto internazionale pubblico*, 3rd ed., Milano: A. Giuffrè.

Barassi, L. (1914) *Istituzioni di diritto civile*, Milano: F. Vallardi.

Barassi, L. (1915) *Il contratto di lavoro nel diritto positivo italiano*, 2nd revised ed., Milano: Società editrice libraria.

Barassi, L. (1935) *Il diritto del lavoro*, Milano: A. Giuffrè.

Barassi, L. (1941) *Istituzioni di diritto privato*, Milano: A. Giuffrè.

Bartolomei, A. (1914) *Lezioni di filosofia del diritto*, Napoli: L. Alvano.

Battaglia, F. (1939) *Scritti di teoria dello Stato*, Milano: A. Giuffrè.

Battaglia, F. (1940) *Corso di filosofia del diritto*, Vol. 2, Roma: Società Editrice del Foro italiano.

Behrend, F.H. (1905) *Die Stiftungen nach deutschen bürgerlichen Recht*, Marburg: Oscar Ehrhardt.

Bekker, E.I. (1910) *Grundbegriffe des Rechts und Missgriffe der Gesetzgebung*, Berlin and Leipzig: W. Rothschild.

Bergbohm, K. (1892) *Jurisprudenz und Rechtsphilosophie*, Leipzig: Duncker & Humblot.

Berolzheimer, F. (1906) *System der Rechts- und Wirtschaftsphilosophie*, 3rd ed., München: C. H. Beck.

Bernatzik, E. (1890) 'Kritische Studien über den Begriff der juristischen Person und über die juristische Persönlichkeit der Behörden insbesondere', *Archiv für öffentliches Recht* 5: 169–319.

Betti, E. (1920) *Il concetto della obbligazione costruito dal punto di vista dell'azione*, Pavia: Tipografia Cooperativa.

Betti, E. (1927) 'La creazione del diritto nella "iurisdictio" del pretore romano', in *Studi di diritto processuale in onore di Giuseppe Chiovenda nel XXV anno del suo insegnamento*, Padova: CEDAM.

Betti, E. (1943) *Istituzioni di diritto romano*, 2nd ed., Padova: CEDAM.

Bianchi, F.S. (1901) *Corso di diritto civile*, 2nd ed., Torino: UTET.

Bierling, E.R. (1894) *Juristische Prinzipienlehre*, Freiburg im Breisgau-Leipzig: J. C. B. Mohr.

Biscaretti di Ruffia, P. (1938) *Contributo alla teoria giuridica della formazione degli Stati*, Milano: A. Giuffrè.

Biscaretti di Ruffia, P. (1939) 'Sull'esistenza di "Unioni non internazionali fra Stati" diverse dagli "Stati di Stati"', in *Scritti giuridici in onore di Santi Romano*, Padova: CEDAM.

Biscaretti di Ruffia, P. (1946) *Lo Stato democratico moderno nella dottrina e nella legislazione costituzionale*, Milano: A. Giuffrè.

Bobbio, N. (1936) 'Istituzione e diritto sociale: Renard e Gurvitch', *Rivista internazionale di filosofia del diritto* 16.

Bobbio, N. (1943) *Scienza e tecnica del diritto*, Torino: Istituto Giuridico della R. Università.

Bonfante, P. (1915) 'Le obbligazioni naturali e il debito di giuoco', *Rivista del diritto commerciale* 13 (2), part 1.

Bonucci, A. (1915) *Il fine dello Stato*, Roma: Athenaeum.

Bonucci, A. (1920) 'Ordinamento giuridico e Stato', *Rivista di diritto pubblico* 12.

Breschi, B. (1914) *La volontà dello Stato nell'ordine giuridico internazionale*, Roma: Athenaeum.

Breschi, B. (1920) *La società delle nazioni: l'ordinamento positivo e la natura giuridica*, Firenze: A. Vallecchi.

Brugi, B. (1907) *Introduzione enciclopedica alle scienze giuridiche e sociali nel sistema della giurisprudenza*, Milano: Società editrice libraria.

Brunetti, G. (1913) *Norme e regole finali nel diritto*, Torino: Unione Tipografico-Editrice Torinese.

Brunetti, G. (1920) *Scritti giuridici varii*, Vol. 3, Torino: Unione Tipografico-Editrice Torinese.

Calamandrei, P. (1929) 'Regole cavalleresche e processo', *Rivista di diritto processuale civile* 6(2).

Calamandrei, P. (1934) *Studi sul processo civile*, Vol. 3, Padova: CEDAM.

Cammarata, A.E. (1925) *Contributi ad una critica gnoseologica della giurisprudenza*, Roma: Fratelli Treves.

Cammarata, A.E. (1926) *Il concetto del diritto e la 'pluralità degli ordinamenti giuridici'*, Catania: N. Giannotta.

Capograssi, G. (1936) *Alcune osservazioni sopra la molteplicità degli ordinamenti giuridici*, Sassari: Gallizzi.

Capograssi, G. (1937) *Il problema della scienza del diritto*, Roma: Societá Editrice del Foro italiano.

Capograssi, G. (1939) 'Note sulla molteplicità degli ordinamenti giuridici', *Rivista internazionale di filosofia del diritto*.

Caristia, C. (1919) *Saggio critico sul valore e l'efficacia della consuetudine nel diritto pubblico interno*, Macerata: Tipografia Economica.

Caristia, C. (1935) *Corso di istituzioni di diritto pubblico*, 3rd ed., Catania: Studio editoriale Moderno.

Carlini, G. (1938) 'Diritto', in *Nuovo Digesto Italiano*, Vol. 4, Torino: UTET.

Carnelutti, F. (1915) *La prova civile: Parte I*, Roma: Athenaeum.

Carnelutti, F. (1939) *Metodologia del diritto*, Padova: CEDAM.

Carnelutti, F. (1940) *Teoria generale del diritto*, Roma: Societá Editrice del Foro italiano.

Cassola, O. (1941) *La recezione del diritto civile nel diritto canonico*, Tortona: Tipografia San Giuseppe.

Cathrein, V. (1913) *Filosofia morale*, Firenze: Libreria editrice fiorentina.

Cavaglieri, A. (1933) *Lezioni di diritto internazionale privato*, 3rd ed., Napoli: Casa Editrice A. Rondinella.

Cereti, C. (1925) *L'ordinamento giuridico internazionale*, Genova: Stab. grafico A. Lombardo.

Cesarini Sforza, W. (1929) 'Il diritto dei privati', *Rivista italiana per le scienze giuridiche* 4(1–2).

Cesarini Sforza, W. (1930) *Lezioni di teoria generale del diritto*, Padova: CEDAM.

Cesarini Sforza, W. (1933) 'La teoria degli ordinamenti giuridici ed il diritto sportivo', *Il foro italiano* 53.

Cesarini Sforza, W. (1939) 'Ordinamenti giuridici' in *Nuovo digesto italiano*, Torino: UTET.

Checchini A. (1921) *Dal comune di Roma al comune moderno: studio storico-dogmatico*, Cagliari: Società tipografica sarda.

Checchini, A. (1937) *Introduzione dommatica al diritto ecclesiastico italiano*, Padova: CEDAM.

Chiarelli, G. (1931) *La personalità giuridica delle associazioni professionali*, Padova: CEDAM.

Chiarelli, G. (1936) *Lo Stato corporativo*, Padova: CEDAM.

Chiovenda, G. (1913) *Principi di diritto processuale civile*, 3rd ed., Napoli: N. Jovene e C.

Chironi, G.P. (1903) *Colpa extra-contrattuale*, Vol. 2, Torino: Fratelli Bocca.

Chironi, G.P. (1906) *Colpa extra-contrattuale*, Vol. 2, new edition, Torino: Fratelli Bocca.

Chironi, G.P. (1912) *Istituzioni di diritto civile italiano*, Torino: Fratelli Bocca.

Cicala, F.B. (1909) *Rapporto giuridico diritto subiettivo e pretesa: profilo di una nuova costruzione teoretica*, Torino: Fratelli Bocca.

Cicu, A. (1914) *Il concetto di 'status'*, Napoli: N. Jovene e C.

Cicu, A. (1915) *Il diritto di famiglia*, Roma: Athenaeum.

Ciprotti, P. (1941) *Contributo alla teoria della canonizzazione delle leggi civili*, Roma: Universitarie.

Cornaggia Medici, G. (1933) *Lineamenti di diritto ecclesiastico italiano*, Milano: Hoepli.

Costamagna, C. (1929) *La teoria delle istituzioni sociali*, Modena: Editore Società Tipografica Modenese.

Coviello, N. (1915) *Manuale di diritto civile italiano: parte generale*, Milano: Società editrice libraria.

Coviello, N. (1916) *Manuale di diritto ecclesiastico*, Roma: Athenaeum.

Coviello, N. (1922) *Manuale di diritto ecclesiastico*, 2nd ed., Roma: Athenaeum.

Coviello, N. (1925) *Manuale di diritto civile italiano: parte generale*, 2nd ed., Milano: Società editrice libraria.

Crisafulli, V. (1935) *Sulla teoria della norma giuridica*, Roma: Anonima Romana Editoriale.

Crisafulli, V. (1941) *Per la determinazione del concetto dei principi generali del diritto*, Pisa: Arti grafiche Pacini Mariotti.

Criscuoli, G. (1922) 'La discrezionalità nelle funzioni costituzionali', *Annali della Facoltà di Giurisprudenza dell'Università di Perugia* 3.

Croce, B. (1915) *Filosofia della pratica*, Bari: Giuseppe Laterza & figli.

Croce, B. (1945) *Teoria e storia della storiografia*, Bari: Giuseppe Laterza & figli.

Crosa, E. (1941) *Diritto costituzionale*, Torino: Unione Tipografico-Editrice Torinese.

Cuche, P. (1913) 'Du rapport de dépendance, élément constitutif du contrat de travail', *Revue critique de législation et de jurisprudence*.

Dallari, G. (1911) *Il nuovo contrattualismo nella filosofia sociale e giuridica*, Torino: Unione Tipografico-Editrice Torinese.

D'Avack, P.A. (1937a) *Chiesa, Santa Sede e Città del Vaticano nel jus publicum ecclesiasticum*, Firenze: Casa Editrice Poligrafica Universitaria di C. Cya.

D'Avack, P.A. (1937b) *Corso di diritto ecclesiastico italiano*, Firenze: Casa Editrice Poligrafica Universitaria di C. Cya.

D'Avack, P.A. (1939) 'La posizione giuridica del diritto canonico nell'ordinamento italiano', in *Scritti giuridici in onore di Santi Romano*, Padova: CEDAM.

De Crescenzio, N. (1899) 'Obbligazione' in *Enciclopedia giuridica italiana*, Milano: F. Vallardi.

D'Eufemia, G. (1931) *Le fonti del diritto corporativo*, Napoli: Detken & Rocholl.

De Francisci, P. (1924) *Il trasferimento della proprietà: storia e critica di una dottrina*, Padova: Litotipo.

Del Giudice, V. (1915) *Il diritto ecclesiastico in senso moderno: definizione e sistema*, Roma: Tipografico Editrice Nazionale.

Del Giudice, V. (1924) 'Il diritto dello Stato nell'ordinamento canonico', *Archivio giuridico Filippo Serafini* 91(1).

Del Giudice, V. (1933) *Istituzioni di diritto canonico*, Milano: A. Giuffrè.

Del Giudice, V. (1939) *Corso di diritto ecclesiastico*, Milano: A. Giuffrè.

Del Giudice, V. (1944) *Nozioni di diritto canonico*, Milano: A. Giuffrè.

Delos, J. (1931) 'La théorie de l'institution', *Archives de Philosophie* 1: 87–153.

De Luca, L. (1943) *Rilevanza dell'ordinamento canonico nel diritto italiano*, Padova: CEDAM.

Del Vecchio, G. (1905) *I presupposti filosofici della nozione del diritto*, Bologna: N. Zanichelli.

Del Vecchio, G. (1921a) 'Moderne concezioni del diritto', *Rivista internazionale di filosofia del diritto*, a. I, fasc. 3–4.

Del Vecchio, G. (1921b) *Moderne concezioni del diritto*, Genova: Tipografia Sociale.

Del Vecchio, G. (1929) 'Sulla statualità del diritto', *Rivista internazionale di filosofia del diritto* 9(1).

Del Vecchio, G. (1935) *Saggi intorno allo Stato*, Roma: Istituto di Filosofia del Diritto.

Del Vecchio, G. (1936) *Lezioni di filosofia del diritto*, Roma: Rivista internazionale di filosofia del diritto.

De Ruggiero, R. (1915) *Istituzioni di diritto civile*, Napoli: L. Alvano.

De Ruggiero, R., Maori, F. (1945) *Corso di istituzioni di diritto privato*, Milano-Messina: G. Principato.

Desqueyrat, A. (1935) *L'institution, le droit objectif et la technique positive: essai historique et doctrinal*, Paris: Librairie du recueil Sirey.

Diana, A. (1905) 'La sentenza straniera e il giudizio di delibazione', *Rivista di diritto internazionale* 3 (1–3).

Diena, G. (1913) 'Considerazioni critiche sul concetto dell'assoluta e completa separazione fra il diritto internazionale e l'interno', *Rivista di diritto pubblico* 1.

Diena, G. (1914) *Principi di diritto internazionale*, Vol. 2, Napoli: L. Pierro.

Diena, G. (1917) *Diritto internazionale privato*, Milano and Roma: Dante Alighieri.

Donati, D. (1906) *I trattati internazionali nel diritto costituzionale*, Torino: Unione Tipografico-Editrice Torinese.

Donati, D. (1909) 'Gli organi dello Stato e il diritto internazionale', *Rivista di diritto pubblico e della pubblica amministrazione in Italia*.

Donati, D. (1910) *Il problema delle lacune dell'ordinamento giuridico*, Milano: Società editrice libraria.

Donati, D. (1914) 'Stato e territorio', *Rivista di diritto internazionale*.

Donati, D. (1921) 'La personalità reale dello Stato', *Rivista di diritto pubblico*.

Duguit, L. (1901) *L'État, le droit objectif et la loi positive*, Paris: Fontemoing.

Duguit, L. (1913) *Les transformations du droit public*, Paris: Librairie A. Colin.

Duguit, L. (1927) *Traite de droit constitutionnel*, Paris: Boccard.

Ehrlich, E. (1913) 'Der praktische Rechtsbegriff', in *Festschrift für Ernst Zitelmann*, München-Leipzig: Duncker & Humblot.

Enneccerus, L. (1911) *Lehrbuch des bürgerlichen Rechts*, Marburg.

Esposito, C. (1930) *Lineamenti di una dottrina del diritto*, Fabriano: T.E.S.A.

Falchi, A. (1914) *I fini dello Stato e la funzione del potere*, Sassari: Tipografia Ditta G. Dessi.

Falco, M. (1938) *Diritto ecclesiastico italiano*, Padova: CEDAM.

Fedozzi, P. (1905) *Il diritto processuale civile internazionale*, Bologna: N. Zanichelli.

Fedozzi, P. (1938) 'Introduzione al diritto internazionale e parte generale', in P. Fedozzi, S. Romano (eds) *Trattato di diritto internazionale*, Padova: CEDAM.

Fedozzi, P. (1940) 'Introduzione al diritto internazionale e parte generale', in P. Fedozzi, S. Romano (eds) *Trattato di diritto internazionale*, Padova: CEDAM.

Ferrara, F. (1915) *Teoria delle persone giuridiche*, Napoli: E. Marghieri.

Ferrara, F. (1921) *Trattato di diritto civile italiano*, Roma: Athenaeum.

Ferrara, F. (1938) 'Le persone giuridiche', in Vassalli, F. (ed.) *Trattato di diritto civile italiano*, Torino: UTET.

Ferrara, F. Jr. (1939) *Lezioni di diritto commerciale*, Firenze: Casa Editrice Poligrafica Universitaria di C. Cya.

Ferrara, F. Jr. (1945) *La teoria giuridica dell'azienda*, Firenze: Editrice Il Castellaccio.

Filomusi Guelfi, F. (1917) *Enciclopedia giuridica*, Napoli: N. Jovene e C.

Fleiner, F. (1913) *Institutionen des deutschen Verwaltungsrechts*, Tübingen: J. C. B. Mohr.

Fragapane, G. (1944a) *Lo stato di diritto*, Milano: A. Giuffrè.

Fragapane, G. (1944b) *Il sistema gradualistico delle fonti normative*, Milano: A. Giuffrè.

Friedberg, E., Ruffini, F. (1893) *Trattato del diritto ecclesiastico cattolico ed evangelico*, Torino: Fratelli Bocca.

Gangi, C. (1945) *Il matrimonio*, Milano: A. Giuffrè.

Gentile, G. (1916) *I fondamenti della filosofia del diritto*, Pisa: F. Mariotti.

Geny, F. (1914) *Science et Technique en droit privé positif*, Paris: Librairie de Recueil Sirey.

Ghirardini, C. (1914) *Il diritto processuale civile internazionale italiano*, Spoleto: Panetto & Petrelli.

Giacchi, O. (1937) *La giurisdizione ecclesiastica nel diritto italiano*, Milano: Vita e pensiero.

Giannini, M.S. (1939) *L'interpretazione dell'atto amministrativo e la teoria giuridica generale dell'interpretazione*, Milano: A. Giuffrè.

Gierke, O. von (1895) *Deutsches Privatrecht*, Vol. 1, Leipzig: Duncker & Humblot.

Gierke, O. von (1902) *Vereine ohne Rechtsfähigkeit nach dem neuen Rechte*, Berlin: H.W. Müller.

Greco, P. (1942) 'Profilo dell'impresa economica nel nuovo codice civile', *Atti della Reale Accademia delle scienze di Torino* 77.

Grispigni, F. (1942) *Corso di diritto penale*, Padova: CEDAM.

Grotius, H. (1925) *De Jure Belli ac Pacis Libri Tres*, Oxford: Clarendon Press.

Gueli, V. (1942) *Regime politico e ordinamento del governo*, Milano: A. Giuffrè.

Gurvitch, G. (1932) *L'idée du droit social*, Paris: Librairie de Recueil Sirey.

Gurvitch, G. (1935) *L'expérience juridique et la philosophie pluraliste du droit*, Paris: Pedone.

Hauriou, M. (1916) *Principes de droit public*, Paris: Librairie de Recueil Sirey.

Hauriou, M. (1925) 'La théorie de l'institution et de la fondation. Essai de vitalisme social', *Cahiers de la Nouvelle Journée*, 4 (La cité moderne et les transformations du droit): 2–45.

Hauriou, M. (1929) *Précis de droit constitutionnel*, 2nd ed., Paris: Librairie de Recueil Sirey.

Hegel, G.W.F. (2008) *Outlines of the Philosophy of Right*, Oxford: Oxford University Press.

Heiner, F. (1912) *Katholisches Kirchenrecht*, Paderbon: F. Schoningh.

Hobbes, T. (1909) *Leviathan*, Oxford: Clarendon Press.

Hold von Ferneck, A. (1903) *Die Rechtswidrigkeit*, Jena: Fischer.

Invrea, F. (1935) *La parte generale del diritto*, Padova: CEDAM.

Jannaccone, C. (1936) *I fondamenti del diritto ecclesiastico Internazionale*, Milano: A. Giuffrè.

Jellinek, G. (1880) *Die rechtliche Natur der Staatenvertrage: ein Beitrag zur juristischen Construction des Völkerrechts*, Wien: Holder.

Jellinek, G. (1887) *Gesetz und Verordnung: Staatsrechtliche Untersuchungen auf rechtsgeschichtlicher und rechtsvergleichender Grundlage*, Freiburg im Breisgau: J. C. B. Mohr.

Jellinek, G. (1908) *Die sozialethische Bedeutung von Recht, Unrecht und Strafe*, Berlin: O. Häring.

Jellinek, G. (1912) *Sistema dei diritti pubblici subbiettivi*, Milano: Società editrice libraria.

Jellinek, W. (1914) *Allgemeine Staatslehre*, 3rd ed., Berlin: Häring.

Jemolo, A.C. (1915) *Esiste un diritto dei fedeli al Sacramento?*, Milano: Società editrice libraria.

Jemolo, A.C. (1916) *L'amministrazione ecclesiastica*, Milano: Società editrice libraria.

Jemolo, A.C. (1923) 'Il valore del diritto della Chiesa nell'ordinamento giuridico italiano', *Archivio giuridico* 90(1).

Jemolo, A.C. (1933) *Lezioni di diritto ecclesiastico*, Città di Castello: Società anonima tipografia Leonardo Da Vinci.

Jemolo, A.C. (1945) *Corso di diritto ecclesiastico*, Roma: Tipografia dell'Università di Roma.

Jhering, R. von (1895) *Jahrbücher für die Dogmatik des bürgerlichen Rechts*, I, Jena: Fischer.

Jhering, R. von (1897) *Der Zweck im Recht*, I, Leipzig: Breitkopf und Härtel.

Kelsen, H. (1911) *Hauptprobleme der Staatsrechtslehre, entwickelt aus der Lehre vom Rechtssatz*, Tübingen: J. C. B. Mohr.

Kelsen, H. (1913a) 'Über Staatsunrecht', *Zeitschrift für das Privat- und öffentliche Recht der Gegenwart* 40.

Kelsen, H. (1913b) 'Zur Lehre vom öffentlichen Rechtsgeschäfte', *Archiv für öffentliches Recht* 31.

Kelsen, H. (1920) *Das Problem der Souveränität und die Theorie des Völkerrechts*, Tübingen: J. C. B. Mohr.

Kelsen, H. (1925) *Allegemeine Staatslehre*, Berlin: J. Springer.

Kelsen, H. (1927) *Les rapports de système entre le droit interne et le droit international public*, Paris: Hachette.

Klein, P. (1903) 'Die Revisibilität des Internationalen Privatrechts', *Zeitschrift für internationales Privat- und öffentliches Recht* 8.

Laband, P. (1911) *Das Staatsrecht des Deutschen Reiches*, Vol. 1, Tübingen: J. C. B. Mohr.

Lasson, A. (1882) *System der Rechtsphilosophie*, Berlin: Guttentag.

Laun, R. (1913) 'Eine Theorie vom natürlichen Recht', *Archiv für öffentliches Recht* 30.

Leontovitsch, V.V. (1937) 'Die Theorie der Institution bei Maurice Hauriou', *Archiv für Rechts- und Sozialphilosophie* 30(2).

Leontovitsch, V.V. (1941) 'La teoria della istituzione di Hauriou e il suo significato per il diritto costituzionale', *Bollettino dell'Istituto di Filosofia del Diritto della Regia Università di Roma* 19(2).

Lessona, C. (1910) *I diritti dei soci nelle associazioni private*, Milano: F. Vallardi.

Lessona, S. (1943) *Istituzioni di diritto pubblico*, Roma: Societá Editrice del Foro italiano.

Levi, A. (1914) *Contributi ad una teoria filosofica dell'ordine giuridico*, Genova: Formiggini.

Levi, A. (1920) *Filosofia del diritto e tecnicismo giuridico*, Bologna: N. Zanichelli.

Levi, A. (1924) *Saggi di teoria del diritto*, Bologna: N. Zanichelli.

Levi, L.R. (1938) 'Sull'approvazione degli statuti degli enti pubblici', *Rivista di diritto pubblico*.

Longhi, S. (1927) *Gli imperativi della carta del lavoro*, Roma: Edizioni del Diritto del lavoro.

Maggiore, G. (1916) *Il diritto e il suo processo ideale*, Palermo: Orazio Fiorenza.

Maggiore, G. (1921) *Filosofia del diritto*, Palermo: Orazio Fiorenza.

Maggiore, G. (1922) 'L'aspetto pubblico e privato del diritto e la crisi dello Stato', *Rivista internazionale di filosofia del diritto* 2–3.

Maggiore, G. (1925a) *Filosofia del diritto*, Palermo: Orazio Fiorenza.

Maggiore, G. (1925b) *Diritto penale*, Bologna: N. Zanichelli.

Maggiore, G. (1937) *Principi di diritto penale*, Vol. 1, Bologna: N. Zanichelli.

Maiorca, C. (1933) *Il riconoscimento della personalità giuridica degli enti privati*, Palermo: Tipografia Michele Montaina.

Manzini, V. (1933) *Trattato di diritto penale italiano*, Torino: UTET.

Marinoni, M. (1910) *La rappresentanza di uno Stato da parte di un altro Stato e le relazioni giuridiche cui da origine*, Venezia: Istituto veneto di arti grafiche.

Marinoni, M. (1912) 'Dell'annessione della Tripolitania e della Cirenaica', *Rivista di diritto e procedura penale*.

Marinoni, M. (1913a) *La responsabilità degli Stati per gli atti dei loro rappresentanti secondo il diritto internazionale*, Roma: Athenaeum.

Marinoni, M. (1913b) 'La natura giuridica del diritto internazionale privato', *Rivista di diritto internazionale*, 2 (3–4).

Marinoni, M. (1914) 'Della condizione giuridica degli apolidi secondo il diritto italiano' *Atti del Reale Istituto veneto di scienze, lettere ed arti*, anno accademico 1913–1914, Vol. 73, Part 2.

Marinoni, M. (1916) 'L'universalità dell'ordine giuridico statuale e la concezione del diritto internazionale privato', *Rivista di diritto pubblico*, Part 1.

Mastino, G. (1923) *Analisi critica delle più recenti teorie sul concetto e i caratteri della legge in senso materiale*, Cagliari: Premiata tipografia Giovanni Ledda.

Mayer, O. von (1895) *Deutsches Verwaltungsrecht*, München-Leipzig: Duncker & Humblot.

Mayer, O. von (1917) *Deutsches Verwaltungsrecht*, 2nd ed., München-Leipzig: Duncker & Humblot.

Mayer, O. von (1934) *Deutsches Verwaltungsrecht*, 3rd ed., München-Leipzig: Duncker & Humblot.

Mazzoni, G. (1934) *L'ordinamento corporativo*, Padova: CEDAM.

Merkel, A. (1885) *Juristische Enzyklopädie*, Berlin und Leipzig: de Gruyter.

Merkel, A. (1890) *Elemente der allgemeinen Rechtslehre*, in F. von Holtzendorff (ed.) *Encyklopädie der Rechtswissenschaft*, Vol. 5, p. 594.

Messina, G. (1904) *I concordati di tariffe nell'ordinamento giuridico del lavoro*, Milano: F. Vallardi.

Messineo, F. (1943) *Manuale di diritto civile e commerciale*, Padova: CEDAM.

Meyer, G. (1899) *Lehrbuch des deutschen Staatsrechtes*, Leipzig: Duncker & Humblot.

Miceli, V. (1906) *La norma giuridica*, Palermo: A. Reber.

Miceli, V. (1914) *Principii di filosofia del diritto*, Milano: Società editrice libraria.

Miceli, V. (1923) 'Le distinzioni nel dominio del diritto', *Rivista internazionale di filosofia del diritto* 3(1).

Miele, G. (1936) *Le situazioni di necessita dello Stato*, Padova: CEDAM.

Miele, G. (1945) *Principi di diritto amministrativo*, Pisa: Tornar.

Monaco, R. (1932a) 'Solidarietà e teoria dell'istituzione nelle dottrine di diritto internazionale', *Archivio giuridico*.

Monaco, R. (1932b) *L'ordinamento internazionale in relazione all'ordinamento statuale*, Torino: Istituto Giuridico della R. Università.

Monaco, R. (1938) 'I regolamenti interni degli enti internazionali', *Jus gentium. Annuario italiano di diritto internazionale* 1.

Monaco, R. (1945) 'Ordinamento giuridico', in *Dizionario pratico del Diritto privato*, Vol. 4, pp. 519–522.

Morelli, G. (1933) 'Limiti dell'ordinamento statuale e limiti della giurisdizione', *Rivista di diritto internazionale*, 25(4).

Morelli, G. (1941) 'I limiti della giurisdizione italiana nel nuovo codice di procedura civile', *Rivista di diritto processuale civile* 18(2).

Mortati, C. (1949) *La Costituzione in senso materiale*, Milano: A. Giuffrè.

Nawiasky, H. (1913) 'Forderungs- und Gewaltverhältnis. Ein Beitrag zum allgemeinen Teil des privaten und öffentlichen Rechts', in *Festschrift für Ernst Zitelmann*, München-Leipzig: Duncker & Humblot.

Niedner, J. (1915) 'Recht und Kirche', in *Festgabe der Leipziger Juristenfakultat für Dr. Rudolph Sohm zum 8. Juli 1914*, München-Leipzig: Duncker & Humblot.

Orestano, F. (1941) *Filosofia del diritto*, Milano: Fratelli Bocca.

Orlando, V.E. (1926a) 'Stato e diritto (Ordinamento giuridico-Regola di diritto-Istituzione)', *Rivista di diritto pubblico*.

Orlando, V.E. (1926b) 'Recenti indirizzi circa i rapporti fra diritto e stato: ordinamento giuridico, regola di diritto, istituzione', *Rivista di diritto pubblico e la Giustizia Amministrativa* 7.

Orlando, V.E. (1940a) 'Ancora del metodo in diritto pubblico con particolare riguardo all'opera di Santi Romano', in *Scritti giuridici in onore di Santi Romano*, Padova: CEDAM.

Orlando, V.E. (1940b) *Diritto pubblico generale: scritti varii, 1881–1940*, Milano: A. Giuffrè.

Orlando, V.E. (1941) *Filosofia del diritto*, Milano: Fratelli Bocca.

Ottolenghi, G. (1902) *Intorno ai fonti del diritto internazionale pubblico: appunti critici in ordine ad alcune teoriche della dottrina tedesca*, Torino: Unione Tipografico-Editrice Torinese.

Ottolenghi, G. (1913) *Sulla funzione e sull'efficacia delle norme interne di diritto internazionale privato*, Torino: Unione Tipografico-Editrice Torinese.

Panunzio, G. (1931a) *Studi di diritto pubblico in onore di Oreste Ranelletti*, Vol. 2, Padova: CEDAM.

Panunzio, G. (1931b) 'La pluralità degli ordinamenti giuridici e l'unità dello Stato', in *Studi filosofico-giuridici dedicati a Giorgio Del Vecchio*, Vol. II: 223–245, Modena: Editore Società Tipografica Modenese.

Paresce, E. (1935) 'Diritto, norma, ordinamento', *Rivista Internazionale di filosofia del diritto* 14(3).

Passerin d'Entrèves, A. (1934) *Il negozio giuridico: saggio di filosofia del diritto*, Torino: R. Gayet.

Perassi, T. (1937) *Lezioni di diritto internazionale*, Roma: Societá Editrice del Foro italiano.

Perassi, T. (1938) *Introduzione alle scienze giuridiche*, Roma: Societá Editrice del Foro italiano.

Pergolesi, F. (1938) *Istituzioni di diritto corporativo*, Bologna: N. Zanichelli.

Perozzi, S. (1906) *Istituzioni di diritto romano*, Firenze: G. Barbera.

Perozzi, S. (1912) *Precetti e concetti nella evoluzione giuridica*, Roma: Bertero.

Perreau, E.H. (1913) 'Les obligations de conscience devant les tribunaux', *Revue trimestrielle de droit civil* 12.

Perticone, G. (1938) *La théorie du droit*, Paris: Hermann & C.

Petrone, I. (1897) 'Contributo all'analisi dei caratteri differenziali del diritto', *Rivista italiana per le scienze giuridiche* 23.

Petrone, I. (1905) *La fase recentissima della Filosofia del diritto in Germania*, Pisa: E. Spoerri.

Petrone, I. (1910) *Il diritto nel mondo dello spirito: saggio filosofico*, Milano: Libreria Editrice Milanese.

Piccardi, L. (1939) 'La pluralità degli ordinamenti giuridici e il concetto di rinvio', in *Scritti giuridici in onore di Santi Romano*, Padova: CEDAM.

Piola, A. (1937) *Introduzione al diritto concordatario comparato*, Milano: A. Giuffrè.

Polacco, V. (1915) *Le obbligazioni nel diritto civile italiano*, Vol. I, Roma: Athenaeum.

Planiol, M. (1913) 'L'assimilation progressive de l'obligation naturelle et du devoir moral', *Revue critique de legislation et de jurisprudence* 42.

Presutti, E. (1917) *Istituzioni di diritto amministrativo italiano*, 2nd ed., Roma: Athenaeum.

Preuss, H. (1899) *Gemeinde, Staat, Reich als Gebietskörperschaften*, Berlin: J. Springer.

Pufendorf, S. (1688) *De jure naturae et gentium libri octo*, the translation of the edition of 1688.

Radbruch, G. (1914) *Grundzüge der Rechtsphilosophie*, Leipzig: Verlag von Quelle & Meyer.

Ranelletti, O. (1912) *Principii di diritto amministrativo*, Napoli: L. Pierro.

Ranelletti, O. (1942) *Istituzioni di diritto pubblico*, Padova: CEDAM.

Ravà, A. (1911) *Il diritto come norma tecnica*, Cagliari: Dessì.

Ravà, A. (1914) *Lo Stato come organismo etico*, Roma: Athenaeum.

Ravà, A. (1937) *Istituzioni di diritto privato*, Padova: CEDAM.

Ravà, R. (1933) *La teoria della pluralità degli ordinamenti giuridici e le associazioni sindacali*, Firenze: Poligrafica universitaria.

Redenti, E. (1905) *Il contratto di lavoro nella giurisprudenza dei probiviri*, Milano: F. Vallardi.

Redenti, E. (1911) *Il giudizio civile con pluralità di parti*, Milano: Societá editrice libraria.

Redenti, E. (1916) *Intorno al concetto di giurisdizione*, Napoli: N. Jovene e C.

Regelsberger, F. (1893) *Pandekten*, Leipzig: Duncker & Humblot.

Rehm, H. (1899) *Allgemeine Staatslehre*, Freiburg im Breisgau: J. C. B. Mohr.

Renard, G. (1930) *La theorie de l'institution*, Paris: Librairie de Recueil Sirey.

Riva Sanseverino, L. (1938) *Corso di diritto del lavoro*, 2nd revised ed., Padova: CEDAM.

Rocco, A. (1933) *Lezioni di diritto penale*, Roma: A. Sampaolesi.

Romano, S. (1945) *Note sulle obbligazioni naturali*, Firenze: G. C. Sansoni.

Romano, S. (1901) 'L'instaurazione di fatto di un ordinamento costituzionale e la sua legittimazione', *Archivio giuridico 'Filippo Serafini'* 9(3).

Romano, S. (1902) 'Osservazioni preliminari per una teoria sui limiti della funzione legislativa nel diritto italiano', *Archivio del diritto pubblico e dell'amministrazione italiana* 1(4).

Romano, S. (1905) 'Sulla natura dei regolamenti delle Camere parlamentari', *Archivio giuridico Filippo Serafini* 4(1).

Romano, S. (1908) 'Il comune: parte generale', in *Trattato di diritto amministrativo*, Vol. 2., Milano: Società editrice libraria, 1908.

Romano, S. (1910) 'Lo stato moderno e la sua crisi', *Rivista di diritto pubblico* 3.

Romano, S. (1912) *Principii di diritto amministrativo italiano*, Milano: Società editrice libraria.

Romano, S. (1925a) 'Di una particolare figura di successione di Stati: a proposito dell'annessione di Fiume', *Rivista di diritto internazionale* 17(3).

Romano, S. (1925b) *Osservazioni sulla completezza dell'ordinamento statale*, Modena: Università degli Studi.

Romano, S. (1937) *Corso di diritto amministrativo*, Padova: CEDAM.

Romano, S. (1944) 'A proposito dell'impresa e dell'azienda agricola', *Rivista di diritto agrario*, 23.

Romano, Salvatore (1945) *Principii di diritto costituzionale generale*, Milano: A. Giuffrè.

Romano, S. (1949) *Corso di diritto internazionale*, 4th ed., Padova: CEDAM.

Rosmini, A. (1841) *Filosofia del diritto*, Milano: Boniardi-Pogliani.

Rosmini, A. (1843) *Filosofia del diritto*, 2nd ed., Milano: Boniardi-Pogliani.

Rotondi, M. (1942) *Istituzioni di diritto privato*, Milano: Ambrosiana.

Rovelli, F. (1931) 'Su la statualità del diritto e la distinzione fra diritto e morale', in *Studi di diritto pubblico in onore di Oreste Ranelletti*, Vol. 2, Padova: CEDAM.

Ruffini, F. (1924) *Corso di diritto ecclesiastico italiano*, Vol. 1, Torino: Fratelli Bocca.

Sägmüller, J.B. (1909) *Lehrbuch des katholischen Kirchenrechts*, Freiburg im Breisgau: Herdersche Verlagshandlung.

Salemi, G. (1930a) *Le circolari amministrative*, Palermo: A. Reber.

Salemi, G. (1930b) 'Il PNF e il suo diritto', *Il diritto del lavoro* 4.

Salemi, G. (1935) *Corso di diritto corporativo*, Padova: CEDAM.

Salvioli, G. (1914) *Sulla teoria dell'accordo in diritto internazionale: note critiche*, Napoli: F. Lubrano.

Scaduto, F. (1904) 'Competenza civile sugli atti ecclesiastici', *Giurisprudenza Italiana* 1.

Schenk, W.-R. (1914) 'Die Abgrenzung des öffentlichen und privaten Rechts', *Öesterr. zeitschrift*.

Scherer, R. (1866) *Handbuch des Kirchenrechts*, Graz: U. Moser.

Schiappoli, D. (1913) *Manuale di diritto ecclesiastico*, Napoli: L. Pierro.

Schmitt, C. (1934) *Über die drei Arten des rechtswissenschaftlichen Denkens*, Hamburg: Hanseatische Verlagsanstalt (trans. Joseph W. Bendersky (2004) *On the Three Types of Juristic Thought*, Westport, CT: Praeger).

Schmitt, C. (1939) 'Führung und Hegemonie', *Schmollers Jahrbuch* 63: 513–520.

Scuto, C. (1941) *Istituzioni di diritto privato*, Napoli: R. Pironti.

Sebastianelli, G. (1905) *Praelectiones iuris canonici*, Romae: Lit. Spellani.

Seidler, G. *Das juristische Kriterium des Staates*, Tübingen: J. C. B. Mohr.

Simoncelli, V. (1890) *Le presenti difficoltà della scienza del diritto civile*, Camerino: Tipografia Savini.

Simoncelli, V. (1917) *Lezioni di diritto ecclesiastico*, Roma: Sampaolesi.

Sinagra, V. (1935) *Principii del nuovo diritto costituzionale italiano*, Napoli: Athenaeum.

Sohm, R. (1892) *Kirchenrecht*, Leipzig: Duncker & Humblot.

Sohm, R. (1915) 'Weltliches und geistliches Recht', in *Festgabe der Leipziger Juristenfakultät für Dr. Rudolph Sohm zum 8. Juli 1914*, München-Leipzig: Duncker & Humblot.

Stammler, R. (1911) *Theorie der Rechtswissenschaft*, Halle: Buchhandlung des Waisenhauses.

Stampe, E. (1905) 'Rechtsfindung durch Interessenabwägung', *Deutsche Juristen-Zeitung* 10: 713.

Stutz, U. (1905) *Die kirchliche Rechtsgeschichte*, Stuttgart: Ferdinand Enke.

Tedeschi, G. (1929) 'Volontà privata autonoma', *Rivista internazionale di filosofia del diritto* 9(6).

Tezner, F. (1914) 'System der obrigkeitlichen Verwaltungsakte', *Öesterr. Zeitschrift*.

Thon, A. (1878) *Rechtsnorm und Subjektives Recht. Untersuchungen zur Allgemeinen Rechtslehre. Neudruck der Ausgabe*, Weimar: H. Böhlau.

Thudicum, F. von (1887) *Deutsches Kirchenrecht*, Leipzig: Duncker & Humblot.

Triepel, H. (1899) *Völkerrecht und Landesrecht*, Leipzig-Tübingen: J. C. B. Mohr.

Tuhr, A. von (1910) *Der Allgemeine Teil des Deutschen Bürgerlichen Rechts*, Berlin: Duncker & Humblot.

Vacchelli, G. (1904) 'Sulla competenza dell'autorità giudiziaria in rapporto agli atti dell'autorità ecclesiastica', *Societá Editrice del Foro italiano* 29(1).

Valeri, G. (1945) *Manuale di diritto commerciale*, Firenze: Editrice Il Castellaccio.

Vanni, I. (1906) *Lezioni di filosofia del diritto*, Bologna: N. Zanichelli.

Vassalli, F. (1932) *Lezioni di diritto matrimoniale*, Padova: CEDAM.

Verdross, A. (1914) 'Konstruktion des Völkerrechts', *Zeitschrift für Völkerrecht* 8.

Volpicelli, A. (1929) 'Santi Romano', *Nuovi studi di diritto, economia e politica* 2(1): 7–25.

Wernz, F.X. (1905) *Ius decretalium*, Romae: ex Typographia Polyglotta.

Wernz, F.X. (1938) *Ius Canonicum*, Romae: Apud Aedes Universitatis.

Weyr, F. (1908) 'Zum Problem eines einheitlichen Rechtssystems', *Archiv für öffentliches Recht* 23.

Weyr, F. (1913) 'Über zwei Hauptpunkte der Kelsenschen Staatsrechtslehre', *Zeitschrift für das Privat- und Öffentliche Recht der Gegenwart* 40.

Weyr, F. (1914) 'Zum Unterschiede zwischen Öffentlichem und privatem Recht', *Österreichische Zeitschrift für öffentliches Recht* 1.

Windscheid, B., Kipp, T. (1906) *Lehrbuch des Pandektenrechts*, Vol. 1, Frankfurt: Rütten & Loening.

Zanobini, G. (1915) *Norme interne di diritto pubblico*, Milano: Società editrice libraria.

Zanobini, G. (1936) *Corso di diritto ecclesiastico*, 2nd ed., Pisa: Vallerini.

Zanobini, G. (1942) *Corso di diritto corporativo*, 6th revised ed., Milano: A. Giuffrè.

Zanobini, G. (1949) 'Stato', in *Enciclopedia del diritto*, Vol. XXIII, Milano: Giuffrè.

Zanzucchi, M.T. (1942) *Il nuovo diritto processuale civile*, 2nd ed., Milano: A. Giuffrè.

Ziccardi, P. (1943) *La costituzione dell'ordinamento internazionale*, Milano: A. Giuffrè.

Zitelmann, E. (1897) *Internationales Privatrecht*, Leipzig: Duncker & Humblot.

Index